THE ART OF WITNESSING

Francisco de Goya's *Disasters of War*

The Art of Witnessing

Francisco de Goya's *Disasters of War*

MICHAEL IAROCCI

UNIVERSITY OF TORONTO PRESS
Toronto Buffalo London

Toronto Buffalo London
utorontopress.com
Printed in the U.S.A.

ISBN 978-1-4875-4378-5 (cloth) ISBN 978-1-4875-4379-2 (EPUB)
ISBN 978-1-4875-4527-7 (paper) ISBN 978-1-4875-4380-8 (PDF)

Toronto Iberic

Library and Archives Canada Cataloguing in Publication

Title: The art of witnessing : Francisco de Goya's Disasters of war / Michael Iarocci.
Other titles: Francisco de Goya's Disasters of war
Names: Iarocci, Michael P., author.
Series: Toronto Iberic ; 77.
Description: Series statement: Toronto Italian studies | Includes bibliographical references and index.
Identifiers: Canadiana (print) 20220398623 | Canadiana (ebook) 20220398704 | ISBN 9781487543785 (cloth) | ISBN 9781487545277 (paper) | ISBN 9781487543792 (EPUB) | ISBN 9781487543808 (PDF)
Subjects: LCSH: Goya, Francisco, 1746–1828. Disasters of war. | LCSH: Goya, Francisco, 1746–1828 – Criticism and interpretation. | LCSH: War in art.
Classification: LCC NE2062.5.G6 A47 2023 | DDC 769.92–dc23

We wish to acknowledge the land on which the University of Toronto Press operates. This land is the traditional territory of the Wendat, the Anishnaabeg, the Haudenosaunee, the Métis, and the Mississaugas of the Credit First Nation.

This book has been published with the help of a grant from the University of California–Berkeley.

University of Toronto Press acknowledges the financial support of the Government of Canada, the Canada Council for the Arts, and the Ontario Arts Council, an agency of the Government of Ontario, for its publishing activities.

Canada Council for the Arts
Conseil des Arts du Canada

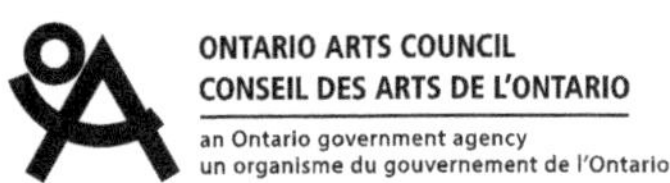

Funded by the Government of Canada
Financé par le gouvernement du Canada

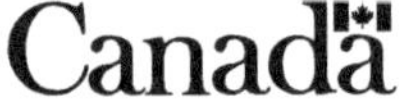

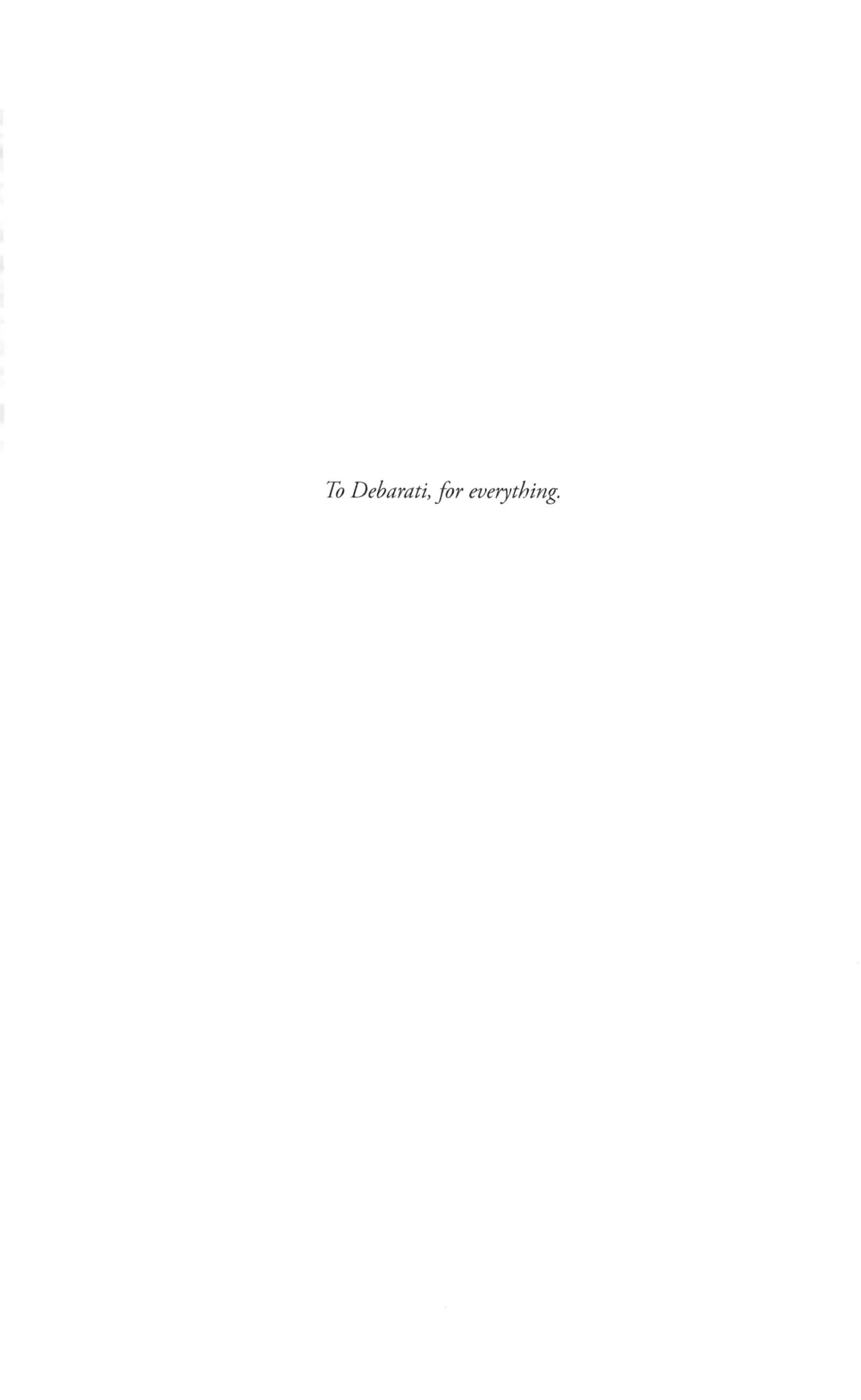

To Debarati, for everything.

Contents

Introduction: Viewing, Reading, Witnessing 3

Beginnings 11

Preface (1863): Image of an Artist 16

1 Tristes presentimientos de lo que ha de acontecer 21

2 Con razón o sin ella 25

3 Lo mismo 29

4 Las mujeres dan valor 35

5 Y son fieras 39

6 Bien te se está 43

7 Qué valor! 49

8 Siempre sucede 53

9 No quieren 57

10 Tampoco 61

11 Ni por ésas 65

12 Para eso habéis nacido 71

13 Amarga presencia 77

14 Duro es el paso! 81

15 Y no hay remedio 87

16 Se aprovechan 93

17 No se convienen 99

18 Enterrar y callar 103
19 Ya no hay tiempo 109
20 Curarlos y a otra 115
21 Será lo mismo 119
22 Tanto y más 121
23 Lo mismo en otras partes 123
24 Aún podrán servir 129
25 También éstos 131
26 No se puede mirar 137
27 Caridad 141
28 Populacho 145
29 Lo merecía 147
30 Estragos de la guerra 153
31 Fuerte cosa es! 159
32 Por qué? 163
33 Qué hay que hacer más? 167
34 Por una navaja 171
35 No se puede saber por qué 173
36 Tampoco 175
37 Esto es peor 181
38 Bárbaros! 187
39 Grande hazaña! Con muertos! 191
40 Algún partido saca 193
41 Escapan entre llamas 199
42 Todo va revuelto 201
43 También esto 203
44 Yo lo vi 207
45 Y esto también 209
46 Esto es malo 213
47 Así sucedió 215

Afterword 219

Notes 225

Bibliography 263

Index 271

THE ART OF WITNESSING

Introduction: Viewing, Reading, Witnessing

This book is about the experience of viewing and reading Francisco de Goya's renowned print series, *The Disasters of War*. Widely acknowledged as a major turning point in the history of visual depictions of war, Goya's *Disasters* remain a touchstone today for any serious engagement with the violence of war and the questions raised by its artistic representation. The print series departs from the largely idealizing, heroic portrayals of warfare that had dominated prior European art, and it brings images of war's unvarnished brutality to viewers at close range. Goya focuses on the atrocities of the Peninsular War (1808–14), one of the bloodier chapters of the Napoleonic Wars that swept through Europe in the wake of the French Revolution. His subject belongs to a pivotal moment in European history, a moment that in many ways ushered in the modern era, and the cost of the wars in lives lost was extraordinary. Historical estimates of the total death toll across the continent during the Napoleonic Wars range from five to seven million dead. Only the even more extensive, industrialized killing of the twentieth century's two World Wars would make such numbers pale by comparison. Still, the Napoleonic Era often continues to be remembered today in terms of heroic grandeur rather than the violence, suffering, and death to which Goya's work testifies.

Known in Spain as the War of Independence, the Peninsular War was a distinctively cruel chapter of the Napoleonic conflict because, in addition to armies confronting one another on fields of battle, it also involved a civilian, guerrilla insurrection against foreign occupation. Napoleon's troops had initially entered Spain as an ally, under the pretence of invading Portugal, and by the time the emperor's true intentions had become clear, key Spanish cities were already under occupation. Madrid became a flashpoint, and civilians famously took up arms against the Grande Armée when the news broke that the Spanish monarchy was being whisked away. Two of Goya's most well-known paintings, *The Second of May 1808 in Madrid* and *Executions of the Third of May, 1808*, commemorate the uprising and its suppression. Although Napoleon had been careful in trying to set up his brother Joseph as the new legal monarch of Spain, broad swaths of the civilian populace rejected "the usurper king," and important portions of the population engaged in active resistance against the occupying army.

The distinction between soldier and civilian often fell by the wayside, unleashing forms of violence that were unconstrained by the conventions of traditional warfare. Napoleon's troops were ruthless in their treatment of non-professional enemy combatants, and Spanish guerrillas who caught straggling imperial soldiers or their collaborators were equally merciless. Civilian population centres regularly came under siege and bombardment, and mass executions were not uncommon. The military theorist Carl Von Clausewitz later came to call this new, modern form of warfare "total war," in order to distinguish it from earlier, more codified forms of armed conflict. As the Peninsular War drew to a close, 6 to 10 per cent of Spain's total population had died as a result of fighting, famine, and related disease. By comparison, Britain, France, and the United States each lost less than 2 per cent of their respective populations over the course of all of the Second World War.

This is the macabre world of modern violence from which Goya's prints emerged, and it is his primary subject. By most counts, the prints we have come to know as *The Disasters of War* were made during the war years, between 1810 and 1814, but they were not published until 1863, some thirty-five years after the artist's death. In its first edition the series consisted of eighty prints, and it was organized into three basic thematic groups. The first depicts the horrors of wartime violence in its many forms, the second portrays the famine and disease that accompanied the conflict, and the third gathers together allegorical images on the political aftermath of the war in Spain. In this book I focus on the first group of prints (Prints 1–47), which constitute just over half of the *Disasters*. They form a clearly bounded subdivision within the series as originally published, they take up the violence of armed conflict in all of its gruesome immediacy, and they are among the most widely reproduced prints in the series. They are also the prints in which Goya reflects most intensely, I think, on the quandaries posed by making and viewing art when the subject is war's horrors.

In what follows I take the reader through these *Disasters*, slowly, image by image, in order to probe the meanings of Goya's famous prints while reflecting on the way various facets of his artistry shape the viewing and reading experience in subtle and often unexpected ways. By artistry, I should make clear that I mean to designate a broad array of creative activities that have not always been discussed together in appraisals of Goya's work. That Goya was, first and foremost, a visual artist and thinker needs little explanation, and this facet of his print series has rightly received the lion's share of commentary since the series' first publication. Artistry in the *Disasters*, however, extends well beyond the making of his images, to the captions he wrote for each print, and to the organization of the series itself. Images, words, and sequence together play an important role within the experience of viewing and reading the *Disasters*, and much of what follows is an attempt to describe how these different forms of creativity contribute to the richness of his prints. My references in this book to *viewing and reading* the prints are consequently meant to remind readers that Goya's prints are both a visual and a verbal experience.

I do not mean to minimize the importance of the visual in the *Disasters* in the least, but I do wish to underscore that Goya's images consistently present themselves with words that shape and complicate the viewing experience in significant ways. The earliest critics of the series recognized this facet of his artistry, and twenty-first-century readers familiar with the *New Yorker* magazine's weekly caption contest are no doubt attuned to the power of words to shape the way we look at images. While philosophers and theorists have long quarrelled over the relationship between words and pictures, in the pages that follow, I hope to persuade readers that Goya's artistry in the *Disasters* rewards attention to both. Often, as we will see, his prints convey meanings that neither pictures nor words can impart by themselves.

Attention to words and images, however, poses its own challenges for readers who do not understand the original Spanish words one sees in each print. Many of Goya's captions are difficult to translate. They are highly idiomatic. Their tone is frequently ironic, sarcastic, or otherwise resistant to straightforward reading, and several captions contain puns and other forms of word play. The captions are also often deliberately ambiguous when it comes to questions of voice (who speaks?) and address (to whom?). Many captions deliberately play with more than one possible meaning. Native speakers of Spanish have not always been of one mind about how to read them, and the one-line English translations that usually accompany modern editions of the *Disasters* have been hard pressed to convey the richness and nuance of the originals. The most widely available English-language edition of the prints contains outright mistranslations. As a result, many anglophone viewers of the *Disasters* have not had access to the full significance of Goya's captions and the various ways they engage his images. I have attempted to address this challenge by discussing the captions at length.

To the extent that we usually conceive of reading in terms of sequence – first this word, then the next – my reference to viewing and reading is also a way of signalling the importance of the sequential presentation of the *Disasters*. Goya spent considerable time ordering and reordering his prints, and readers have noticed that many of the captions accompanying his images only make sense in the context of those that immediately precede them. Nevertheless, there is no strong consensus about the significance of Goya's sequence and the weight it should be given in interpreting his prints. For some, the collection known as *The Disasters of War* is a convenient way of organizing prints that were made independently, at different times, and possibly with different motivations. For others, Goya's sequence is a medium of expression in its own right, and while each print can be viewed as a more or less independent work of art, the series as a whole is also an artwork calling for attention to the role played by individual prints within the larger structure. In what follows I will be exploring this latter approach as it pertains to the forty-seven prints Goya dedicated to the violence of war.

Beyond questions raised by the posthumous publication of the *Disasters*, a good part of the difficulty in deciding how to take in the print series stems from the peculiar kind of narrative Goya constructed when he sequenced his images. While there is little or no continuity as one turns from print to print – the series is not the equivalent of a graphic novel – Goya's sequence does nevertheless give form to a basic story. It begins with a foreboding print that references the moments before the outbreak of war, it portrays fighting and famine, and it ends with allegorical prints that speak to the political climate that followed the defeat of the French and the restoration of Spain's absolutist monarch, Ferdinand VII. Broadly speaking, Goya organized a viewing and reading experience that simulates movement through historical time. No print represents a particular day, month, or year, but each of the *Disasters* represents a moment within an itinerary that aims to mimic movement through the war years themselves. The protagonist of that movement is the viewer, who is positioned as a witness travelling through time. Movement from print to print approximates the experience of witnessing different scenes of violence, one after another, during times of war. Much of this book is an attempt to describe that experience.

I will consequently turn frequently to the effects that Goya's prints produce by virtue of their position within the sequence. My hope is to show how, beyond basic thematic divisions or clusters, Goya worked with the viewing order of his images for expressive effect. The meaning of images is shaped by the context in which they are viewed, and throughout the *Disasters* Goya deliberately manipulated the sequence so as to produce meanings that no single print could convey on its own. Print series were commonly bound together as albums in the nineteenth century, and another important facet of viewing and reading *The Disasters of War* is the book form itself. His depictions of violence famously position viewers at close range, but Goya's prints are also intimate in another sense. They were made to be held closely, the way one holds a book or, increasingly today, a digital tablet or smartphone. The experience of moving from one print to the next as one turns the page is an important part of taking in Goya's *Disasters*. Exhibits in which framed prints are displayed on walls, books that reproduce a handful of prints, and web resources in which a selection of images is offered can be illuminating points of entry into the *Disasters*. My interest here, however, has been to imagine and partially recreate the *Disasters* in book form in order to explain more fully the role that sequence – turning from one print to the next – plays in shaping the viewing and reading of Goya's prints.

Thanks to the painstaking work of several generations of art historians, we have a relatively clear picture of the history of the making of the *Disasters*, a detailed understanding of Goya's creative process, and a thorough account of the circumstances that led to the publication of the first edition. Goya was First Court Painter in Madrid in the spring of 1808 when the Spanish people rose up in arms against the Napoleonic armies. The artist lived through the six years of war that followed in relative comfort, and he was especially savvy at navigating through Madrid's changing political circumstances. He had ample opportunity to hear about many of the forms of violence and suffering he would depict in the *Disasters*, and he travelled to Zaragoza to survey the damage the city had suffered during its first siege. While depicting the unheroic truth of war's brutality was central to Goya's agenda, however, the *Disasters* are much more than acts of visual testimony, and scholars have noted that Goya's relationship to witnessing in the *Disasters* is rarely a straightforward affair.

The artist's activities during the war years make clear that he was neither an outright supporter of the Bonaparte régime nor a fervent insurgent against the French imperial order. Like many civilians of his class, he took a largely pragmatic approach to getting through the war years, and his adaptation to the changing political winds of the conflagration in Spain is more complex than the political labels that have often been applied to him. A supporter of enlightened reform, he witnessed the extraordinary violence that Napoleon unleashed in the name of such reform. An admirer of national tradition and the Spanish popular classes, he also saw terrible atrocities committed by the people in the name of Spanish nationalism. At times seemingly critical of the Spanish aristocracy, he was deeply enmeshed in the social world of his patrons. An associate of Spanish supporters of the French, the so-called *afrancesados*, he would see many of his acquaintances persecuted mercilessly as traitors to Spain when the conflict ended. Immediately following the war, Goya himself would have to prove that he had not been a collaborator as the returned Spanish king, Ferdinand VII, instituted a regime more repressive and reactionary than those that had immediately preceded him. It is no surprise then that Spanish terms like *ilustrado* (enlightened), *afrancesado* (Frenchified), *liberal*, or *patriota* do not adequately account for the complexities of Goya's life experience.

The clearest, most forceful expression of Goya's feelings about the war is in fact to be found in the *Disasters* themselves, where his critique of the violence unleashed in Spain – and indeed the violence of war as such – is remarkable precisely because of his refusal to identify consistently with any given faction. Goya understood fully the ways in which political and religious sectarianism can lead to and sustain horrific violence. His critical stance in the series is grounded in a cosmopolitan humanitarianism that decries *all* of the rationales that contending parties marshal in order to justify the violence they inflict on one another during times of war. In this sense, as we will see in the pages that follow, Goya's *Disasters* are first and foremost a moral critique, a macabre satire of war. His prints do not aim to depict actual, historical events, the way history painting does. He portrays historically representative forms of violence, examples of the kinds of brutality that routinely took place during the conflagration. At the same time, the events Goya portrays are situated within distinctively abstract times and spaces. They unfold in an "anytime" and "anyplace" that give the *Disasters* a modern and at times even contemporary feel. The prints of course belong to their age, but precisely because of Goya's subject, their relationship to history is not easily reduced to a handful of years, a decade, or a century for that matter. The fact that they continue to speak to our present in so many ways is telling.

As I have already suggested, Goya's series is also one of the earliest important artworks of the modern era to reflect on the quandaries of making and viewing art when terrible brutality is the primary subject. While the *Disasters* have often been compared to the photojournalism of war, Goya's prints are not documentary in the sense that war photography aims to be. The print series shares with much war photography a moral indictment of the violence, but it does not depict what was actually there, in front of Goya's eyes, at some point in time. The images, the captions, and the sequence that we call *The Disasters of War* were all laboriously constructed slowly, after the fact, and Goya repeatedly signals their fabricated, artificial nature in intriguing ways. The experience of viewing and reading the *Disasters* is consequently one in which we are invited to look at the horrors while simultaneously being reminded that we are looking at an image. We see terrible violence, but we are at the same time prompted not to forget that we are looking at a picture.

It seems an odd gesture. Why remind the viewer of art's artifice, of its constructed nature, in a project that aims to exhibit and critique the truth of war's horrors? The answer lies, I think, in the moral sensibility that informs the *Disasters* more generally. As an artist who lived through the war years, Goya would have been acutely aware of the profound difference between actual violence and the representation of violence in an artwork. He also came of age in an era that increasingly understood images as well-crafted illusions, and he used terms like "invention" and "caprice" to characterize his work. While he clearly believed in art's power to convey urgent truths – the *Disasters* are his most eloquent testament to such belief – he also understood, perhaps more clearly than many an artist before him, the limits of pictorial representation when it comes to the subject of war's horrors. For this reason, as we will see, many of his prints play in pointed ways with the distinction between viewing actual violence and viewing violence in an image. In doing so, Goya's *Disasters* are, historically speaking, an early attempt to reflect on the ethical challenges that arise in the making and the viewing of violent images. What does it mean to make such art? What does it mean to view it?

Central to such problems and to Goya's artistry throughout the *Disasters* is the illusion of witnessing. While all pictorial representations create a hypothetical or notional viewer, not all pictures call to us primarily as witnesses. We do not usually say, for example, that we *witness* a still life, a portrait, or a landscape. In the *Disasters*, however, our looking is made to carry the moral weight of witnessing.

Pictorial illusion is, by and large, the illusion of witnessing, and we will often be positioned in ways that raise questions about who we are, or who we believe ourselves to be, when we look at images of violence. At the same time, many of Goya's prints will subtly remind us of the virtual nature of our witnessing. While each image will assign us a viewing place within the scene, we will also be prompted in various ways to remember that we are not actually there, but rather here, on this side of the image, viewing and reading. The fact that we routinely hover between these two ways of looking at images becomes especially charged when the subject is horrific violence, and, as I hope will become clear in what follows, Goya's *Disasters* engage the complexities of our looking in extraordinarily rich and suggestive ways.

The structure of this book closely follows that of the series. It begins with two short essays ("Beginnings" and "Preface"), in which I explore how the front matter to the first edition, reproduced in many subsequent editions, subtly shapes the viewing experience. The book then proceeds systematically through the first forty-seven *Disasters*, and it concludes with a brief Afterword. The goal of organizing the book this way has been to recreate the experience of viewing and reading the series as I comment on it. Although readers can jump to individual images as they see fit, proceeding sequentially will be the best way to understand how the order of the prints contributes to their meaning. I should also add that I have restricted myself to the prints dedicated to wartime atrocities rather than the entire series because it is in these images that Goya most keenly reflects on the relationship between violence, on one hand, and making and viewing images, on the other. The artist's depictions of famine and his allegorical commentaries on the restoration of the Spanish monarchy are equally rich, and I would encourage readers to view them after reading this book in order to appreciate Goya's engagement with these other important themes.

I accompany each print – at times a small group of prints – with a short interpretive essay that combines visual analysis, textual commentary, and observations on the print's position in the sequence in order to highlight and explore the meanings that these three phenomena together generate. Across the essays readers will also note a series of recurring themes: the importance of self-reflection, the complex interplay of thought and feeling within the viewing experience, the dense, conceptual play elicited by the captions, and the way Goya's prints work with the twofold nature of images as both scenes to be witnessed and pictures to be looked at. Each interpretive essay is accompanied by a second, briefer set of notes and comments at the back of the book. Notes are intended to give readers a brief sketch of the critical reception of each print, bibliographic references for further reading, and more detailed discussion of key issues raised by the print in question. They do not aim to be exhaustive. I have intentionally given more weight to Spanish sources in the notes, and I have relied strongly on Spanish bibliographers. This is not only because Spaniards were writing about Goya long before he was discovered by the rest of Europe, but also because Spanish sources have often been sidelined within much of the tradition of English-language commentary on the *Disasters*. For this reason, I have also taken the liberty of translating all citations into English. I have placed the Notes at the back of the book intentionally, in order to privilege the immediacy of the viewing and reading experience for those moving through the series sequentially.

For viewers coming to *The Disasters of War* for the first time, I have tried to provide a useful introduction to the complexity of Goya's prints and the viewing experiences they organize. For those already familiar with the series, I offer, not a radically new take on the print series, but an invitation to look again with fresh eyes. Central to such a revisiting is the idea that moral self-reflection was as important to Goya as the denunciation of the violence he depicted, and that the artist's understanding of images as both worlds to be entered imaginatively and pictures that exist within our own, everyday worlds was an important part of his approach to depicting wartime atrocities. I hope that in the aggregate these analyses persuade viewers to revisit some of the commonplaces about Goya and his artistry in *The Disasters of War*.

A final note regarding language and terminology. When I refer to the *Disasters*, in italics, I mean to designate the print series that Goya created. The word "disasters," without italics, is meant to refer to the calamities represented within the prints. By "image" I mean the pictorial component of each print, while "caption" singles out the verbal component. When I use the word "print" without further distinctions, I mean to evoke both the image and caption together. Beyond these basic distinctions, I have deliberately attempted to avoid excessively specialized terms. *The Disasters of War* were intended for a broad public. Their form as prints that could be mechanically reproduced on large scales speaks to this public vocation, and I have aimed for the language in this book to address a similarly broad readership. More specialized terms and commentary can be found in the Notes. The images reproduced here come from the 1863 first edition. The size of original prints averages 5 ½ by 7 ½ inches, or 14 by 19 centimetres, with captions in script below each image. For the purposes of reproduction here, the prints have been reduced in size. The blank margins around each image have not been reproduced, and captions with modernized spelling appear as chapter headings.

Beginnings

Beginnings are strange creatures. To begin an artwork in pictures and words, as Goya does in *The Disasters of War*, is not only to begin the showing and the telling, but also to decide where things begin and where they might go. Beginnings make real some possibilities and so, by definition, abandon others. In order to begin, other possible beginnings must be put aside. Creative expression has always been informed in important ways by this tension between the opening and closing of possibility. Artists and writers speak to the experience regularly when they refer to the creative process in terms of decisions. The words crossed out on a manuscript or deleted from the computer screen, the brush strokes that were painted over, the studies that preceded a sculpture, the early proofs of an engraving: these phenomena point to the intimate relationship between making, on one hand, and roads not taken, on the other. To begin to make is to dwell in this difficulty.

Practically speaking, however, beginnings tend not to linger on this dimension of the creative act. They are most often too busy with the task of beginning, and they get on with it, as it were, by saying what all beginnings must tacitly say, echoing the old Latin *incipit*: it begins here. In doing so, beginnings draw attention away from their origins within a realm in which they themselves were still one of any number of unrealized possibilities. Beginnings usually entice us to forget that it could indeed have begun elsewhere or otherwise. They make such forgetting easy. "It begins here" tells us there is no need to look elsewhere. More importantly, the statement performs what it says. Beginnings begin things. As we begin things, then, it may be worth asking about the beginnings of *The Disasters of War*.

The question is by no means an easy one. One can always imagine beginnings in more than one way. We might, for example, locate the beginnings of Goya's war images in large-scale historical phenomena (the Enlightenment, the French Revolution, Napoleonic imperialism, or the Peninsular War). Beginnings might also be found in the more specific, Spanish face of that history (the machinations within Spain's royal family, the installation of Joseph Bonaparte on the throne, the popular uprisings, the battles, the famines, the restoration of absolutism).

In a more biographical register, one could look to Goya's life story for possible beginnings (his early years and training as an artist, the various phases of his art making, his position as court painter, his prior printmaking, his experience of the war years). Another approach to the prints' beginnings would focus on their physical making (the years or months in which individual engravings were made, the preparatory drawings, an examination of the various working proofs Goya produced, a piecing together of his early ideas about sequencing the images, the various states of the work before publication). These are all equally compelling and ultimately intertwined places to begin. Scholarly work on the print series has followed many of these paths, and we will be turning to such contexts frequently over the course of this book. For the story of viewing and reading that I will be telling in what follows, however, we will begin literally, with the title page of the first published edition of Goya's print series: "*The Disasters of War*. Collection of eighty plates invented and engraved, with aquatint, by Don Francisco Goya. Published by the Royal Academy of Fine Arts of San Fernando. Madrid. 1863." The page is undoubtedly a beginning of sorts. Although not of Goya's making – it and the title it bears were created by the Royal Academy long after the artist's death – it identifies the work as it is still known today, and it creates a set of expectations, sketching for readers what lies ahead. Front matter like this title page begins to shape our sense making, even when the artist did not produce it. For most Spanish speakers at the mid-century, the word *desastre* would have meant "misfortune, unhappy and lamentable event," a definition to which the 1852 edition of the Spanish Royal Academy's dictionary adds the Latin words *calamitas* and *infortunium*. Still hovering around the concept, however, would have also been the older, etymological understanding of disaster as a kind of un-starring, a disruption of the world's natural order, a catastrophic falling away from the way things ought to be. The title page also specifies that the prints have been invented, a word that at the time immediately denoted making – the way an inventor makes (Lat. *invenire*) – and afterwards, in a second sense, the making-up that has subsequently become associated with fiction and imaginative art (Lat. *fingere*). In addition, this page identifies the specific kind of making involved, which in Goya's case in fact covers a range of techniques, many not named explicitly, including etching, dry point and burin engraving, lavis, and aquatint. Then comes the familiar trio: author, publisher, and date.

Beginnings address the fact that we inevitably form an idea or hypothesis about the road ahead and that this idea, shifting and provisional as it might be, strongly shapes the way we engage the arts. We adjust our expectation according to our conceptions of what it is that we are engaging all the time: news report, poem, text message, sculpture, advertisement, tweet, novel, textbook, etching. How we read and look depends on what we believe ourselves to be taking in. Beginnings know this, and they seek to shape the process in subtle ways. The information conveyed by the title page of *The Disasters of War* establishes a rudimentary interpretive

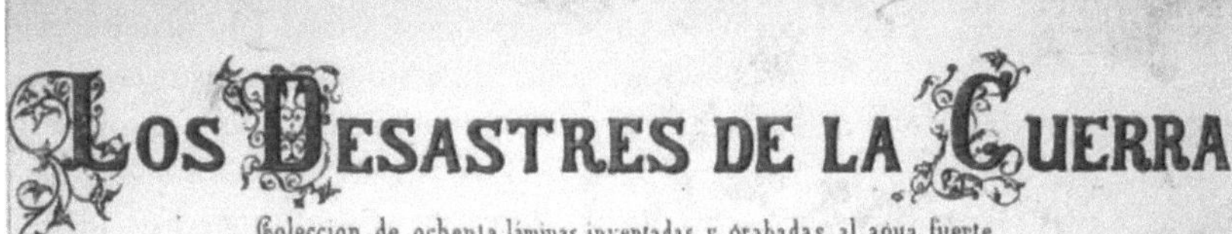
LOS DESASTRES DE LA GUERRA

Coleccion de ochenta láminas inventadas y grabadas al agua fuerte

POR

DON FRANCISCO GOYA.

Publícala la R.l Academia de Nobles Artes de San Fernando.

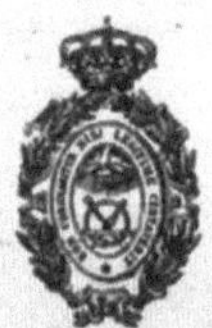

MADRID.

1863.

framework for the series. The page quietly offers early instruction in how to approach the images that will follow. It sets up the prints as representations of something generic, the disasters of war, rather than something historically specific. Goya's prints do of course famously offer semblances of moving through the violence and aftermath of the Napoleonic occupation of Spain (1808–14), and earlier provisional titles point to this dimension of his work. Whoever decided on this title, however – it was most likely a member of the Royal Academy – chose to emphasize the universalizing dimensions of Goya's prints rather than the historical moment that inspired them. The opening words of the series prompt readers to see the historical world that will appear in many of Goya's images as a vehicle through which the artist is also addressing something else, something that inhabits a different order of time and place, a phenomenon that is both ancient and urgently contemporary. The title suggests that Goya's images are something more than historical testimony in the conventional sense of the word. It announces that what we will be encountering is a mode of reflecting on a difficult subject, a form of thinking in images and words about something named *The Disasters of War*.

At the same time, careful attention to this title yields an early warning against believing we might fully know what that something is. As will often be the case with Goya's prints themselves, rather than pinning things down, the opening page sends readers along paths that branch and multiply. The title initially seems to point unambiguously to those disasters that are specific to war, the ones that belong to it, the ones that war is especially adept at unleashing in contrast to other forms of disaster. But the words could also be saying something else: the disasters of war, for example, as opposed to the glories of war, which would have been a far more common nineteenth-century formulation. The title would in this sense name the disastrous face of war, the one that even today most states prefer not to show their citizens. One can also read the title as a reference to the disasters that befall war, the disasters on which war itself, however we think of it, founders; or the title could refer to a subset of events, disasters, positioned as special kinds of occurrences during times of war. In such readings, the concept of war and the concept of disaster qualify each another in intricate ways, even as they stand at a slight distance from one another. In another moment, however, the very distinction between the two concepts seems to collapse. The disasters of war can also mean the disasters *that are* war, as if to underscore that this is what war in fact is, a series of disasters.

In putting these and other meanings into motion, the title complicates any easy understanding of what *The Disasters of War* designates. The various meanings of the title suggest that the subject of the prints that follow may be just that, a *what* that can never be entirely pinned down. We call it war and think we understand, but Goya's is in many ways an elusive subject, and it often unfolds at the limits of moral understanding. He will be after this subject, with words and images, throughout the series, and so will we, as viewers of those images and readers of those words. If beginnings shape things by subtly starting to define the subject of our viewing and reading, this beginning also does so by shaking up conventional certainties. It tells us that Goya's subject is something that words only begin to name, and it cautions us about taking for granted that we know fully what that subject is.

Titles, however, do not just allude to the subject of a work. They also name the work itself, and on this count at least, things seem clearer. What is designated by the title, *The Disasters of War*, is quite simply the published series of prints. Still, there is something intriguing in the fact that the title simultaneously names two different realms: the world created *within* the prints, where we will grapple with understanding the disasters of war, and this other world, the one in which we are viewing images and reading, a world in which *The Disasters of War* is the title of a collection of prints. The phenomenon tells us something important about the experience of engaging semblances of the world. It reminds us that there is a twofold process involved in the activity, a simultaneous "inhabiting" of more than one domain. It draws on our capacity to see and at times to dwell imaginatively within the works we take in without forgetting entirely that we are actually also here, looking at images. Goya understands this dual nature of images intimately. It is central to his artistry, and as we will see he works with it in fascinating ways over the course of *The Disasters of War*.

Preface (1863): Image of an Artist

Following the title page of the first edition is a Preface commissioned by the Royal Academy of Fine Arts of San Fernando, and it too aims to make a claim on our viewing and reading. It consists of a brief series of comments about the work along with a short biography of the artist. The text is somewhat dated, remaining within Spain's nineteenth century in a way that the prints themselves, which continue to speak to the present, do not. For that very reason, however, the Preface offers intriguing insights into the historical context in which *The Disasters of War* first became public. Goya had spent his last years in Bordeaux among Spanish exiles, and he died in the French city in 1828. As most scholars of his work have speculated, his prints on the war and its aftermath probably remained unpublished during the first half-century for political reasons. His highly critical and decidedly anti-patriotic perspective on the Napoleonic conflagration would certainly have been politically unwelcome in both Spain and France during the years immediately following the war. Within the Spanish context this would have been particularly true of the final images of the series, which unflinchingly satirize the reactionary political order that triumphed under the restored monarchy of Ferdinand VII.

The critical thrust of *The Disasters of War*, however, was not limited to the traditionalist monarchic absolutism that followed Napoleon's defeat. With strange foresight, the print series also struck at what would become one of the central myths of the political forms that followed absolute monarchy; that is, the grand myth of the nation. Over the course of the first half of the 1800s, the tale of heroic popular resistance to Napoleonic imperialism had become the very touchstone of modern Spanish nationalism. Reinvigorating age-old notions of Spanish identity, the epic of the people's heroic struggle against foreign invasion was among the most broadly disseminated narratives of national belonging in Spain throughout the 1800s. The Second of May, which commemorated the popular uprising against the French, was Spain's national holiday until 1958. In many regards it was a celebration on par with Bastille Day in France or the Fourth of July in the United States. Goya's prints, by contrast, were unambiguously critical of national myths.

His images and words pointed to forms of violence and suffering that dismantled the rhetoric of heroic patriotism. Against the backdrop of the nineteenth-century cult of the nation, Goya's prints were untimely, uncomfortable forms of demystification. If one imagines for a moment an artist decrying the violence that is celebrated in, say, the US national anthem, one might get a sense of how much of an outlier the Goya of the *Disasters* was within the nationalism of the mid-1800s.

The publishers of the 1863 edition of *The Disasters of War* consequently must have faced something of a conundrum. How to celebrate Goya as a Spanish artist when nationalism was clearly an object of criticism within the print series? Their solution was simple and ingenious. In an astute act of public relations, the Preface to the first edition deftly sidesteps Goya the critic and satirist. The profound analyst of war makes no appearance either. In place of this figure, the Academy delivers a safer, national Goya. Readers are reminded of the artist's renown; they are also assured that Goya holds an honoured place within the national tradition of Spanish painting; and they are informed that he was an utterly unique artist, having "adopted a way of seeing in the arts which nobody possessed before him, and perhaps nobody will follow afterwards."

In effect, Goya is packaged for public consumption as a celebrated artist, a creator with great powers of imagination, and a patriot at that. Fame and artistic merit take centre stage within this story, while the fact that the series is a thoroughgoing denunciation of war remains safely in the wings. We read that that what distinguishes the series is its "novelty in the topics, originality in the characterizations, brilliance in the compositions, valour and self-assurance in the chiaroscuro, decision and even delicacy in the draughtsmanship." Praise similarly extends to Goya's talent as a writer of captions. "The legends on each plate" – readers learn – "are an additional facet of the author's genius … A short phrase, a single word, reveal in their very brevity the fleeting idea that his mind conceived in one moment and his hand represented in little more than another." Novelty, originality, brilliance, imagination, fleeting impressions, spontaneous creation. In this account, Goya is not only a patriot but also a romantic genius whose work the Academy has taken the task of making public out of a sense of duty to the nation, "with the confidence that it will merit a favourable reception by lovers of the Spanish Arts." An impressive feat of image management, the formulation takes Goya out of the political history he lived in order to secure his place within the world of the arts, a parallel world imagined to exist at some remove from the here and now.

When the Preface turns to Goya's biography, a similar process of careful selection is at work. Readers learn of the artist's early tutelage, of his studies in Rome, and of his cartoons for the Royal Tapestry Factory. They encounter the Goya of the religious frescos, the talented portraitist, and the painter of Spain's popular classes. His earlier printmaking is also acknowledged, although its satirical dimensions are not. As the life story winds down, readers additionally learn that Goya himself was a member of the very Academy that is now publishing his prints. The biography closes with two sentences. The first one reads: "He was court painter for King Charles IV from April 1789 on, and he was the first among this group in October 1799." The second, final line of the biography adds: "He died in Bordeaux at eighty-four years of age [he was actually eighty-two], on April 16, 1828." A summary reading of this closing could easily miss the narrative sleight-of-hand. Between the two sentences that wrap up Goya's life are some twenty-nine years that simply fall out of – or, to be more precise, never make it into – the biography. Not by coincidence, they are precisely the years of political upheaval, occupation, and war, the years of a restored, reactionary monarchy, and the years of Goya's later departure from his homeland for Bordeaux. The story that most seems to matter when it comes to *The Disasters of War* is literally left between the lines by the Academy so that Goya can take his place within the history of art as a famous, highly talented patriot.

The reasons for such an omission are not difficult to imagine. By the closing years of the eighteenth century, Goya's association with enlightened reform was well known. Among his acquaintances were some of the more famous thinkers and writers of the Spanish Enlightenment, and many of them – Jovellanos, Iriarte, Moratín – had in fact openly supported the Bonapartist regime in Spain in the belief that it was the most efficient way of achieving reform. While Goya was publicly guarded on the matter during the Napoleonic period, his social ties to Spanish supporters of the new monarchy were by no means a secret. In addition, as was required of all members of the Court, he had sworn an oath of allegiance to Joseph Bonaparte. Whatever his convictions at the outset, however, the war years transformed him. Although he never actively fought the French occupation, Goya was not an overt advocate of the regime either. The violence and suffering of the Peninsular War made it difficult to hold abstract allegiances for long, and there was the very pressing question of how to navigate his personal circumstances as court painter. Goya's activities during the period in fact speak to his practical adaptation to shifting regimes of power. He was neither a patriotic resistance fighter nor an outright collaborationist. He took commissions from the new king, Napoleon's brother Joseph, but when the French were defeated and British troops entered Madrid, he also painted portraits of their general, the future Duke of Wellington.

Goya in fact negotiated his circumstances between 1808 and 1814 sufficiently well enough to be reinstated as a court painter when Ferdinand VII returned to the capital. Royal favour, however, was no longer forthcoming, and as the closing, allegorical images of the *Disasters* themselves reveal, the political distance between monarch and painter could not have been greater. Most of Goya's commissions after Ferdinand's return did not come from the royal house. With the fall of Spain's Liberal Triennium in 1823 it became clear that constitutional liberalism had no future under Ferdinand, and it was at this point that Goya left the country for France, pointing to medical reasons for his travel. Just how motivated by politics that final move was is difficult to say. Many of his acquaintances – the so-called *afrancesados* – had by the 1860s been written out of Spanish history as traitors to the nation, and although Goya's political trajectory had not been identical to theirs, it had in the end converged with them in Bordeaux. What called for careful management as *The Disasters of War* first went to press in 1863 was the fact that Spain's most famous painter of the modern era had left his homeland and died among a circle of *afrancesado* friends.

Like the title page, the Preface aims to condition our viewing and reading, in this case by constructing a very particular image of the artist. Such images often accompany and subtly guide our approach to artworks. If we resist one image, we usually replace it with another. I have just contrasted the Academy's patriotic, romantic Goya, for example, with the image of Goya in Bordeaux. Artist images are in fact interpretive maps, keys to further understanding, and such images are also paradoxically the result of artworks themselves. A Velázquez emerges out of *Las Meninas*, a Cervantes out of *Don Quixote*. The Goya of the Academy's Preface is one thing. The Goya of my commentary on the Preface is another. Whatever our understanding of Goya, however, viewing and reading *The Disasters of War* will involve potentially modifying that understanding. The experience of an artwork inevitably informs our understanding of its maker.

This is so in part because there is something within the activity of reading and looking at pictures that subtly works on us as we take things in. We are porous creatures, and what we let in can change us. What to let in and how to let it in are never trivial questions. They are fundamental to the activities of viewing images and reading. Critical viewing and reading, for example, requires the ability keep our guard up as we take things in, and it is an especially important skill in contemporary culture, where so much of what wants to get in is not necessarily working in our interest. The experience of engaging art, however, also requires the ability to lower the guard, to give oneself over to what one sees or reads with some measure of abandon. The objects and experiences we have traditionally associated with the arts ask this of us, and we miss much of what they have to offer if we do not heed the call.

Serious engagement with art seems to require the ability to shuttle back and forth between this open disposition, on one hand, and critical distance on the other. At times we can give ourselves over so thoroughly that we seem to forget where we are. We say we are lost in a painting, absorbed by a novel or poem, so gripped by a film that we almost lose sight of our surroundings. Even so, we retain some awareness that we are viewing or reading. At other times, however, the knowledge that we are looking at an image can itself become the object of our attention. This is especially true when artists create images of the world that invite us to indulge in their illusions and, at the same time, prompt us to reflect on our own activity as viewers. Goya is among such artists, and as we shall see, one of the things his images do to us repeatedly is to play with our viewing and reading. It is a serious form of play. His work will invite us to inhabit the disasters of war, to imagine for a moment that we are there, but it will also find ways of reminding us once and again that we are also here, looking at a series of prints. The first print is a good example.

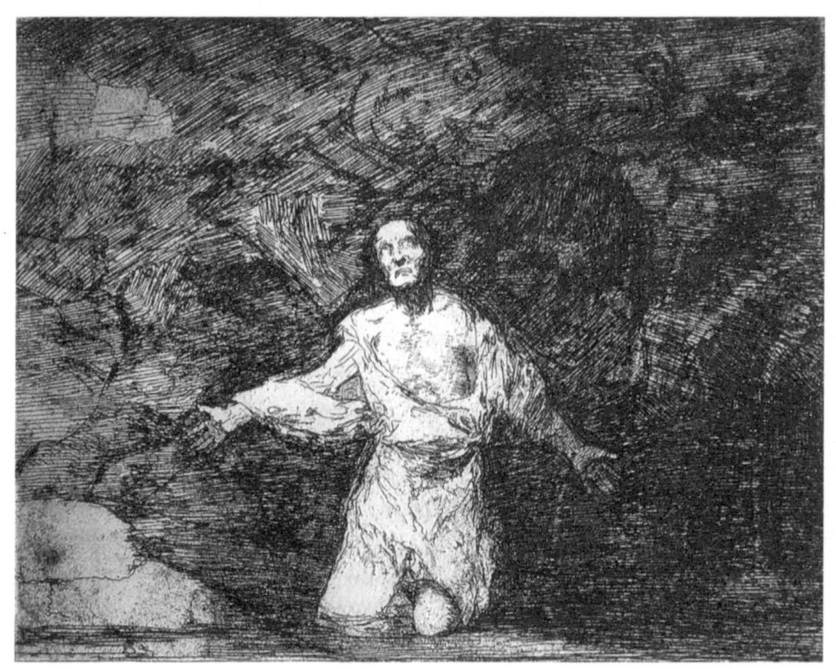

1
Tristes presentimientos de lo que ha de acontecer

A man kneels before us, his arms stretched out to his sides in what appears to be a supplicant's pose. His head tilts slightly, and he looks to the sky with eyes turned upward and to his left. His gaze betrays something verging on fear. His clothes are torn, and his torso is exposed. He is alone, and in darkness. His location is difficult to pinpoint, but there are reasons to believe it is outside, perhaps on a mountainside. One can make out stones to his right, in the foreground with him, and larger, less defined masses, perhaps boulders, off to his right and behind him. What little light there is comes from behind us, to our right, and its source appears to be the place to which the man has turned his gaze, a place that he can see but that we, who are looking at him, cannot. The caption reads "Sad presentiments of what is to come to pass." War's disasters begin with presentiments of their arrival.

Presentiment has a long history of entanglement with conceptions of an order beyond the here and now, a realm in which the future can be gleaned before it begins to take form in the material world as an unfolding present. From the Greek oracles through the prophets of the major religious traditions, foreseeing the future has conventionally been bound up with conceptions of the otherworldly. The verb *to divine* speaks to this proximity. Presentiment, however, is more nebulous than divination. Neither prophetic vision nor the result of revelation, presentiment is a feeling, a bodily sensation. It belongs to the world of the senses, the very world that eighteenth-century science, moral philosophy, literature, and the arts had explored insistently as the flip side of abstract reason. Presentiment is a knowing that comes from feeling. In a modern, secular understanding, it has very much to do with the here and now. It is a form of knowledge that arises from an especially refined sensitivity to the present, a feeling of the present that is so attuned to it – in a way that abstract thinking cannot be – that it begins to detect signs of the future within it.

Goya's print works with both ways of understanding presentiment in this opening image and its caption. The man who in darkness turns his head towards the light clearly echoes a well-known Christian theme, and one can recognize the iconography of martyrdom in the supplicant's pose. To the extent that martyrdom is understood within Catholic theology as a reenactment of the foundational sacrifice of Christ, the image ultimately points, as more than one scholar has noted, to the story of Agony in the Garden. Given the importance of Gethsemane as a paradigmatic scene of grappling with the knowledge of impending suffering and death, it is no surprise that Goya would draw on its symbolism. Religious allusion in the *Disasters*, however, is rarely a straightforward affair. If the image draws on the visual codes of Christian art, it also stages a powerful contrast. The man kneeling in the darkness is not Christ or a Christian martyr, and while viewers might momentarily associate this scene with the biblical story in which Jesus asks God to spare him from his fate if possible, the analogy only goes so far. The parallels are quickly undone by the knowledge that for this man "what is to come to pass" is not a redemptive sacrifice in accordance to a divine plan. What awaits him is to experience the disasters of war, events in which Goya will find nothing redemptive. Nowhere in the images that follow will Goya point to the divinity that gives the suffering in Gethsemane its meaning. This is a strange and modern Gethsemane, a scene of impending suffering without the promise of redemption.

At the same time, if we recall the years leading up to the war in Spain, the image also points to the experience of historical presentiment. The Napoleonic Wars had swept across most of Europe long before Spain became one of its theatres, and it was the first war to become a "media event" within the growing world of print journalism. With Napoleon at the centre of what at the time seemed an invincible modern empire, the possibility of warfare was an ever-present danger for most European powers. Spanish diplomacy took place under increasing French pressure in the years before the Peninsular War, and French troops entered and began to occupy Spain under the pretence of supporting an earlier invasion of Portugal. When open conflict finally erupted in 1808, one could easily see what had led to it. In this sense the presentiments evoked by the man in this first print point to the historical experience of feeling that war, with everything it means, is on the way. The logic of war is often at work long before it shows its face. Events lead up to it, and those interested in waging it almost always dress it in the guise of inevitability. War's coming is not difficult to detect if one is attuned to the signs, and although human beings ultimately decide to make war, its advent can feel like fate in the classical sense. It can present itself as an impersonal force that has little to do with what you, or I, or this man surrounded by darkness might want. "What is to come to pass," which can also be translated as "what *must* come to pass," conveys this sense of the unavoidable.

The sad presentiments, however, do not simply name what the man with whom we might momentarily identify is feeling. One of the things captions traditionally also do is to identify the subject of an artwork, much like a title. "Sad presentiments of what has to come to pass" is, among other things, the name of the image we have before us. If we step outside its illusion – the one in which there is a man on a Gethsemane-like mountainside, in darkness – the caption names the representation of sad presentiments themselves. Within this framework, the man is not experiencing presentiments; he and the other elements of the image *are* the presentiments. He is allegorical and the composition in its entirety is an attempt to make visible something – presentiments – that technically speaking cannot be seen. The white figure in the foreground against an almost entirely black background becomes a visual analogue of presentiment, a way of representing in visual terms the experience of feeling the future from within a present in which future time is almost entirely opaque. The relatively undefined shapes within the background do something similar. Like the future we might begin to feel before it has arrived, these shapes are difficult to make out. Barely visible on the right half of the print, they show more of themselves on the left, but even there, it is like feeling one's way in the darkness, which is to say that it is like presentiment.

The image also exemplifies presentiment in a very different sense. This is the first of a series of prints, and within this context the caption tells us that this first image is a visual presentiment of subsequent images. "What is to come to pass" now refers quite literally to the *prints* that will follow this one. The man with tattered clothes, an exposed body, and an incipient expression of suffering on his face is, visually speaking, a presentiment of things to come. *The Disasters of War* will be littered with images of bodies, clothed and unclothed, and with the depiction of myriad forms of suffering. This image is the first glimpse of others that are on their way. What was a vague sense of the future for the man is, for us in the present, a history that has passed, and unlike the man, we know that this is the first image within a series and that others await. The caption plays with the difference between the man's world and ours, and it speaks to both.

In retrospect it becomes clear that the caption has worked and reworked our viewing experience from various angles. The "sad presentiments" have named multiple facets of the image: the quasi-Christian Agony in the Garden, the feeling that war is on its way, the experience of vaguely making things out within the image, and the knowledge as readers of *The Disasters of War* that this image is the first in a sequence. The same is true of "what is to come to pass." It names the knowledge of death's coming exemplified by biblical narrative, the seemingly unstoppable historical forces that lead to war, and the image sequence itself, which "is to come to pass" for us as readers. The richness of the print is linked to the caption's many possible references and the way they take us through numerous dimensions of the image. Without the caption we would have a very different and by comparison conceptually impoverished first image. Similarly, a different caption – one, for example, that did not speak on so many levels – would alter the experience of looking at the print entirely. This is the sense in which Goya's artistry in *The Disasters of War* is both verbal and graphic, and, as the Academy noted when the series first went to press, he is a master of captioning.

Goya understands that words coupled with images can create effects that neither medium can achieve by itself, and he will often deliver captions that call attention to and then probe the complexities of the images he has made. One of his strategies, already on display in this first image, consists in writing captions that speak *within* the illusion they address while simultaneously speaking *to* the image as an image. Goya depicts presentiment within the image, and at the same time the image is itself a visual presentiment of things to come. We will return to this technique more than once as we move through the series, and the significance of this double voicing will grow in proportion to the disasters we take in.

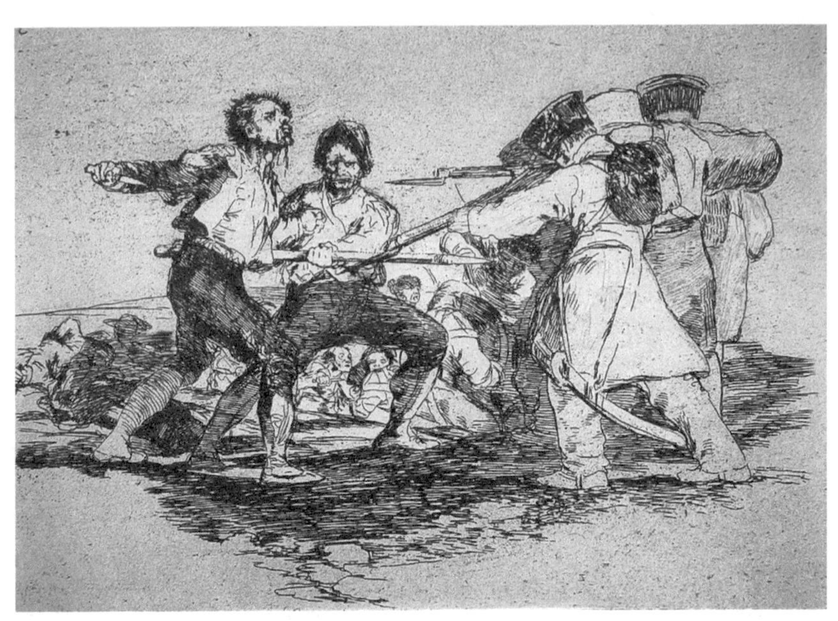

2
Con razón o sin ella

The time of presentiments is over, and the feared future has arrived, at close range. We are only a few feet away from people who are killing each other. On the right, uniformed imperial soldiers hold a firing line that has become slightly irregular in the mêlée. Their backs are turned to us, we cannot see their faces, and it is difficult to know their number. There are at least four of them in the section of the line we can see. The firing line, however, runs perpendicular to our plane of sight, and it could extend beyond what we see, as far back, for example, as the crowd in the background, further downhill, which is also fighting. What is happening within the multitude is difficult to discern, but closer to us the details are painfully clear. On the left, two Spanish partisans, whose faces we do see, attempt to stand their ground. There is little doubt about who has the upper hand. The Spaniards are not soldiers, and they have no rifles. One holds a knife as blood gushes from his face. The other awkwardly wields a crude spiked stick. Further to the left and slightly behind the man with the knife a body has already fallen. Poorly armed and unorganized, the partisans are not likely to last long. We are probably looking at their last moments.

Goya's composition makes literal the idea of two opposing forces at battle: the bilateral symmetry of the image, with a centre axis that runs through most of the weapons in the foreground, accentuates the terms of the conflict, while the crowd in the background gestures to more inchoate forms of violence. At the same time, the pitting of disciplined professional soldiers against poorly armed civilians is rich with symbolism. Goya often represents French firing lines in ways that highlight the impersonal, logically organized, repetitive, and almost machine-like quality of such formations. (The tendency would be developed masterfully in his most famous painting of the war, *Executions of the Third of May, 1808*.) Napoleon's armies had become famous for revolutionizing warfare. Enlightened reason had been brought to bear on questions of logistics, organization, strategy, and tactics in order to found what most historians consider a distinctively modern science of warfare. There is something coldly efficient and even technological in this firing line. Formations are, after all, technologies of war. In contrast, the Spaniards appear to belong to a more primitive, agrarian world, a world of unmechanized, rural modes of violence.

Anonymous moderns are dispatching more primitive natives, and this way of depicting imperial violence is intertwined with the history of the Napoleonic Wars themselves. For France, the wars were struggles of and for an emergent modern world. Bonaparte's empire was propelled, symbolically at least, by the idea of defending and expanding the legal, political, and social order that had begun to take shape in the wake of the French Revolution. Like later modernizing empires, Napoleonic France framed its conquests as wars of emancipation. The rationale for invading its neighbour to the south was, nominally, to liberate a purportedly backward Spanish people from the shackles of their *ancien régime*. Elsewhere in Europe, the Grande Armée had from time to time been greeted as an army of liberation, and Napoleon expected something similar in Spain. To his surprise, however, Spaniards for the most part did not look upon the armies that moved into their country as instruments of emancipation. Across the Spanish political spectrum, the majority of the population instead came to see them as forces of occupation and dominion.

Broadly shared national resistance to foreign occupation in turn gave birth to a new, particularly modern form of armed conflict. While armies would continue to battle it out in the traditional sense, what was distinctive in Spain was the important role of guerrilla warfare, the ad hoc militarization of a hostile native population against the occupier. In the face of a superior, more modern army, the Spanish populace coupled traditional forms of fighting with a new unconventional form of engagement. They waged a war of attrition, quickly coming together to attack when the opportunity presented itself, and just as quickly disbanding into civilian invisibility as required. The word "guerrilla" literally meant "small war." It designated the loosely organized bands of partisans against the French, and its entry into the modern European lexicon dates from these years. Guerrilla warfare, however, also implied an important shift of perspective for the occupying army. All civilians became potential enemy combatants, and they were treated accordingly. Goya locates the violence of most of *The Disasters of War* within this new form of warfare, which blurs the distinction between civilian and soldier. It is the historical frame of reference for this image of poorly armed civilians who are about to be finished off by professional soldiers.

The caption, which explores the meaning of what is happening in the scene, literally reads, "With reason or without it." The rich ambiguity of the original version, however, is difficult to convey in English. In Spanish and the Romance languages more generally, an extraordinarily wide-ranging number of idiomatic expressions involve the word "reason," and Goya's caption plays with them. "To have or not to have reason" is the way one expresses being right or wrong, for example. Reason can also be involved in expressions of understanding, where acting "with reason" means acting comprehensibly. Idioms constructed with the word also address questions of justice and justification: to do something "with or without reason" can mean to act justly or unjustly. "To give the reason" of a thing means to explain it. "To give somebody else reason" means to agree with them, to acknowledge that they are right. "The reason of state" refers to law and government. Then there is the mental faculty of reason, whose presence or absence conventionally governs the distinction between the sane and insane. This is a small sampling of the possibilities Goya evokes by writing a caption that withholds the additional linguistic contexts that would restrict its meaning in Spanish. The caption makes the meanings proliferate, and to approximate the game Goya is playing, we need to imagine an ambiguous, short caption that says many things at once: "right or wrong," "rational or not," "just or unjust," "with cause or without," "legal or illegal," "understandable or not," "sane or insane."

Across this wide range of possibilities, however, the caption does make one thing clear. The with-or-without-it formula underscores that what we see in the image has little to do with the words, concepts, and meanings we might supply. What the men are doing in fact undoes these very categories. The violence renders terms like reason, sanity, justification, and cause meaningless. Their presence or absence does not matter. The killing is happening anyway. This notion acquires an additional, ironic edge if we combine it with the knowledge that, as we have just seen, Napoleonic imperialism justified itself precisely in the name of a new regime of reason, politics, and law. Reason, which was to have set men free, has become an instrument of imperial violence. Professional soldiers are killing poorly armed civilians, and they are doing so in the name of liberty, equality, and fraternity. In short, the print points to the self-cancelling effect of violence in the name of reason; the killing, the caption suggests, discredits whatever justification might be brought to it.

Powerful as all of this is however, it seems to remain within an indictment of what *the soldiers* are doing. The image clearly elicits sympathy for the Spanish partisans. We see their faces and their suffering, not those of the machine-like French soldiers who are about to mow them down. Goya's prints were originally aimed at a Spanish public for whom sympathy for fellow countrymen would have been second nature. Within the national narrative of the conflict, the French were unambiguously the enemy. They had invaded and occupied the country, deposed the Spanish monarchy, and set up their own regime under Napoleon's brother Joseph. The Preface to the first edition voices the common understanding of the war as an "unjust foreign invasion, which sought to humiliate." If Goya had been the patriot the Preface made him out to be, this image would be in line with such sentiments, and its critique of the violence would be informed by his own national bias. The image would be one more example of the familiar story that all political communities tell themselves, the tale in which a foreign *they* is barbaric or especially cruel, while the domestic *we* – usually understood as an innocent victim – remains above scrutiny. Goya is indulging this sentiment, to be sure, but it is not, as one might imagine, to reinforce us-and-them narratives of belonging. The print prompts viewers to abhor what the soldiers are doing, and Goya makes sure that we see that these are *French* soldiers killing poorly armed *Spanish* civilians. He does this, however, because he knows that we are looking at images, and he knows that at some point we will turn the page.

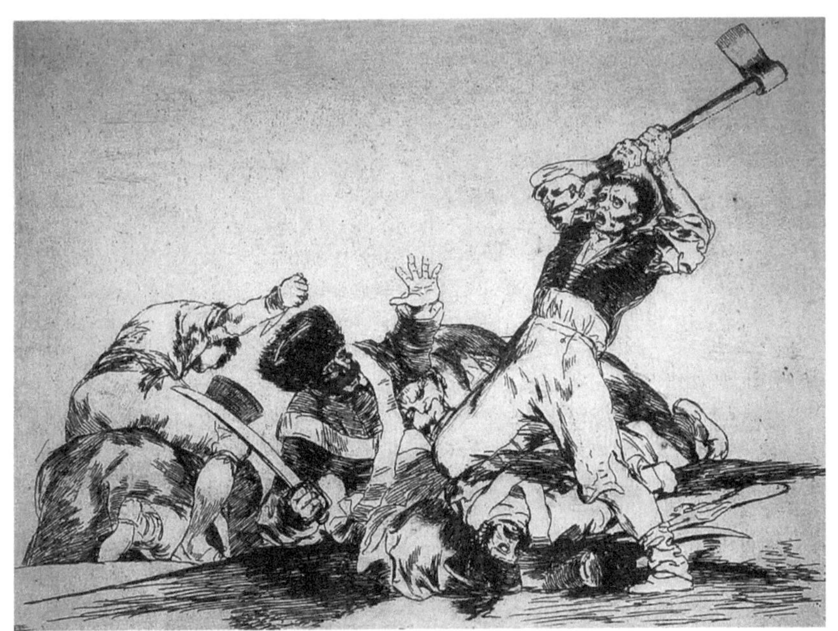

3
Lo mismo

When we do, everything seems to have has changed. On the right, precisely where the French firing line was in the previous image, a Spanish partisan now stands, straddling a dead, uniformed body. He has taken a back swing with an enormous axe, and we see him just as he about to bring it down on a soldier with the full force of his upper body. In his face, a hollow, distant, even dazed expression, with gaping mouth, suggests little or no feeling, as if he is elsewhere, gone in the moral sense. The soldier who will receive the blow has fallen. Turned towards the man with the axe, he sees what is coming, and his left hand, which Goya has placed at the very centre of the image, is extended in a desperate defensive gesture, a gesture that is perhaps also a last plea. To the left of this soldier and slightly further back, a second partisan rides on top of another soldier who appears to be trying to crawl away. The partisan wields a knife that he holds high and, like the man with the axe, he is about to plunge it into his opponent. Neither soldier has long to live. The strong diagonal line that Goya has used to organize the composition – from upper right to bottom left – conveys both the movement of the blows to come and the superior position of each partisan above his respective foe. The caption to this image, in which the tables have turned so drastically, reads: "The same thing." Goya allowed and even fed Spanish national sentiment in the previous image, but it was a set-up, a way of making the dismantling of the national "we" here all the more forceful.

Again, Goya's caption plays with its readers. In this case, the game involves telling us that we are looking at "the same thing" while showing us something patently different. Not only is the image obviously not the same, in the sense that we are now looking at a different print, but within the violent world it depicts, things have also changed drastically. Spanish partisans were dying in the previous print. Now they are killing. We would consequently have to conclude that the caption proposes a general equivalence rather than a literal sameness. "The same thing" conveys the idea that although the two images look different, they in fact depict the same phenomenon, and what is obviously the same in this regard is the killing and the dying. In order for us to read both images as depictions of the same thing, however, another shift must also take place: the markers of the difference that defines the two sides of the conflict, the very markers that sustained a nationalist reading in the previous image, need to fall away. We still see French imperial uniforms, and we still recognize Spanish partisans, but the caption tells us that it makes no difference. As a result, there can no longer be an easy identification with one side or the other. A national *we* would have to acknowledge that in the killing, *we* and *they* are the same.

The meaning of Goya's caption, however, does not stop there. "The same thing" does not simply suggest that the two images are equivalents, or that both sides of the conflagration are equally violent. "The same thing" also says something like the Latin *ibidem* or the colloquial English *ditto*. It refers not only to the previous image but also to its caption, meaning that we are to carry over "With reason or without it," and everything it implies, to this image as well. Even if a national "we" were to read the second image as saying something like "they kill, we kill, it's all the same," the repetition of the caption makes clear that it is not just in the killing that the two sides are the same. It asserts that Spanish killing is equally absent of any reason, justification, or cause. Defence of the nation against foreign occupation, for example, would simply be one more reason and would not justify or explain what is happening in the image. If we recall the strength of nineteenth-century nationalism and in addition consider the fact that Spain's "War of Independence" against Napoleonic France was the very touchstone of Spanish national sentiment throughout the 1800s, we might begin to grasp how radical Goya's gesture in these two prints is. Together they underscore that whatever reasons either side might offer to justify things, those reasons become emptied of any meaning in the face of the disasters they have helped to unleash. It is an extraordinarily powerful indictment of bellicose nationalism.

Through the sequence Goya makes a strong moral claim. In effect, he argues that *no justification* can legitimate the violence he depicts. At the same time, the caption points towards a more philosophical acknowledgment that something within the violence itself exceeds explanation. History will only take us so far. Despite the markers that point to the general historical context of the Napoleonic invasion, *The Disasters of War* are not the equivalent of historical snapshots. Conventional historical approaches to the prints can often miss this facet of Goya's work. The two regimes of justification that Goya critiques in this sequence, for example, belong to orders of time that extend well beyond the Napoleonic Wars. On one side, universalizing, cosmopolitan, secular ideals. On the other, the claims of national, religious, or ethnic identity. The opposition has informed numerous conflicts throughout the modern era, within states and between them, and one can recognize the pattern across the globe today. Insofar as the French Revolution and the Napoleonic Wars were, for most historians, bloody inaugurations of Europe's modern era as such, it should come as no surprise that Goya's critique continues to have a contemporary resonance. The disasters with which he grapples take place at the threshold of a modern political world to which we continue to belong in fundamental ways.

In addition, while one can situate war's disasters within historical time, they also unfold within a cyclical time of recurrence. We find them throughout the record of human existence, and as the news on any given day confirms, they are happening now. They are always disturbingly new and at the same time the repetition of an age-old phenomenon. Perhaps for this reason, troubling as Goya's images may be, most viewers find something deeply familiar within them as well. While we rarely dwell on it, recognition often accompanies our other responses to the *Disasters*. Recognition that this is what human beings can do to one another, recognition that they have done so throughout history, and recognition that somewhere they are doing it today. Goya's critique of the rationalizations that typically accompany war dismantles the respective agendas of Napoleonic imperialism and Spanish nationalism, but its scope extends beyond this historical context to something more fundamental: the *we* and *they* of political life as such and the justifications that political communities of every kind construct in order to legitimate or otherwise excuse the disasters they inflict on one another.

The Disasters of War also quite literally belong to our time in a subtler way that it will be important to recall as we proceed. To put it plainly, when we take in an image, the past momentarily becomes part of our present. Reading and looking at images happen in the unfolding of present time. We engage objects made years or centuries ago, and they become experiences that take place in the here and now of our experience. I am writing these lines on a foggy April afternoon in Northern California, some months or years before the image of my writing on an afternoon becomes, for a moment, part of your present as you read these lines. In a similar way, to take in Goya's prints is to bring his images of the disasters of war out of the historical moment of their making and into the present of our viewing and reading. Goya constructs many of his images as virtual present moments. The prints invite viewers to enter them as *something that is happening*: a man in tattered clothes is kneeling in the darkness, a firing line of soldiers is killing Spanish partisans, civilian combatants are dispatching French soldiers with crude weaponry.

Much of the urgency of Goya's work comes from this illusion of viewing moments as if they were in the present, and the suggestion of moving through time as we progress from one image to the next depends on the conceit. Turning from print to print aims to mimic the experience of time as a succession of present moments. Such movement also underscores how important sequencing can be to the artistry of *The Disasters of War*. Meaning is contextual, and sequence signifies. This dimension of Goya's art can vanish when individual prints are excerpted from the series or discussed without reference to what comes before and after them. Sequencing generates important layers of meaning. To move from the first print to the second is to experience a transition from the time of presentiments to the time of the disasters proper. To turn from the second to the third is to entertain momentarily a Spanish nationalist reading and then see it expressly dismantled. No single print conveys any of this by itself. The experience is produced by the sequence, or more precisely, by our viewing and reading the images in succession. Goya's prints often exploit this expressive potential of sequence in order to orchestrate particularly powerful experiences. Sequencing allows Goya to communicate complex ideas across groups of images. Individual prints can turn out to be the first moment within more lengthy expressions, and a thought or theme will often traverse two or more images that are linked to one another through the captions. At other times, to turn the page feels more like starting a new sentence.

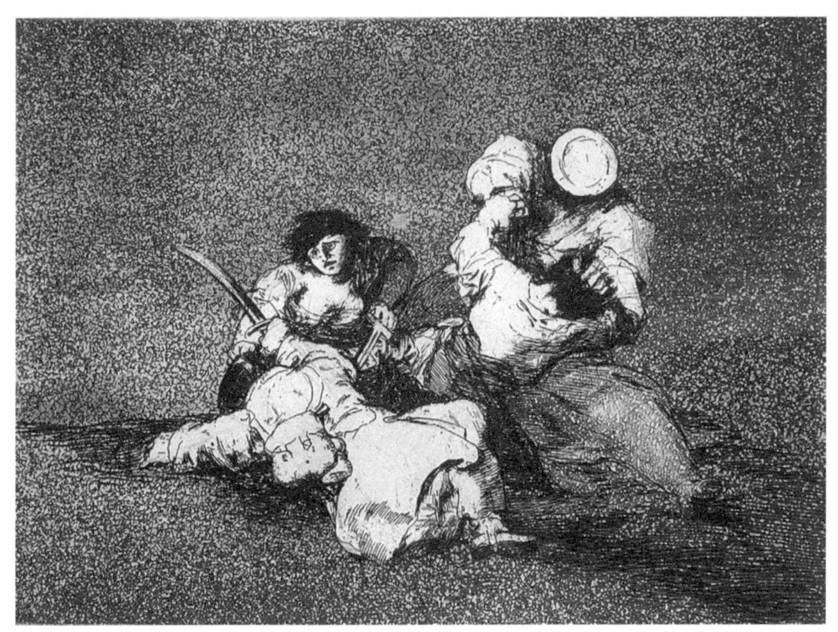

4
Las mujeres dan valor

From the critique of war's rationalizations, we turn to two women struggling against imperial soldiers. On the right, one of them grapples hand-to-hand with a man who has her by the hair. Their arms are locked, her back is to us, and he looms over her. His head tilts down, and we see only the top of his uniform hat. The suggestion of another woman, presumably dead, angles out to the right from behind him. To the left of this pair, another woman fights against a second soldier. He has slumped towards her on the ground, extending his sword in her direction as he dies. She has found her mark first, and her sabre angles down and into the soldier's torso. Each pair in the image inverts the other. On the right the advantage seems to go to the soldier, and the woman is falling before him. On left the woman has the upper hand, and it is the soldier who falls in front of her. In contrast to the previous two images, however, the outcome of the fighting here remains unclear. Instead of signalling an impending fate for one side or the other, the image underscores the struggle itself.

Few details aside from those pertaining to the fighting vie for visual attention. There is the suggestion of a ground, which slopes down from left to right, but the rest of the image is awash in a blur of grainy darkness which envelopes the lighter-toned combatants. Throughout *The Disasters of War* attention to place will often be minimal. The details of a recognizable place are not the priority. As we have already seen, there is something decidedly out of place and out of time about Goya's subject. When and where these women are matters very little in comparison to what is happening, and the relatively abstract space they inhabit conveys the idea. In addition, such space reminds readers, who might be caught up in the illusion of seeing women struggling against soldiers, that they are looking at an image. Goya will often set naturalistic figures against minimally naturalistic or overtly abstract backgrounds. It is one of the many ways he plays with the twofold nature of our viewing, inviting us to see men and women struggling while reminding us at the same time that we are within the space and time of an image. Placing these women in a carefully rendered, realistic space governed by traditional notions of perspective would produce an entirely different and perhaps less powerful effect.

Given the preceding images and captions, which are so thoroughly critical of the attempt to rationalize war's disasters, one might expect similar commentary here. This image does after all depict more of "the same thing," which is to say violence "with or without reason." The caption, however, appears to take us in a radically different, even diametrically opposed direction. It reads, "The women give courage," or more generically, "Women give courage." Goya's critique of war's senselessness appears to yield here to rallying around courageous women combatants. Images of courageous woman have long been a mainstay of wartime propaganda, and they accompanied the Peninsular War on both sides of the conflict. Typically, such images aim to mobilize viewers by trading on traditional assumptions about gender. For women, such images are a call to rise above their everyday roles as the supposedly weaker, peaceful, nurturing sex, and the convention prompts men to action by threatening gender shame. If women can fight and die, then men, the putatively stronger, more courageous sex, have no excuse. The fighting woman is in this regard a powerful symbol that exploits traditional gender stereotypes, and it appears to be a strange departure from the critical framework established in the opening sequence of the series.

Viewers of the *Disasters* consequently confront a fundamental interpretive question early in the sequence. Is Goya's position on war morally consistent, or does he decry the horrors of war in one moment only to celebrate patriotic heroism in the next? Scholars of his work have not always been of one mind on the matter. In this print and several that follow, however, I hope to persuade readers that Goya does not adopt an inconsistent moral position on the violence he depicts. Things are not always as they initially seem, and as a consummate satirist, Goya is particularly attuned to the power of irony. While he evokes the tradition of the courageous woman in this print, for example, he also alters its conventional meanings in fundamental ways. We need only look at the women once more. There is nothing particularly heroic or exceptional in their postures or demeanours. The woman on the right appears about to be overcome, and the expression on the face of the woman on the left, the only face Goya allows us to see, is hardly heroic in any conventional sense of the word. There is sadness in her eyes, something bordering on melancholy. Viewers steeped in religious iconography might even find an ironic echo of the Pietà in this distraught woman with a slumped male body before her. Sword still in hand, however, she makes a rather strange, grieving Madonna.

Those familiar with Goya's Black Paintings may also recognize in her face an expression much like the one the artist would later give another, biblical female combatant in his *Judith and Holofernes*. Whatever her symbolic status, this is not the face of heroic determination we might expect from a more traditional image of feminine courage. If there is courage here, it is courage without heroic grandeur. The women are fighting for their lives. There is nothing more than the struggle itself, and we already know from the preceding prints that on a grander scale the fighting is senseless, devoid of reason or justification. What initially seemed a rehearsal of the convention of feminine courage turns out to be an ironic, critical commentary after all, a subtle dismantling of that very convention. This – the print conveys – is what struggling women actually look like. Significantly, neither the image nor the caption communicates this critique by itself. It emerges from the gap between what the caption says and what we in fact see, a gap that takes place in the experience of trying to put the two together as we read.

Goya has in addition crafted an intriguingly open-ended caption. It stipulates that the women *give* courage, but it does not signal *to whom* such courage is given. Within the world depicted, the words would potentially describe anybody who was there, anyone who saw these women struggling and was moved to courage. In this sense the print points to what wartime combatants have repeatedly confessed: that it is not the greater political cause that prompts people to rise to the moment of battle. What is called courage is often the simple, largely unconscious response of seeing that people with whom one shares deep bonds are in peril. You are there, you see the women struggling, and you are moved to courage. Like the fighting that prompts it, courage happens with or without reason. An immediate, urgent response to the moment of war's disasters, it can eclipse fear and the desire for self-preservation. It is an almost instinctive reaction to others in a pressing moment of danger.

If we were there, the caption suggests, we would be moved to courage. And yet, Goya's caption also makes room for a group of viewers who could not be more distant from that time, its demands, and its dangers. The unspecified *to whom* of the women's courage giving includes us, here, looking at a print that represents women fighting. Within the world depicted, the caption would not be ironic and we ourselves might be moved to courage. Instead, while we may have momentarily engaged the fantasy of being there, we know ourselves to be on this side of the illusion, contemplating a print that scoffs gently at the conventions of representing feminine fighting in heroic terms. The caption speaks within the world represented and to us as viewers of images. Its irony trades on the difference between imaginatively being there and being here, looking at a print.

A similar game is under way when it comes to pinning down the imagined speaker of these words. Who "says" this caption? The simplest answer is Goya himself, but the artist often adopts voices that are not entirely his own. While he can write in the conventional voice of an artist labelling his image, in many prints he also plays with other voices. One can imagine men saying "The women give courage" on the field of battle, near the struggle that has been depicted. Fellow combatants of any gender might say this to one another to keep their spirits high. Once again, however, if we leave the illusion and consider the image against the historical backdrop of similar images, the caption echoes what wartime propagandists have routinely made of representations of fighting women. It becomes the quotation of a cliché. We say the words to ourselves as we read the caption, but only to find an image that is at odds with it. The fact that the print would fail if judged as a piece of wartime propaganda is telling. If heard on the field of battle the words might be earnest, but here, as we contemplate an image that does not in fact instil courage, the irony becomes apparent, especially in the wake of what we have already seen. Whether considered in terms of imagined speakers or imagined viewers, the caption plays with the levels of our viewing and reading, and there is an additional wrinkle. The words, it turns out, have been the first half of a compound sentence that does not finish until we turn the page.

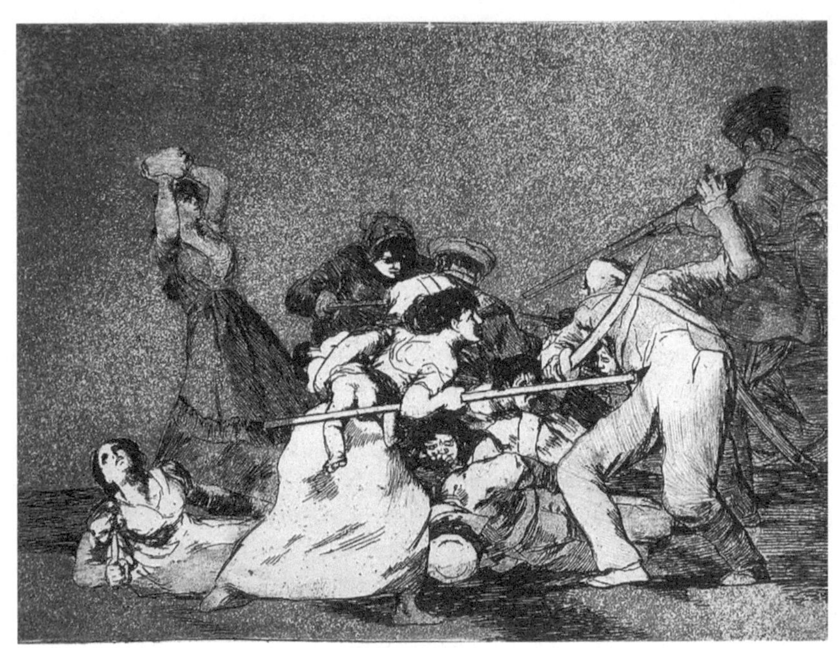

5
Y son fieras

"The women give courage," "and" – we now read – "they are wild beasts." The fighting women have multiplied from two to four. In the foreground, with her head at the centre of the image, a barefooted woman holds an infant over her left hip as she lunges at a soldier with the lance she wields in her right arm. She has caught her opponent at the waist, and the soldier falls from us dramatically with knees bent and head thrown back, a body in the process of becoming lifeless. To the left and behind the fighting mother, a second woman has fallen, clenching a dagger. As she agonizes, she looks skyward with what seems like determined resignation. Behind her, a third woman has lifted a boulder above her head with both hands, and she is about to hurl it at the remaining soldiers, who occupy the right side of the image. In the background, just left of centre, a fourth woman stabs at another soldier with her sword. Between these women and a sole, remaining soldier who stands to the far right, aiming his musket in their direction, the bodies of imperial troops have begun to form a pile. The tide of battle appears to favour the women.

They have been rendered naturalistically, but it quickly becomes apparent that several of the women are also well-known icons: the ferociously protective mother, the dying martyr, the Amazon-like woman of strength. In some cases, symbolism even overrides the demands of pictorial naturalism. The fighting mother is compelling, for example, but not especially realistic. With infant in one arm and lance in the other, her semblance stretches credibility, but what Goya sacrifices on this front he gains in terms of overall impact. The shorthand of infant and lance visually joins motherhood and killing into a powerful synthesis, and the angle of the infant's body and the falling soldier echo one another in an eerie juxtaposition of young life and the moment of death. Other figures follow a similar pattern. The woman with the dagger is not just one more woman dying; her martyr's pose signals sacrifice and firmness of commitment to the end. The woman with the boulder also seems to exceed a merely realistic understanding; what she is doing connotes physical power. The least obviously symbolic of the four is the woman with the sword, who leans into her victim with an intimacy reminiscent of her counterpart in the previous image. Still, in the aggregate there is something strongly iconic about these women. We might initially indulge the illusion of real women fighting soldiers, but in the next moment we would have to recognize that we are also looking at feminine archetypes.

In fact, this image seems to convey precisely the larger-than-life, heroic quality that was so strangely absent from the previous one. The caption, however, makes clear that Goya is continuing to play with our viewing. In the preceding print, the non-heroic appearance of the women was at odds with the courage evoked by the caption. Here, the visual codes with which the women are depicted do indeed signal feminine courage, but now the caption undercuts the heroic archetypes. These seemingly courageous women are "wild beasts," we are told, and the reference to animals is not arbitrary. While it echoes common expressions that identify violent or otherwise uncivil behaviour – from the colloquial "you are an animal!" to the more erudite tradition of *homo homini lupus est* – it also reworks the conventional meaning of courage in fascinating ways.

For much of its history, courage was conceived as a distinctively human capacity. It was one of the four cardinal virtues within Roman Catholicism (Lat. *fortitudo*), and it was commonly understood as strength of will and resolve in the face of difficulty and danger. In its classic formulations, courage was imagined as a higher, human faculty that could tame baser, animal instincts. Goya's caption turns such conceptions on their head, signalling that the violence depicted here belongs to a primal, instinctive, animal world. It has little to do with the higher faculties. It is more immediate, even visceral.

The caption also retroactively alters the meaning of the previous print. Whatever our understanding of the courage-giving women in the preceding image, such understanding must now be coupled with the assertion that they too are wild animals. As was the case in the transition from Print 2 to Print 3, what is set up in one print is dismantled or altered radically in the next. The demystification of courageous heroism in "The women give courage" now becomes more pointed. What we call courage, the sequence implies, is actually instinctual, animalistic violence. In fact, an alternate translation of the caption is "And they are feral." The original Spanish, *fieras*, can be read as either a plural noun (wild animals) or as a plural feminine adjective (wild, feral, fierce).

This association with the animal world is additionally emphasized by prevailing conceptions of gender that at the time imagined the feminine as natural, instinctive, embodied, and animal-like, in contrast to masculine reason. Goya's demystification draws on these misogynistic conventions. A man with infant in tow, for example, would not convey animal instinct in quite the way Goya's fighting mother does, precisely because of the conventional linking of women, instinctive parental protection, and the animal world. In one interpretation of Prints 4 and 5, courageous women have been revealed to be, not the proxy men they seemed to be, but animals after all. The broader message conveyed here, however, concerns the effects of the violence, which makes the distinction between the human and the animal senseless. In doing so, this sequence echoes the earlier moments in Prints 3 and 4 in which the distinction between reason and unreason crumbled in the face of the killing and the dying. War's disasters, Goya signals, are events that undo the humanist pieties that would have us believe ourselves – men or women – to be fundamentally reasonable creatures who live at some remove from the animal world.

The prominent role of gender within the world of the *Disasters* comes to the fore early within the series. Much as it still is in many parts of the world today, the nineteenth-century battlefield was conventionally imagined as a masculine sphere of conflict, with women typically cast either in secondary, supporting roles or as exceptional feminine heroes. The reality of women's involvement in wartime violence, however, has always been more complex than the way it has subsequently been imagined and represented. The participation of women, particularly working-class women, in the Spanish struggle against Napoleonic occupation has been well documented, and Goya makes visible the complexities of their involvement in war's disasters. Over one-third of the prints include women, as both victims and perpetrators of violence, and, as is the case here, women are often the primary subjects. In addition, as we will see in subsequent prints, Goya's work will often reveal the deeply gendered nature of warfare itself. His prints highlight the fact that men and women are swept into war in different ways and that the bodily consequences of the violence we call war vary accordingly.

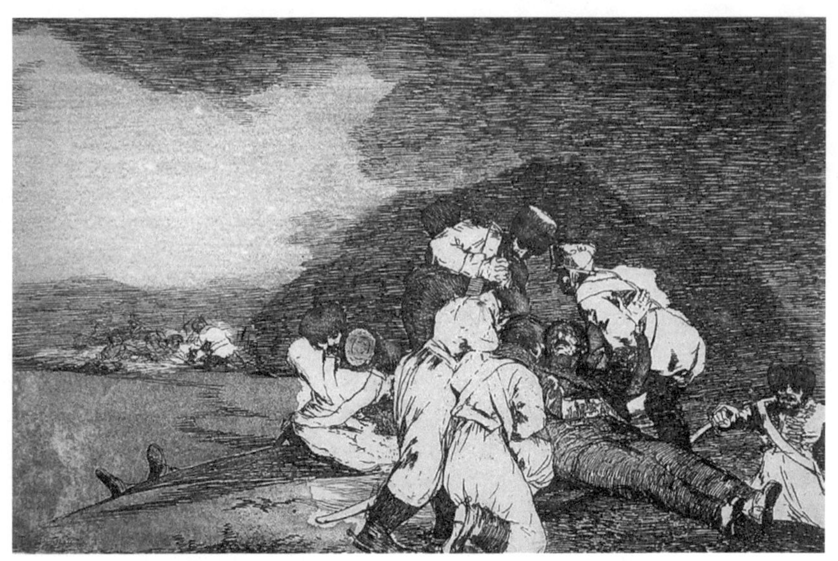

6
Bien te se está

A momentary reprieve from scenes of active battle. French troops huddle around a casualty who leans back in shadows. A soldier to the right of the wounded man supports him, holding his arm. To the left, three additional men are part of an impromptu sort of vigil. The first, on bent knee in the foreground, has lowered himself in order to be at eye level with the fallen man. A second soldier stands next to him, leaning in with his head inclined. Both have their backs to us, and although we cannot see their faces, their poses suggest that they are looking at the wounded man, perhaps offering words of encouragement or solace. Above and behind them, a third soldier stands with his hands clasped. He is praying for the fallen officer, whose face we see but cannot make out fully. What we do see clearly, because it is in the light, is the wounded man's hand, held up against the side of the soldier supporting his arm. There is still life in the hand, along with the suggestion of pain in the open palm and extended fingers. As was the case in Print 3, the image draws masterfully on the expressive quality of the human hand. Here, the man's hand is the only limb that escapes the penumbra surrounding his body. He has fallen, literally and symbolically, into a shadow world that tellingly contrasts with the lighter tones in which those around him, who have been spared his fate, have been rendered.

As we saw in Print 1, Goya often imbues the tonal contrasts inherent to his medium with symbolic dimensions. Black, white, and the greys in between find analogues within the world of the disasters themselves, where life, death, and various gradations of violence and suffering come into intimate contact with one another. If the fallen man hovers between darkness and light, he is also suspended between the world of the living and the dead. In a world before antibiotics, wounds were serious, life-threatening events. Wartime death often came slowly, after the heat of battle, and its arrival was as much a function of poor medical attention and infection as it was of the wounds themselves. Such suffering belongs to time scales that are not easily rendered in scenes of conflict, and Goya seems to register the dilatory quality of suffering here. His subject is the aftermath of battle, not the spectacle of its violence. The wounded man is agonizing, and while the final outcome for him is uncertain, it does not look promising.

While the fallen soldier and his attendants make the strongest initial claim to our visual attention, they by no means fill the frame. They do not even fill the right side of the print. Whatever its pathos, the group scene has been positioned within a broader landscape. From the lower right corner, another soldier approaches, as if from battle, sword still in hand. To the left of the group, a second casualty is held up by a fellow soldier, and further to the left still, two feet break the horizon line of the hillock that defines the foreground. The feet intimate that a man lies on his back, downhill, out of sight, lifeless and unattended, and Goya makes a subtle link between this man, whom we do not see, and the wounded man on the right. He has positioned both sets of feet symmetrically along the arched outline of the hillock – they are odd, mirror-like images of one another. The composition in fact offers a suggestive series of more general contrasts between the left and right halves of the image. On one side a cadaver, out of sight and alone, against the backdrop of light grey fields and a sky delivered in the print's brightest tones. On the other side, a wounded man, in sight and accompanied, against the backdrop of the print's darkest mass. Differences of technique reinforce the basic contrasts: on the left, the telltale granular quality and tonal variations of aquatint; on the right, the tightly packed, dark horizontal lines of more conventional engraving.

From a technical point of view, the dark mass behind the men provides contrast for the scene in front of it, but the mass is expressive as well as functional. Like many of Goya's backgrounds, it defies easy naturalistic interpretations, hovering somewhere between mountain and dark cloud on the horizon. Whatever its status, there is something foreboding about the way it looms behind the wounded man and his friends, the way its shape vaguely echoes the shape of the hillock, and the way its darkness dialogues with the pall surrounding the man. If the aftermath of battle has been cast in gloom, this dark mass is its tonal anchor. In addition, Goya's composition suggests that what is happening in front of the mass, in the foreground, may also be going on elsewhere. On the horizon in the distance, just to the left of the mass, other figures have gathered, and although we cannot make out what they are doing with certainty, the vaguely sketched body closest to the darkness is angled in precisely the same way as the soldier holding the wounded man in the foreground. Whether it is ongoing battle or another group of wounded men, the parallels suggest the idea of repetition.

The caption to this image of the wounded, the dead, and those left to face them could not be more jarring. It reads: "It serves you right." In the original Spanish, "you" is in the singular form and directed at an individual. Its most obvious, immediate reference is the wounded man. But who, one might ask, would say such a thing to a man who has been wounded, to a man who may in fact be dying? The caption invites us to consider the possibilities. Among the most plausible is that the words represent the voice of the enemy, especially an enemy whose hatred has eclipsed any sense of compassion. In such a reading, the caption expresses the typically hardened celebration of another's suffering that is one of the hallmarks of enmity, and there are linguistic reasons to believe that the caption's speaker belongs to the popular classes. The standard order of pronouns in Spanish calls for "bien se te está," but the caption transposes them to "bien te se está," a variation typical of the rural and popular speech of Goya's home region of Aragón. The effect, which has been lost in English translations, is to turn the caption into the citation of the colloquial speech of an "everyman."

Stepping outside the scene for a moment, one might also imagine Goya himself speaking the caption to the man. If it were the case, we would again have to ask the question of moral consistency. Does Goya decry war's senselessness in the opening images of the series only to rant like an enemy against a wounded man? If this is Goya's voice, it seems more productive to imagine a distinctively ironic tone here. As we have seen, the *Disasters* go out of their way to dismantle the justifications that would have us believe suffering such as this man's serves anybody right (Prints 2 and 3). For readers attuned to what has come before, this is no earnest expression. It speaks with sarcasm in what amounts to an ironic inversion of the compassion the scene might elicit. Whether imagined in Goya's voice or not, it is a verbal expression of enmity whose contrast with the suffering we see is meant to disturb.

Stepping back into the scene, however, it is clear that the words have also been assigned a very specific position. These are not the words of just any enemy. "It serves you right" would logically have to come from someone looking at the man's suffering; not his fellow soldiers but an additional person who has also been assigned a place within the image, someone who occupies the very position we do when we too look at the fallen soldier. Goya has written a caption whose most logical site of enunciation is the place of the notional viewer, and in doing so he raises the question of any viewer's relationship to the subject depicted. Who are we when we look at the wounded man and his comrades? How would we respond to the scene? If we were there, Goya suggests, we would be on one or the other side of the conflagration, and if these men had been killing our fellow countrymen, friends, and loved ones, we too might find ourselves saying "it serves you right."

In effect the caption makes readers momentarily voice an enemy combatant's words as they read the print. It prompts us to confront our own relationship to the scene and the cruel sentiment the words convey. Such an exercise would have been particularly pointed for a Spanish reading public of the 1860s, for whom memory of the Napoleonic invasion and occupation was relatively proximate. More broadly, the caption suggests that any viewer could indeed look at the fallen man as an enemy. As words attached to the place of viewing, the caption plays with the ways we look at the scene, and among other things, it intimates that we may not always be who we like to think we are.

On this side of the illusion, however, things seem qualitatively different. We occupy a space and time that are removed from the man's. He is not our enemy, and compassion seems the more appropriate response to viewing his semblance and the figures attending to him. From our position here, the caption appears to be an ironic negation, not only of the Goya of the earlier prints, or of the care and concern of the soldiers who have gathered around the fallen man, but also of our own, presumably moral reaction to the representation of his suffering. If that is the case, we would have to acknowledge that our seemingly more compassionate response to the man's suffering is only possible because we are *not* there. Within the world depicted, we would be thoroughly conditioned by our position within the conflict. In this sense we have another print that plays with the difference between viewing the image and actually being in the situation depicted.

Goya often challenges the facile moral assumptions that viewers can bring to their viewing. The assumption that we would care for the man if we were there is undercut by the caption, and the assumption that we inhabit a higher moral ground than those involved in the scene is undermined by the fact that we are not there. We are only looking at the scene as if we were. In fact, the print suggests that one of the disasters of war may be the way it produces "it serves you right" within otherwise well-meaning people who find themselves caught up in the violence. It points to the limits of projecting our sensibility as viewers of images into the scenes we imaginatively witness. As we will see in later prints, Goya often short-circuits morally self-righteous responses to the atrocities he depicts by subtly reminding viewers of the differences between actually witnessing violence and looking at images of violence. He wants us to look at the horrors, but across the series he will also prompt us, once and again, to reflect on what it means to confront such horrors in artistic form, as images.

There is also a final irony at work here by virtue of the print's position within the sequence. What initially appeared as a temporary reprieve from the violence depicted in the preceding prints – a break from active killing – has turned out, in the end, to be no reprieve at all. While the scene itself is not violent in the conventional sense, the image and caption together make clear that violence has been at work nevertheless, in the gaze of an imagined enemy witness. Looking, the print teaches, can itself be coloured by animus, and in their power to affect, images can themselves be a form of violence. Goya will return to this idea several times over the course of the print series.

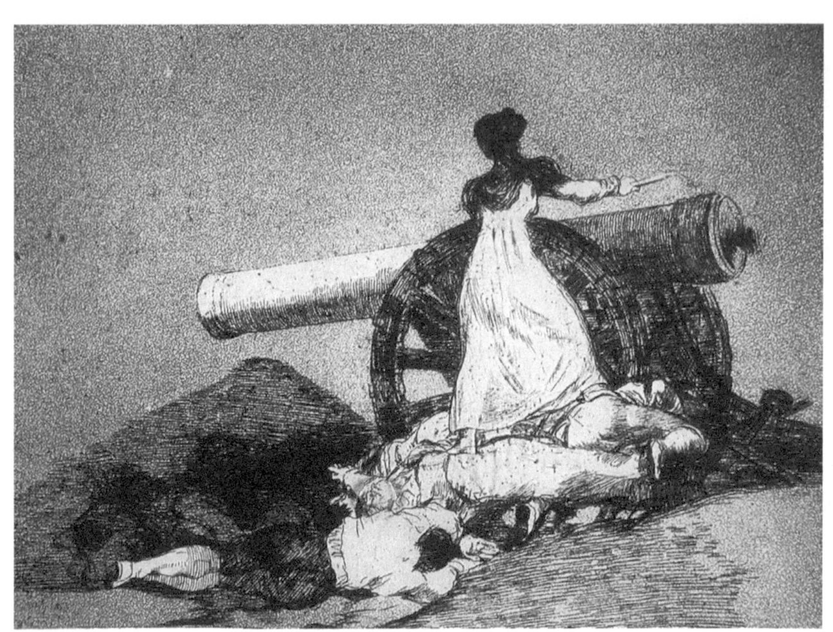

7
Qué valor!

A woman is about to fire a cannon. Cadavers spill down the hillside on which the weapon is perched, and she has had to climb over the dead in order to reach it. She stands unevenly on a pile of bodies. Her back is to the viewer, and she extends a linstock towards the cannon with her right arm. In stark contrast to her white Empire dress, under which the outline of her uneven stance is discernible, her head and shoulders are in dark silhouette. The cannon angles downward slightly, from right to left, towards an enemy somewhere outside the frame. The back end of the artillery piece sits in shadows. The front of the barrel, however, gleams brightly in a tone that eerily matches the woman's dress and the garments of several of the dead. In the background a pyramid-like mass rises beneath the cannon barrel on the left. In front of it, darker shadows suggest more proximate masses that are difficult to make out. A grey sky hovers over the scene, which bears the caption "What courage!"

Within Goya's sequence, this print clearly marks a return to the earlier line of inquiry concerning feminine courage. In fact, it now becomes apparent that the wounded man in the preceding print was a momentary detour within a series dedicated to women combatants. Once again, sequence signifies. With images of fighting women on either side of it, the depiction of the officer in the previous print in effect becomes a parenthetical comment on casualties, a glimpse at what courageous combatants produce. In a similar way, the image we now have before us is also conditioned by context. It would be one thing to view this print on its own, where "What courage!" might stand as a straightforward expression of admiration. It is quite another to turn to feminine cannon-fire after having pondered the wounded officer and the women combatants who preceded him. Given those reflections, context makes clear that the caption to this image is also equivocal, if not downright sarcastic. At the least there is reason to believe that Goya does not identify with the sentiment fully. In the earlier cases, feminine courage was revealed to be unheroic (Print 4) and animalistic (Print 5). Now, in a seemingly explosive culmination, a single figure fires heavy artillery.

For a mid-nineteenth-century Spanish public, the image would immediately have signalled unusual heroism in accordance with the dominant ideas of the day concerning men and women. Much as in Prints 4 and 5, the mere fact of a woman combatant would have been seen as exceptional. From a more contemporary perspective, however, the print also makes visible the presumptions underpinning traditional notions of feminine heroism. As conventionally conceived, womanly courage was ultimately about assuming historically masculine roles. This woman literally stands where a man would normally have been expected, and she wields a weapon that well before Freud was understood as a sign of phallic, masculine power. To be courageous in this regard is, literally and symbolically, to occupy a man's position. Such presuppositions would largely have remained unquestioned for most nineteenth-century viewers.

Many, however, would also have quickly recognized something far more specific than the archetype of feminine heroism. Scholars have noted that Goya's print references one of the most celebrated tales of womanly courage to emerge from the Napoleonic conflagration in Spain. The story began circulating in the immediate wake of the siege of Zaragoza in June 1808. Agustina Raimunda María Zaragoza Domènech (1786–1857) had in fact "manned" the cannon at the city's *Portillo* entrance as Spanish soldiers were fleeing from the defences. Her celebrity was almost instantaneous, and the narrative of Agustina of Aragón or *La Artillera* (the artillery-woman), as she came to be known, quickly became a mainstay of wartime propaganda. In the decades following the war, her image circulated as a romantic icon of national heroism, and she was the subject of a myriad of poems, plays, engravings, and paintings. She was familiar to readers of the English-speaking world through the verses Lord Byron dedicated to her in *Childe Harold's Pilgrimage*. Most educated Spaniards in the first half-century would have known her story, and Goya, himself a native of Aragón, is likely to have first learned of Agustina during a trip to Zaragoza between the first and second sieges of the city.

For those making the connection between the woman in this image and the historical Agustina, the irony of the caption would have been especially pointed, a barb aimed at an icon of national resistance. To achieve the effect, Goya once again plays with the difference between witnessing a scene and looking at a representation. Had viewers actually seen Agustina at the cannon during the siege of Zaragoza, "What courage!" might presumably have been a spontaneous response to the events unfolding before them. To viewers positioned at some historical distance from those events, however, the caption is anything but spontaneous. For those familiar with the deluge of heroic images and narratives concerning Agustina and other women fighters throughout the first half-century, the caption would be recognized as the repetition of a heroic cliché within the new, unabashedly antiheroic context of the *Disasters*. Viewing this print within the sequence highlights its ironic tenor. Heroic nationalism literally becomes something that is out of place given what has come before.

Even on its own, however, this would be a strange depiction of womanly valour. The purported heroine has her back to us, and her head and shoulders are in shadows. Her pose is far more in keeping with the kind of anonymity Goya typically reserves for other perpetrators of violence, as we saw in Print 2. In addition, the faceless woman has no name. Goya does not identify her in the caption – it would have been easy to write "What courage, Agustina!" – and he places her within a setting that is peculiarly devoid of specific visual references to Zaragoza, such as city walls, or the *Portillo* entrance. There is simply the outline of a hillside strewn with bodies, and a dark mound in the distance, a shape that defies an immediate naturalistic understanding. Again, we need only note how unsuccessful the print would be as war propaganda in order to appreciate Goya's irony here.

The print is also another instructive example of Goya's oblique approach to the historical, of the way historical dates, locations, and events yield to a different, more complex sense of time and place. If this is Agustina of Aragón, she is out of place, not only because the heroine has been positioned within a series of images that demystify her heroic status, or because she has been depicted as a faceless, nameless woman, but also because she inhabits a pictorial space that refuses specific historical reference. Within the series, she is one more woman among those who have preceded her. Goya has made room for this woman to be identified as Agustina or any number of wartime heroines, to be sure, but he has not restricted the print's meaning to such figures. Historical reference is secondary to Goya's broader inquiry into the moral meaning of the violence and the meaning of its viewing. Those who know the story of Agustina are likely to recognize her in this print, but in so doing they must also confront the question that Goya's sequence poses. How should one look at *La Artillera*, given what one has already seen, and what should one make of her in light of the disasters to come?

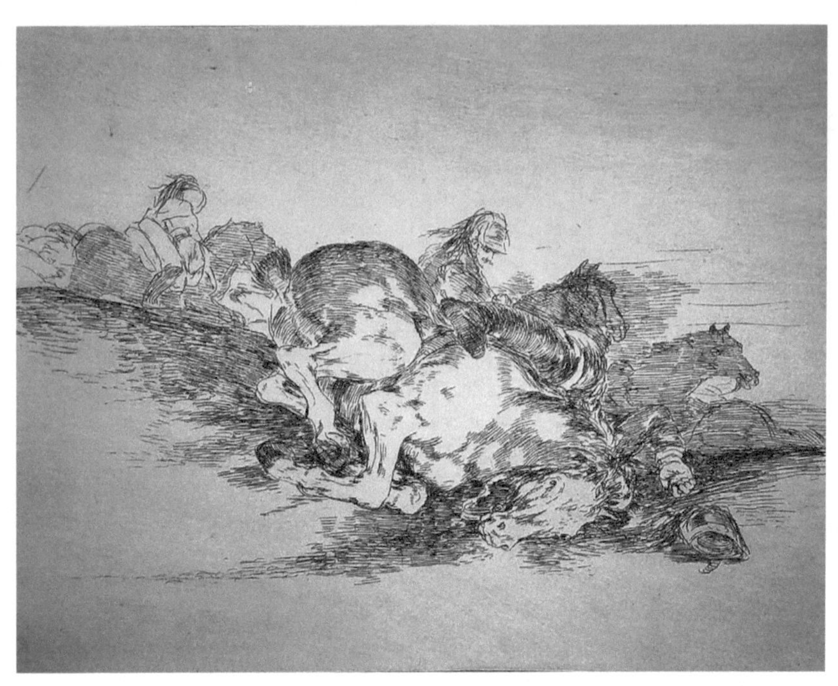

8
Siempre sucede

A horse has fallen. Its body rests, a slumped carcass sloping down a hillock. With crumpled legs before it, the mass of its hindquarters is piled awkwardly uphill from its head and neck. A descending diagonal line organizes the composition from upper left to lower right, heightening the impact of the fall. While the horse, rendered in lighter tones, draws immediate visual attention within the jumble, it quickly becomes apparent that this is not the only lifeless body here. A rider has fallen with his mount, or more accurately, a rider has fallen under it. A dark, booted leg still straddles the horse, its foot resting at the centre of the image. A thigh, part of a torso, and an arm can also be made out behind the horse's neck. The outlines of a human head and face, now turned upside down, are discernible near its mane. The rider's cap has been toppled during the fall, and it lies a short distance from both heads. The soldier is, or was, a member of the cavalry.

In the background, other riders gallop by. Goya has rendered them with far less detail than the fallen horse and rider, not only to suggest the blurred depth of the background, but also in order to convey the riders' movement. He has shaded the galloping horses with the traditional engraving technique of close, parallel, horizontal lines. Shadowy forms around the horses are suggested in the same way, and on the right side of the image a looser band of parallel lines against the sky reinforces the sense of swift movement from left to right. This is either a cavalry charge or a frenzied retreat. Differences in technique once again reinforce thematic elements. Part of the power of this image, for example, stems from the contrast between the sketchy background motion of the living cavalrymen and the more clearly delineated, crumpled stasis of the horse and rider in the foreground. Goya's caption to the scene reads, "It always happens," or in some translations, "This always happens." There is nothing at all uncommon about this, the print asserts, nothing exceptional. It happens all the time. Horses fall, by accident or as a result of battle, and riders are crushed under their weight.

If such deaths are frequent occurrences, however, something about them nevertheless unsettles conventional narratives of the way soldiers perish. To be killed in the heat of battle, struck down by a foe, is one thing. Such a demise at least corresponds to the way cultures typically imagine soldiers *ought* to die. To die mangled under the weight of one's own horse, perhaps the result of an accident, is something altogether different. Heroic tales do not sit easily with what has happened here, and the force of Goya's image is magnified when one recalls the symbolic stature of horses and horsemanship historically, as markers of wealth and signs of social prestige. Words like *chevalier* or *caballero* still remind us that longstanding feudal notions of nobility were initially tied to horses and horsemanship. In Goya's day, equestrian portraits of aristocrats and royals remained a mainstay of European painting, and as First Court Painter the artist knew the genre well. Within the military, horses brought with them rank and social status. The association between horses and wealth remains to this day, and connoisseurs routinely refer to the animals in terms of their nobility. Against such a backdrop, it becomes clear that the image of an awkwardly slumped horse carcass with a crushed rider beneath it is more than a gruesome depiction of death in times of war. It is also a symbolically charged negation of the notion that there is anything at all noble about what has taken place. Today's equivalents are those non-heroic events in which soldiers unexpectedly die: an overturned vehicle, a helicopter crash, friendly fire. In such instances one often senses collective embarrassment or even shame mixed in with the grief over what has happened, but Goya's caption tells us not to fool ourselves. Where there is war, it asserts, this always happens.

The imagined speaker of these words would have to be somebody who *knows* that this always happens, somebody who has presumably seen it happen time and again. It could indeed be Goya himself, or the voice of any veteran familiar with this kind of death. Whoever it is, he or she speaks from experience and appears to address the uninitiated. Within the world depicted, "This always happens" might be spoken to an inexperienced combatant or witness, for example, as a way of explaining things. But the words also clearly address viewers of the print, positioning us as inexperienced witnesses in need of explanations, and they potentially modify our response to the scene. If one has had a strong emotional reaction to the image, for example, "This always happens" tempers the initial response, suggesting that there is in fact nothing particular or exceptional about the scene. It is another example of a caption that is purposefully at odds with the initial emotional charge of the image. The caption's "always" also makes clear that the image is more than the simple record of a single historical event. It instructs viewers that the scene is exemplary, the depiction of something that happens repeatedly. It points to the cyclical repetitions that, as we saw earlier, routinely accompany the disasters of war.

The caption also subtly addresses at least two different dimensions of the image. The words make sense within the scene depicted, but they also make sense as a comment on the image itself. We saw this technique in the opening image of the series (Print 1), where "presentiments" named both the experience of the man depicted and the image itself as a visual presentiment of subsequent images.

A similar game is afoot here: if what "always happens" refers to the sort of death we see here, it also identifies a very different sort of happening. It names our encounter with the image. When we turn to this print, "It always happens." The words address the scene, and at the same time they speak to the part of us that knows we are looking at an image. Deaths like this happen, it suggests, but what is happening here is also an image. For viewers familiar with the long history of largely celebratory or commemorative images of war, there is an additional irony in the caption. While "this always happens" in times of war, deeply antiheroic depictions of scenes such as this one had "happened" relatively rarely in the world of commissioned war art. What is horrifyingly ordinary within the scene depicted is in many ways an extraordinary "happening" in art-historical terms. The caption's irony trades on understanding these two very different kinds of happening.

Finally, there is also a subtle bit of word play in the original Spanish caption, a nuance not easily conveyed in translation. A number of Spanish verbs can communicate the idea of happening – *pasar* for example, or *ocurrir* – and each carries distinctive connotations. Significantly, the verb Goya has chosen for this caption is *suceder*, a word that contains within it the idea of succession, as in *to happen next, to take the place of, or to follow*. He has used a verb that conceives of happening as something sequential. "This always happens" is also, more faintly, "This always follows." The caption refers not only to what we see in the image but also to what has come before, and what has come immediately before this print in Goya's sequence is seemingly the most explosively "heroic" image of *The Disasters of War*. Goya has set up for readers an experience that moves rather jarringly from cannon fire to the abject death of being crushed under one's horse. Even if we overlook the sarcasm of the previous print or minimize its ironies, this caption tells us that what we see here always follows such scenes. It suggests that moments of exhilaration or enthusiasm, the very kind of scene propagandists of war so often exploit, are always followed by the kind of death we have just contemplated. Examination of this print in isolation would miss its expressive force as a commentary on Print 7. Any vestiges of heroism that might have withstood the ironic dimensions of the previous print come tumbling down here, almost literally.

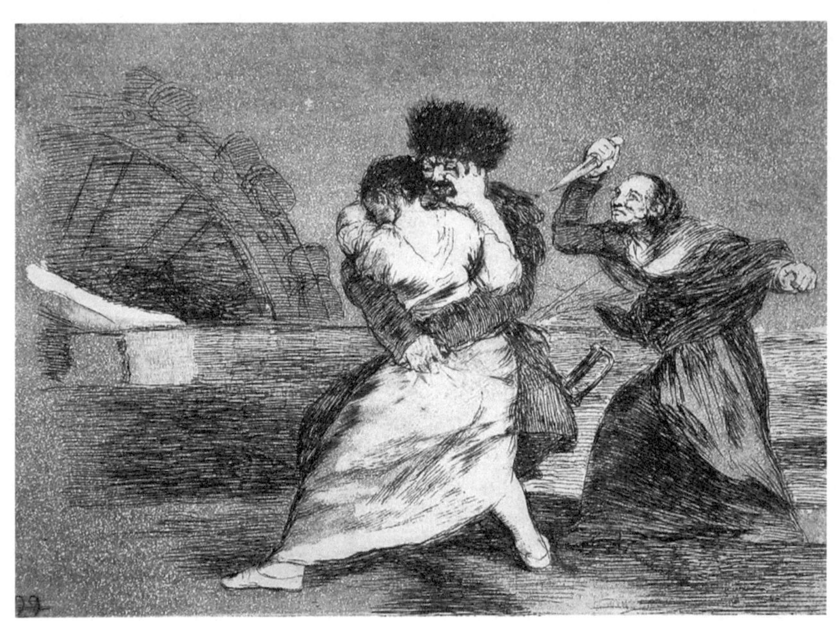

9
No quieren

Again, Spanish women are fighting the enemy. The stakes of the struggle, however, have become more specific than they were in previous prints. The aggression is sexual. At the centre of the image, a woman tries to fend off a soldier who has caught her in a violent embrace. With arms around her and bent legs trying to straddle her lower body, the soldier's intent is clear. His right hand clutches at the woman's dress, which he is beginning to raise, revealing the outline of her buttocks beneath it. She scratches at his face as she turns her head from him, and her stance reveals that she is trying to push herself away. The struggle between the two is visually amplified, not only by the pair's central position within the composition, but also by strong tonal contrasts. In a deft exploitation of the medium's expressive potential, Goya has enveloped the woman's white dress in the darkness of her aggressor's uniform, and shadows border her garment on the ground. Slightly behind and to the right of the struggling couple, an older woman lunges towards the soldier with a dagger in hand, poised to plunge it into his back. He seems unlikely to overcome his victim. The caption reads, "They don't want to."

In this print Goya comments on one of the most common yet routinely hidden faces of war. His subject matter is attempted rape. As previous images began to make clear, wartime violence has conventionally been conceived and waged in strongly sexualized terms, and it has often unfolded within a largely phallic pattern of thinking: transgressing borders in order to penetrate, occupy, and possess can describe both what armies traditionally attempt to do to enemy territory and what rapists try to do to their victims. If earlier prints exhibit the sexualized patterns of thought and behaviour that have traditionally governed the way war is imagined and prosecuted, however, here Goya shows viewers where such patterns routinely lead. For centuries, women of the vanquished were treated as spoils of war, there for the taking, like other enemy possessions. Although a loose body of legal work decrying wartime rape had emerged by the time of the Napoleonic wars, it nevertheless remained a widespread practice. Historians have documented that within theatres of combat such as the Iberian Peninsula, sexual violence and the threat of such violence was an important psychological weapon in the struggle to control a hostile civilian population. The fact that Goya denounces the practice as one of war's disasters is, historically speaking, a relatively novel and modern moral stance on sexual violence.

The print is also one more example of the strange timeliness of many of the *Disasters of War*. War rape is now generally considered a crime under international law, but it is prosecuted very irregularly in comparison to other forms of atrocity. In addition, common as it has been from the 1800s to today, war rape has rarely if ever been part of the public face of war. As tightly interwoven into wartime violence as it is, rape is a dimension of warfare that has routinely been excused, minimized, or rationalized away. This is so in part because shame hovers over it, for perpetrators and victims alike. The raped, we know, come forward in far fewer numbers than victims of other forms of violence, and in the modern era at least, war rapists do not usually boast publicly about their exploits. Rape typically occurs off stage, as it were. Even when it is sanctioned or used systematically, official disavowals usually follow. There is something to be said, then, for the seemingly simple act of making attempted rape visible in a visual idiom that departs from the mythological rapes that had more frequently populated the archive of Western art up to Goya's days. In taking up the subject, Goya shows viewers something that conventional representations of war regularly omit, something that is rarely made visible today.

In this image, Goya situates the attempted rape alongside a river, and he places a watermill in the background. In terms of composition, the watermill clearly provides a visual counterbalance to the woman with the knife, while the river delineates the upper and lower halves of the image. The detail with which Goya has depicted the watermill, however, seems something of a departure from the more abstract treatment of background in the preceding prints. As we have seen, what one usually finds in the background of the *Disasters* are dark masses, undefined shapes, or broad and at times grainy fields of aquatint. Why devote such detail to the watermill and its reflection in a river? It could be that Goya is signalling that the scene is taking place away from public scrutiny, on the outskirts of town, where watermills were typically located. Even so, the image does not deliver the specificities of a distinctive, particular location here. The depiction of place remains general, and it is largely symbolic.

In addition, there are reasons to believe that Goya has set up a fascinating conceptual game within this background. "Water" and "watermill" are the key terms of a well-known Spanish proverb, *llevar el agua a su molino*. Literally translated, the expression means "to carry water to one's mill," and it is a colloquial way of saying "to take advantage of a situation." For readers familiar with the proverb, the water and the mill in the background are a symbolic commentary on what is happening in the foreground. Rape accompanies war, the print suggests, but rape is also a taking advantage of the occasion of war. It is an example of the way words and graphic images become intimately intertwined in Goya, even before one reads his captions.

The print provides another example of the way Goya works with the twofold nature of viewing and reading his prints. On one level this image relies for its effects on our indulging the illusion that we are looking at a would-be rapist and the women who are resisting him. At the same time, however, what we see in the background has been constructed in order to reward a non-naturalistic approach to pictorial space. The viewing experience entails shifting from naturalist illusion to more figurative understandings of what has been depicted. It requires the capacity to respond morally to the terrible immediacy of what is happening in the foreground while adopting a more distanced, conceptual or aesthetic understanding of the image in the background. "Look and be moved," Goya's prints seem to say, "but do not forget the artifice of what you see."

For its part, the caption, "They do not want to," colours the experience of viewing this print in intriguing ways. In a first moment, the words seem almost unnecessary. One can see that the women are resisting and do not want the man to succeed. Why repeat with words what is already evident in the image? More importantly, why raise the question at all? Rape is by definition unwanted. The caption could be an emphatic gesture in which the words and the image reinforce one another, but it seems to do more than merely emphasize what we already see. "They do not want to" is not the same thing as "They are resisting," or "They are fighting." The caption describes the women's internal dispositions, and it comments on something integral to the phenomenon of rape. "They do not want to" expressly relates what we see in the image to questions of feminine will and, more importantly, to the question of feminine desire. In addition to the women's will to resist, the caption addresses the realm of sexual wanting: it asserts clearly that neither woman has any sexual interest in the assailant.

In doing so, Goya's words unequivocally counter the myth of complicity that has historically accompanied and justified rape, the myth, persistent to this day, that women "really want to," even if they resist, and there is another facet of the original caption that is not fully conveyed in English translation. When applied to people, the Spanish verb *querer* in Goya's *No quieren* can communicate not just desire but also affection, as in *te quiero*. "They do not want to" is also, in a fainter, secondary sense, "They do not love." The caption thus intimates that rape – here, attempted rape – is more than a physical assault. Goya's words underscore that rape aims to violate the will, desire, and affective disposition of those whom it targets. A psychologically complex and comparatively modern understanding of sexual violence, the caption also suggests at least one additional idea. Attached to an image in which the aggressor seems unlikely to succeed, Goya's words subtly intimate that these women will not be raped *because* "they do not want to." It seems logical enough: the women are resisting, and it appears that they will not in fact be raped. This depiction of apparently successful resistance, however, is the first moment in a sequence, and the caption is again setting readers up for what will come next.

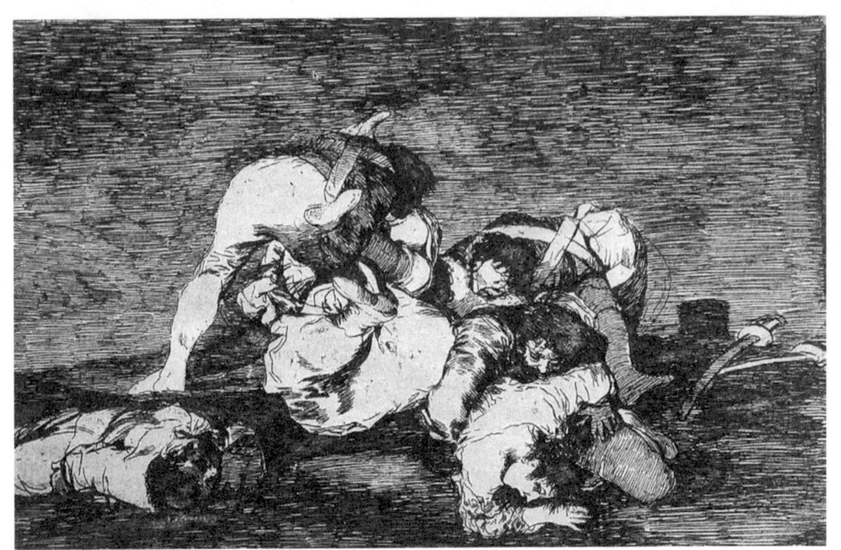

10
Tampoco

More hand-to-hand fighting. Bodies are intertwined, and it takes some time to discern the details of what is happening. There are at least three soldiers here, each violently coupled with a different victim. The first and most dramatic pair occupies the foreground, just right of centre, where a woman in a white dress has been toppled. Like her counterpart in the previous print, her garment contrasts strongly with the darker, menacing tones around her. Her face, in profile, and the position of her arms suggest that she has just hit the ground and is struggling to get her bearings. Her feet dangle in the air, and the diagonal line defined by the lighter tones in the image, from upper left to lower right, accentuates the movement of her fall. The gloved arm of her aggressor dramatically crosses her at the waist, and Goya emphasizes the power of this violent embrace by taking some licence with perspective. The arm is enormous and out of proportion in comparison to other limbs in the image. Behind this couple, to the left, a second soldier, his back to the viewer, hunches over another victim. In contrast to this soldier's solid stance, his victim's legs are up in the air, one on each side of the aggressor. Whoever is on the ground has been thrown back with legs spread apart. The soldier is in fact pinning a leg under his right arm. A third pair, behind and to the right of the couple in the foreground, is more difficult to make out, but something similar appears to be underway. We see a soldier bent over someone, and a woman's leg juts out below him. Goya has again posed the bodies in ways that underscore the sexual nature of the aggression. The struggles here involve raw, bodily force in a macabre kind of wrestling. This is not regular combat. Swords and a hat are on the ground near the horizon line to the right, and other equipment, perhaps a backpack, rests in the foreground to the left. Such elements, which again provide compositional balance, also qualify the narrative in suggestive ways: The soldiers have put their weapons down in preparation for what they are about to do, and the heavy horizontal lines Goya has used to darken background and foreground suggest that they act under cover of darkness.

Like the preceding print, the subject here is attempted rape, but Goya's sequence has once again turned the tables when it comes to likely outcomes. The previous aggressor was moments away from succumbing to the older woman's dagger. These would-be rapists appear to be moments away from realizing their intent. They are in dominant positions vis-à-vis those they assault, and they seem to be overpowering their victims. Perceiving this shift is an important facet of the experience Goya has set up for readers as they turn from the previous print to this one. The earlier caption read, "They do not want to." Here, under such different circumstances, Goya's caption states, "Neither do they." To move from one print to the next is consequently to entertain two radically different imagined outcomes despite the fact that the victims in both cases "do not want to." If the previous print subtly suggested that avoiding rape was somehow linked to such "not wanting," the new caption now utterly dismantles such thinking. The victims here also "do not want to," but their circumstances are different, and by all counts they are about to be raped. Viewing the two prints in sequence prompts the realization that when rape takes place, it has little to do with what the victims want or how strongly "they do not want to." Some of those who resist may in fact evade rape. Others who resist will not. The point is not that resistance is unimportant but rather that, like other disasters of war, rape happens, despite the resistance. In this regard, the sequence takes aim at another longstanding myth concerning rape, the myth still heard in some quarters today that women would not be raped if they simply resisted enough.

The refutation of such an idea emerges from viewing the two prints in sequence, and it is an additional example of what can be lost when Goya's prints are approached in isolation. Like reading, however, sequential viewing is more than the one-way, linear movement it initially seems to be. We usually imagine ourselves moving forward along a time-line, from beginning to end, but the activity also involves repeated backward glances. As we progress, we modify the way we understand what we have already seen. The meaning of resistance to rape in the previous print is subtly altered, for example, by what we have seen here. Such alteration, as we saw in earlier prints, often happens within sequences that are linked together by their captions: Prints 2 ("With reason or without it") and 3 ("The same thing"), Prints 4 ("The women give courage") and 5 ("And they are wild beasts"), or now Prints 9 ("They do not want to") and 10 ("Neither do they"). In each of these groupings, the later print retroactively modifies the meaning of its predecessor.

This back-and-forth movement can also traverse the series more broadly. Looking at these scenes of intended rape, for example, could lead one to reconsider the women combatants viewed earlier. Our initial presumption in viewing Prints 4, 5, and 7 was that the women depicted there were partisans fighting for the Spanish cause. Returning to those images now, however, we might legitimately ask whether the women are not also fighting for something more personal, indeed more intimate, because they know, as we ourselves have just seen, what can befall women who are defeated by enemy soldiers. The earlier images do not suddenly become more obviously about rape than they were before, but the possibility of rape begins to inform these scenes in ways that were not initially apparent. The question of feminine courage that Goya poses in the earlier prints also becomes more complex, and more troubled, by what we have just read. What was presented in terms of courage, it now seems, might also have been a desperate struggle not to be raped. Conversely, the question of courage migrates forward, beyond its initial context. Precisely because we have looked at earlier prints of fighting women, we might ask whether the women we see now, struggling against an aggression that is more obviously sexual, are any less courageous than those who came before them. We might also notice that when rape is more openly the subject, courage disappears from the captions. These are examples of the kinds of visual and conceptual association that Goya's prints set up by virtue of their sequential presentation.

Although such back-and-forth associations often take place just below the threshold of our awareness, they are much more common than one might suspect. The last chapters of a novel prompt readers to reevaluate a character they thought they understood. While listening to a piece of music, you recognize the return of an earlier melody that initially may have seemed unimportant. A poem's closing line suddenly shifts the reader's understanding of everything that has led to it. Even the so-called static arts rely for many of their effects on the simple fact that they too will be experienced over time, the time it takes to walk around a sculpture, for example, or the time it takes to move one's attention from one part of a painting's canvas to another. Whether intuitively or more purposefully, artists inevitably engage the way artistic experience unfolds in time. In *The Disasters of War*, Goya works with it in deliberate ways in order to create multiple, shifting layers of meaning as readers move through the series.

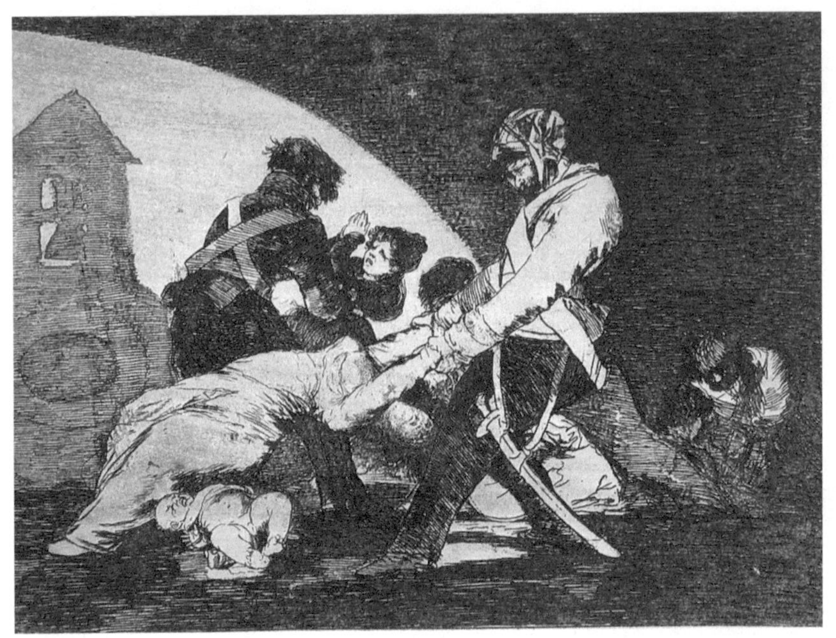

11

Ni por ésas

Yet another scene of sexual violence, and once more soldiers clearly have the upper hand. In the foreground, dramatically, a mother is being dragged backwards by her assailant while her infant lies on the ground. Behind and above them, left of centre, a second woman, her hands together in a supplicant's pose, pleads with a soldier who has her by the arms. Just to the right of her, and behind the soldier doing the dragging, we see the head of a third man. His comrade in the foreground blocks his torso, but his legs are visible in the shadows, where they have been rendered in profile and in a slightly lighter tone that angles down towards the lower right corner of the image. Although easily overlooked, his posture and the crumpled white dress into which he leans suggest strongly that he has mounted his victim and is in the act of raping her. Still further to the right, deeper in shadows and more difficult to see, a fourth woman is on the ground, toppled with her back towards us as an assailant hunches over her. Her head is at his waist in what could very well be forced fellatio, or it could be that he is climbing on top of her. The darkness makes it difficult to know for sure. In contrast to this shadow world, the bell-tower and windowed façade of a church occupy the background to the far left of the image.

Goya's composition masterfully dramatizes the events taking place. The bright, diagonal line, from the mother's foot to her aggressor's shoulder, highlights the forceful movement of this central pair, and irregularities along that line convey poignant nuances: the infant on the ground, now separated from his mother; the tense curves of the mother's legs and arched back as she tries to hold herself up; the head that falls away from an eerily straighter, tauter line running from the woman's shoulder to her assailant's. At the centre of the image, the soldier's gloved hands clasp the mother's wrists. His head is bandaged, but the wound clearly has not diminished him physically. He towers over his victim, and his hands and arms are almost twice as thick as hers. Although he is exerting some effort to pull her back, the task does not appear to be especially difficult. The expression on his face is disturbingly calm, as if he were simply pulling an object across the ground.

A second, strong line of composition, from upper left to lower right, follows the curve of the archway under which the aggression is taking place. This line intersects with the soldier's arm and extends along his sash and down the legs of the man behind him. Echoes of these principal lines can be found elsewhere within the image. The tilt of the pleading woman's body as she tries to back away from her attacker, for example, repeats the angle of the figures in the foreground, reinforcing the sense of movement from left to right. Similarly, the mother's body and head begin to delineate a curve (completed by the aggressor's right leg) that mimics the archway above it. Much of the composition hinges on the intersection of straight and curved lines, as if distilling the sexual aggression into a geometry of the masculine and the feminine.

Equally rich is the symbolism with which Goya imbues tonal contrasts in this image: light and shadow, the public and the hidden, the spiritual and the carnal. Each of these oppositions is organized within the basic tonal division Goya sets up between the left and right sides of the image. In turn, much of the drama of the scene stems from Goya's depiction of movement from one realm to the next. The women's terror and desperation come from an understanding of what awaits them in the shadows, a darkness that is moral as well as physical. It is no coincidence, then, that movement into the gloom is also movement away from the church. As we have already seen, when Goya places well-defined buildings in the background of his *Disasters*, the motivation is often conceptual rather than naturalistic. In this case, the presence of the church establishes a powerful symbolic contrast: extreme moral transgressions are taking place against the backdrop of an institution widely understood at the time to be a societal repository of moral reflection and instruction. The print thus underscores an idea that recurs with regularity across the series as a whole, the notion that the events depicted are moral disasters as much as they are physical catastrophes. While Goya's prints attest to the horrific face of war, they just as frequently point to the broader calamity that accompanies armed conflict: the suspension or outright collapse of the ethics that would normally work to prevent such horrors.

The church takes on additional historical nuances when considered in light of the conflictive relationship between Spanish Catholicism and the Napoleonic regime. While Bonapartist Spain officially maintained Catholicism as the state religion for pragmatic reasons, in practice the imperial army saw the Catholic Church as a bastion of Spain's *ancien régime*, the very reactionary order it sought to dismantle. As later prints in the series record, churches, monasteries, and convents were routinely pillaged, and the clergy themselves were often targeted. Napoleonic secularism fuelled such hostilities, to be sure, but so did the fact that the Spanish Church was a key political actor in the uprisings against Napoleon. Using the power of the pulpit over a largely illiterate populace, the clergy had effectively prompted the masses to wage holy war against the foreign aggressor in what amounted to a modern crusade. The fact that rape in this print is taking place within view of a church resonates with such antagonisms, and it may speak to the soldiers' historic disregard for the institution of the Church in Spain.

The caption to this scene of violence reads, "Not even like that," or "Not even that way." The original Spanish, *Ni por ésas*, is an expression used when an event or effort has made no difference to an outcome. It implies an unalterable state of affairs, and here it refers to the fact that under no circumstances will the rapists be deterred. Not even with a church in sight. Not even if you beg for mercy. Not even if you are a mother with her child. Goya is once more exploiting feminine archetypes to great effect. This time, however, he invokes, not the instinctual, protective ferocity of women as depicted in Print 5, where we saw a very different mother and child, but rather the flip side of the archetype. With the church behind them, the mother and the pleading woman are figures of the feminine sacrosanct, and their function here is to emphasize that in times of war nothing is sacred, set apart, revered, or exempted from violation. As archetypes of the feminine sacred, these figures suggest that, symbolically at least, rape is a kind of desecration.

It also becomes clear retrospectively that this print has been carefully positioned as a third, culminating moment within the series of reflections on rape that Goya was pursuing in the previous two prints. Like the women before them, these women obviously "do not want to," but, in contrast to their predecessors, they are not fighting. The most active of them is pleading, appealing to her aggressor's sense of compassion, and even so, the caption avers, she too will be raped. In this regard, "Not even like that" refers not only to what we see in the image but also to the efforts to avoid rape that we have viewed in the preceding two prints. The sequence thus conveys that neither physical resistance nor appeals to religion, morality, or compassion can guarantee anything when it comes to the question of rape. To read the three prints in sequence is to confront slowly the notion that *nothing* can effectively stop wartime rape, an idea that no single print conveys on its own. The most common English translation of the caption as "Nor these" misses the mark entirely.

The rape sequence is also a revealing example of the way artifice in the *Disasters* raises questions concerning the meaning of what we see. Goya invites us to view his images as if we were witnesses to the violence, but time and again he also pulls us back to the knowledge that we are looking at prints. The initial affective responses his images so powerfully provoke are routinely channelled into more reflective modes of engagement. Sequencing, the word play of the captions, and the non-naturalistic elements of each image beckon readers to deliberate about what they view. While we may momentarily imagine ourselves to be witnessing attempted rape in the preceding images, for example, the experience of seeing three separate rape scenes in a carefully orchestrated sequence draws attention to our activity as we move from one print to the next, adjusting our understanding along the way.

Similarly, as we saw in Print 6, Goya's positioning of the notional viewer raises questions about the act of looking itself. The men in these images *do not want to be seen*. They have searched for the outskirts of the city (Print 9), the cover of night (Print 10), and the shadows under an arcade (Print 11). Within the worlds depicted, how is it then that we have nevertheless come to see them? More disturbingly, who would we have to be in these scenes in order to witness such events? As in earlier prints, the most plausible explanation is that we would be fellow perpetrators or potential victims, which is to say that we would be deeply implicated in the events taking place. If that were not the case, however, if we were unseen bystanders gazing at attempted rape, we would, morally speaking, be involved in a most callous kind of voyeurism. Given such choices, it would be understandable, and far more comfortable, to return our attention to the fact that we are *not* witnesses to rape but rather viewers of images for whom looking without being seen is simply a common pictorial convention. Even so, the uncanny proximity between the position of the voyeur within the scene and our own position here, safely out of sight, looking at a rape scene, is enough to give most viewers some pause.

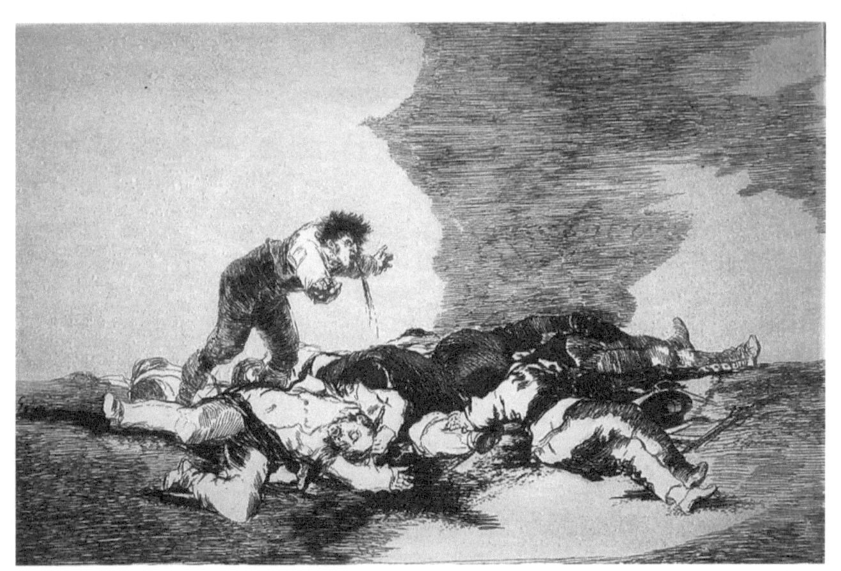

12
Para eso habéis nacido

A group of corpses has been piled in the middle of a stark landscape, and a man leans over them, vomiting. Individual bodies are distinguishable in the foreground, but the mass of corpses becomes darker, more tangled, and less differentiated as it approaches the horizon of the incline on which the dead are strewn. Goya has reserved some of the darkest tones of the print for the bodies at the top of the slope, just below the centre of the image, and the extension of the field of corpses is difficult to determine. In the *Disasters*, horizons often suggest that what we see may be part of something vaster, just out of sight. In contrast to the largely horizontal axes along which the dead are distributed, a single, living figure rises at an oblique angle to them. The upright and the prone, the vertical and the horizontal, the living and the dead. Composition again reinforces thematic contrasts, and in this sense it seems telling that the man standing among corpses does not, indeed cannot, stand upright. Bending over the dead with outstretched arms as he retches, the man's torso eerily echoes the angle that runs from the right knee of the corpse at his feet to the top of the darkened heap. A compositional parallel that links the living and the dead, it brings together two key elements of Goya's subject matter: lifeless bodies and the physical revulsion they produce in those who are left to face them.

A strange, enigmatic sky presides over the scene. The dark, irregular column rising from the horizon behind the corpses could be smoke from a distant fire. If it is smoke, however, there is something odd about the way the column pinches outward on its left side as it rises, something peculiar about the small tongues jutting out from the swaths of shade on the upper right. Such shapes seem to trouble the illusion of smoke, and we could in fact be looking at something else. If the shaded portions above the figures are not a depiction of smoke, but rather the depth of a dark sky, three white clouds quickly come into view: on the left an enormous, billowing cloud with two lobes that run down the centre of the image to the horizon, and on the right two smaller clouds, or more precisely parts of clouds that extend beyond the frame. Even when they are not overtly abstract, backgrounds in the *Disasters* are not necessarily governed by naturalist objectives.

In turning to this field of the dead, viewers again move from a scene of active struggle to a scene belonging to the aftermath of conflict. While Goya will depict scenes of violence as they unfold in the moment, most of the *Disasters* in fact represent the repercussions of such moments. Of the forty-six prints dedicated to the subject of wartime violence, for example, fewer than half depict active, ongoing, or impending fighting. The rest, the majority, represent what is left in the wake of the violence: the wounded officer in Print 6, the crushed rider of Print 8, and now, this field of the dead. By interspersing such scenes with images of violent acts themselves, Goya's sequence organizes an experience that moves back and forth from the time of violence proper to the time of its aftermath. Among other things then, sequence powerfully conveys the "what follows" that we usually name with the word consequence. Sequence in the *Disasters* subtly undoes the fantasy of violence without consequence that accompanies most idealizations of armed conflict. It is one of the ways Goya marks the disasters as *fatal consequences*, the term he used in his working title for the series.

Intriguingly, however, Goya does not present such consequences as the direct result of earlier events portrayed in the series. The pile of bodies depicted here, for example, is not in any obvious way the result of the rape scene that came before it, nor is it linked visually or verbally to any of the scenes we have viewed in the preceding prints. One might conclude that like that of the wounded officer or the crushed cavalier, this kind of scene generally follows the sort of violence we have already viewed, but the print's undefined relationship to earlier *Disasters* also produces another effect. Precisely because it is not expressly linked to the scenes we have already looked at, this image gestures towards a much broader field of violence that remains out of sight. It evokes a violence we have not seen – here, the violence that killed these people – and it suggests that what we do see in the series is in fact a small subset of what is or was "out there." Movement through the series in this regard suggests the limits of individual perspective. During times of war, one comes upon disastrous consequences without necessarily having seen their violent causes.

The suggestion of a violence that remains out of sight is also one of the ways that Goya addresses the artistic challenge posed by the scale of modern warfare as such. The Napoleonic Wars were massive, multi-theatre events that mobilized entire populations, and, as we noted earlier, in Spain the war inaugurated forms of violence that spilled well beyond the traditional battlefield. Violence could erupt anywhere, at any time, and no image or group of images could possibly depict the conflict as a whole, the way a bird's-eye view of two armies confronting one another might have, for example, for earlier forms of warfare. In the face of this challenge, one of Goya's strategies is to create and sequence images in order to point towards that broader whole. By suggesting unseen causes, images such as this one reference a vaster world of violent conflict in a way that more straightforward pictorial representation cannot.

Even as the image subtly alludes to a wider sphere of violence, however, its primary aim is to make visible the bodies of the dead, to put before viewers what armed conflict always produces, regardless of the larger strategic or political objectives that might inform it. Goya's subject is in this sense deeply antiheroic once again. While fighting, killing, and even dying can lend themselves to tales of heroism, corpses do something else. They refuse the heroic, precisely because the animating principle to which one might attach ideals such as heroism is no longer present. Whoever these people were, heroic or not, is gone now. How they died makes little difference to the scene. They have become bodily remains, and much of the power of Goya's image stems from the gruesome details of what naturally happens to bodies once they are no longer alive.

Viewers are sometimes uncertain about why the sole living figure among the dead is vomiting, but the reason would not have been lost on audiences more intimately familiar with death than we generally are today. Bodies decompose fairly quickly, and the stench can be nauseating, particularly when corpses are piled together. This dimension of the image is easy to miss because Goya is working within a visual medium, and viewers must infer the full sensory context. Among other things, the vomiting man is a way of making the stench visible. If we were there, the experience would no doubt involve all of our senses, and we might find ourselves retching as well. Once more then, the difference between actual witnessing and looking at an image comes to the fore, and it raises the question of our relationship to the scene and to the man standing within it. How should we look at this image? Is revulsion a legitimate moral response? If we are disgusted, what does it mean in light of the way the image differentiates us from the nauseated man? If we are not disgusted, what does it mean about us, the visual culture in which we live, and the way we look? By placing a witness within the scene who is viscerally affected by his encounter with the bodies, the image subtly prompts viewers to reflect on their own activity as notional witnesses.

The caption for this scene of death and revulsion reads, "For that you have been born," or, more colloquially, "That is what you were born for." The commentary on the lives that have ended in this field is extraordinarily caustic, and the words engage the image in complex ways. To begin with, the caption approaches what we see by raising the question of why we are born, which is to say the purpose of human life as such. Viewers will no doubt bring to the print their own ideas concerning human purpose, but whatever notions we do bring, they are likely to contrast in fundamental ways with the scene we are viewing. The caption draws on the abyss between our own sense of human purpose, whatever it is, and what we see before us in the image. Goya's words in fact suggest that war is a violent undoing of other conceptions of human purpose. The print intimates that one of the disastrous consequences of war, beyond the bodies themselves, is the way it repurposes human life, the way it sets life on a course that ends in scenes such as this one. In a literal sense, the bodies here *were* born in order to end as they did, and this violent redirecting of human destiny, this snuffing out of other possibilities, is precisely what Goya's caption so bitingly decries. "For that you have been born" encapsulates war's demand that all other human purposes, including life itself, be subsumed to its own, violent ends. A combatant who sees individual lives as something dispensable might speak the words without irony. From our perspective here, gazing at the wasted lives that litter the field, however, they take the form of a biting, critical lament.

Readers may also recognize in the caption an ironic echo of the *memento mori*, the religious injunction to remember that we are all born to die. Within a Catholic theological framework, such remembrance conventionally serves to emphasize the vanity of worldly affairs in light of the ultimate, divine order and judgment believed to await all mortals. The sarcasm of Goya's evocation of the *memento mori* is consequently especially pointed. Rather than symbolizing mortality as a general human condition, these bodies testify to the results of wilful violence, and nothing in the image points to an otherworldly order in which the deaths might be accorded meaning. There is no destiny beyond what we see in the image. In addition, the caption tellingly does not specify that these people were born *to die* (*para morir*), the way one would expect of the classic *memento mori*. It states more ambiguously that they have been born *for that* (*para eso*), where *that* alludes not only to dying but to all of the gruesome details of the scene. They have been born to become what we see: to be killed, to putrefy, to be splattered in vomit. Religious allusion becomes suffused with irony precisely because Goya's visual treatment of his subject is so harrowingly secular.

This print's caption also plays with more than one possibility when it comes to the question of voice. To whom can we attribute "For that you have been born"? It could be that Goya himself is commenting on the senselessness of what he has depicted by feigning to address the dead. (In the original Spanish, the "you" is grammatically plural and informal.) In such a reading, the caption is an apostrophe directed to those no longer present, as if to say, "How can it be that you were born only to die this way?" Another, darker, and perhaps less obvious possibility is that the caption represents the inner voice of the man standing in the field. "For that you have been born" could be the word-thoughts that accompany his retching, perhaps as an expression of his revulsion. A third option, however, involves us as viewers who "pronounce" the words as we read the print. Like the caption to Print 6, which made us address the fallen officer, this caption also has us momentarily address the figures we see. We "say" the caption to them as we look, which raises questions about our own activity as viewers. What does it mean, for example, to be addressing the dead? Who are we when we speak these words? How do we "speak" to them as we read?

Goya creates similar effects through the ambiguity of the caption's address. Within the scene, it seems fairly clear that the words are directed to the dead, but in a second, fainter sense, the plural "you" can also address the viewer. In this reading, "For that you have been born" would be telling us that what we see in the image awaits us as well. Not death in the general sense of the *memento mori*, but the gruesome particulars of wartime death. The prophecy is unsettling, to say the least, and we might ask how anyone could make it, especially in light of the fact that we are here, safely looking at an image. The artist could not possibly know how we will end. Then again, neither can we. Unlike the corpses in the field, our deaths by definition lie ahead, and it would be foolish to pretend that we know the form they will take. Who can say for certain that they will *not* be swept up into the violence of war? How many of those who have died during wartime would have imagined it? By subtly addressing both the figures depicted and viewers themselves, the caption momentarily unsettles the presumed safety of our viewing, as if to say, "Do not deceive yourselves. This could easily happen to you." In terms of voicing and address, then, Goya has crafted a caption that speaks within the illusion and to us as viewers. The result is a layering of meanings that prompts readers to reflect critically on their viewing and on their relationship to what they see.

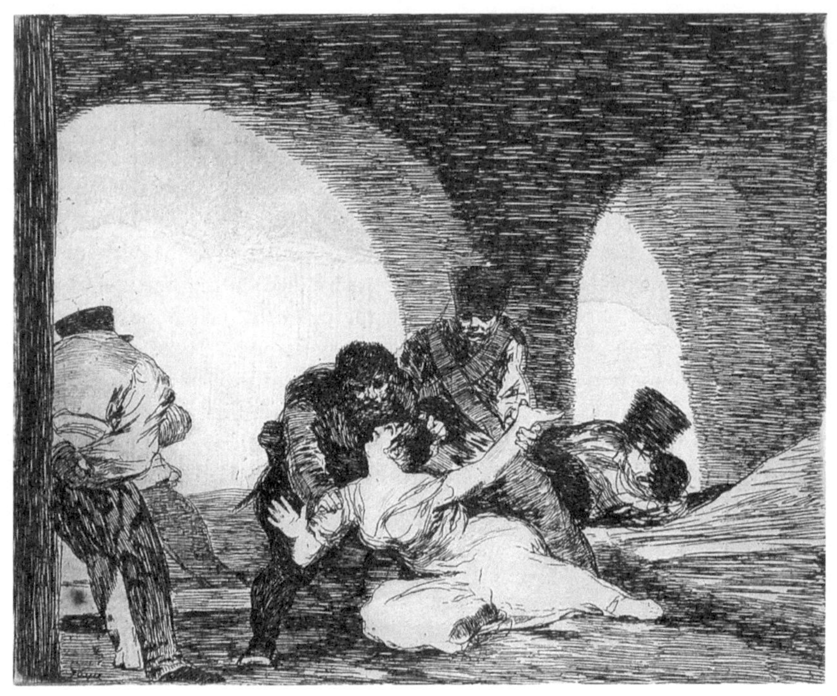

13
Amarga presencia

Two soldiers have seized a woman under an archway. One of them, above her and to the left as we face them, holds her by the hair and shoulder. The other grasps her by the wrist as he stands with legs astride, above her and to the right. Additional figures flank the group on either side. On the far left, a man with hands bound behind him leans against a wall. His back is to us, and he partially blocks our view of another man who stands just outside the arch on the left. To the right of the central group, a third soldier, his hat visible under the second arch, appears to be on top of another woman. The pair is also under the archway, and the darkness that bulges out slightly at the column's base suggests that their lower bodies lie in shadows, behind the figures in the foreground. It is most likely a rape in progress. The woman in the foreground, however, makes the strongest initial claim to our visual attention. With arms outstretched and head tilted back in painful silhouette, she constitutes the emotional heart of the image. Framed by arches to the left and right of her, she, like many of her predecessors, appears in some of the print's brightest tones. Only the light of the world beyond the arches, a world that contrasts starkly with her position in the shadows, competes with the woman's anguished lustre. Darkness and light again take on morally symbolic meaning, much along the lines we considered in Print 11.

In this print Goya also creates a complex sense of pictorial space. There is something strangely flat, for example, about the whiteness beyond the arches. A blankness devoid of figures or strong suggestions of depth, the space challenges the visual habit that would have us see simply sky. Under the archway, things are also less simple than they initially seem. Strange anomalies characterize the perspective governing the depiction of the archway. If the arches are to be understood as aligned within the same plane, for example, the one on the right would from our point of view have to be much more open than it is. Instead, its slant suggests that it pivots away from the plane of the first arch at an angle difficult to reconcile with the perspective traditionally associated with pictorial realism. The result is an oddly bending archway, or perhaps space is bending. More perplexing still is the right base of this arch. Just what is it that angles up and to the right at forty-five degrees, occluding our view of the place where the arch would meet the ground? What purpose would the hint of an unseen incline serve? Such details trouble naturalist illusion. One can interpret them expressively, as markers of a traumatic world gone astray, but such features of the image also subtly remind viewers that the scene is a picture, something constructed for our viewing.

Thematically, the print represents a return to the subject of rape, and this gesture highlights something important about the artistry of sequencing in the *Disasters*. As we have seen, Goya often clusters thematically related prints together, and he frequently uses captions that bind one image to the next: Prints 2 and 3 on the senselessness of violence ("With reason or without it" and "The same thing"), Prints 4 and 5 on womanly valour ("The women give courage" and "And they are wild beasts"), or Prints 9, 10, and 11 on rape ("They do not want to," "Neither do they," and "Not even like that"). At the same time, however, Goya often muddles the boundaries of such clusters for artistic effect. The depiction of women combatants in Prints 4 and 5, for example, seemed to come to an end with the wounded officer in Print 6, but the subject returned, amplified, in the cannon fire of Print 7. Similarly, Goya's reflections on sexual violence in Prints 9, 10, and 11 appeared to subside as we turned to the nauseated man above the field of the dead in Print 12, and yet we find ourselves once again contemplating a print that is about rape. In each of these instances, thematic clusters that seem to come to a close do not in fact put an end to their respective subject matters. The series feigns to move on, but only to return to earlier subjects, as if to make more forcefully the point that *there is no moving on* when it comes to the disasters of war. Atrocities such as rape do not happen a scant few times, at this battle, in that village, or in those pictures we just saw. These and other disasters recur as long as war continues to be waged, and Goya communicates the idea – again an idea that no single print can convey – by returning to certain subjects after subtly having suggested to viewers that they would be moving in a new thematic direction. From the field of the dead we return to impending rape once more.

The caption to this scene, which unfolds under an archway reminiscent of Print 11, reads "Bitter presence." The words seem straightforward enough, but the caption plays with our reading once again. It can refer to any number of elements in the image, and its relative ambiguity prompts readers to entertain numerous possibilities. Rather than immediately pinning things down, "Bitter presence" in effect asks our sense making to roam through the image as we try to assign the words to what we see. From the perspective of the woman in white, for example, the bitter presence undoubtedly refers to her aggressors, whose presence is the source of her affliction. Given the sexual nature of the violence depicted here, the caption could very well name rape itself as an unwanted, violent, bitter presence. This would certainly be the case for the victim in shadows behind the central group. The presence, however, could also refer to the man on the left, the man whose hands are tied behind his back. More than one scholar has suggested that he is a family member, perhaps even the husband of the woman who is going to be raped. If that is the case, the man is a bitter presence for the victim because she knows that a loved one will be watching as she is violated. Alternatively, the words could just as easily apply to the man's own situation as a prisoner forced to be bitterly present for what is about to happen. If witnesses are a bitter presence for the woman, however, the caption might also include the notional viewer, turning our looking into a vexed activity once more.

Still another possibility, given the way Goya's prints often point to our own viewing position, is that the caption refers to the entire scene, the impending violence, the bound man, and the anguished woman, which together are a bitter presence *for us* as imagined witnesses to rape. Like the man on the left, we too are looking and can do nothing to prevent what is about to happen. If the scene is a bitter presence for us, however, we would again need to pose those unsettling questions that have accompanied our viewing in earlier prints. What kind of witnesses would we be if we were in this scene? What would we be doing there? Why would we be in the darkness, under an archway, looking? Whatever our answers, we would also need to note the differences between the bitterness for us as witnesses and its meaning for the woman or the bound man. We might brush such questions aside by returning our attention to the fact that we are not there, looking at impending rape, but rather here, looking at an image. Still, we would nevertheless have to grapple with the way the image positions us as viewers. Even within the framework that approaches the image as an image, the caption remains uncannily pertinent. "Bitter presence" could be telling us that the image itself is an unexpected painful moment within the sequence of prints we have been viewing. We may have thought that we were done with such scenes, yet we confront the persistent presence of rape once more, knowing all the while the profound differences between what bitterness means to us and its meaning for the figures within the scene.

By writing a caption that speaks to so many different facets of the image, Goya again brings the question of meaning to the fore. To look at this image without the caption produces a powerful experience, to be sure, but what the *Disasters* do so well, time and again, is to yoke words to such experiences, words that complicate what we see, or more precisely, words that generate complex understandings of what we see. Given the moral urgency of Goya's subjects, it may seem an odd choice. Why complicate a rape scene with the kind of conceptual play we have just sketched? We cannot know for certain, but one of the effects of such complication is to channel initial viewing responses towards critical deliberation and reflection. Perhaps precisely because of the moral urgency of his subject, Goya's captions routinely provoke thought, even as his images produce other, initially less deliberative responses (horror, disgust, compassion, etc.). Among other things, then, captions spur viewers to reflect critically, both on what they see and on their own activity as they take in the prints. We miss something fundamental about *The Disasters of War* if we take them to be exclusively about presenting the horrors. They do indeed put images of terrible violence before our eyes, with an uncanny intimacy that separates Goya from much of the European visual tradition that preceded him, but making the horrors visible is only one part of his artistry in the series. His prints are also, and just as importantly, extraordinarily sophisticated vehicles for reflecting critically on the act of making and viewing such violence in artistic form.

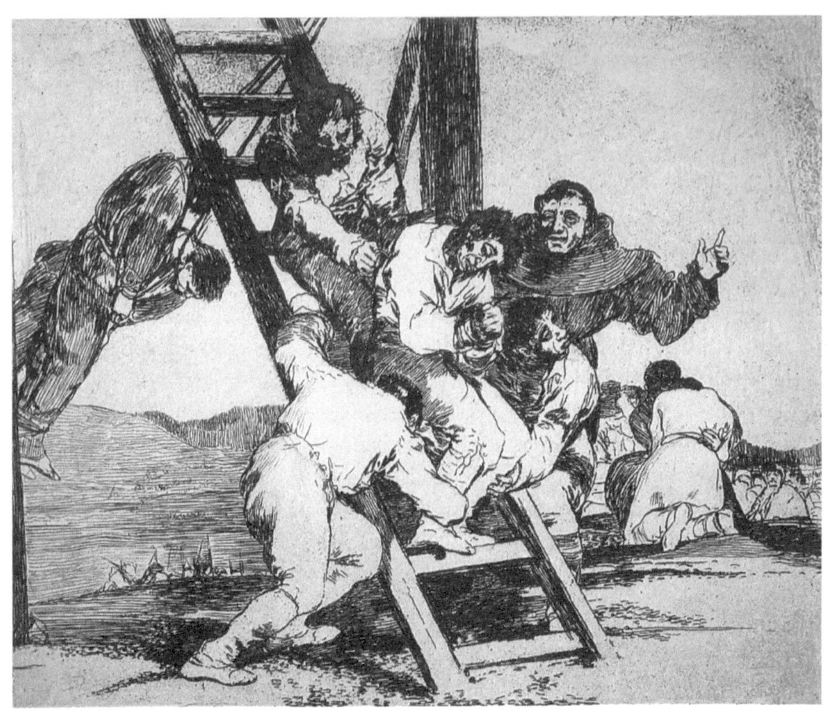

14
Duro es el paso!

A new form of violence. Neither the unbridled aggression of combatants nor the brutality of wartime rape, but more methodical killing: an execution. Prisoners have been condemned, a gallows has been built, and workers are carrying out the punishment. Such executions routinely took place on both sides of the conflagration in Spain, and there has been considerable scholarly speculation on the possible historical contexts to which this print may allude. For some, the image recalls the execution by Spanish authorities of partisans who had slaughtered over three hundred defenceless French residents of Valencia in the summer of 1808. Others argue that this could be the depiction of one of the many executions of French civilians and their Spanish collaborators, the so-called *afrancesados*, by anti-Napoleonic authorities. Still others recall that death by hanging was the most common form of punishment for Spanish guerrilla fighters who were caught by the French.

Taken together, such interpretations offer an intriguing array of historical possibilities. Spaniards, Frenchmen, collaborators, and guerrillas each plausibly occupy the position of the victims for a moment. The very range of possibilities, however, is a useful reminder of the open and relatively undefined status of history in Goya's series. If the victims in this image cannot be linked definitively to any given historical account, such indeterminacy is no accident. Goya could easily have specified things more precisely, either pictorially or with his caption. Instead, the print, like the vast majority of the *Disasters*, knowingly avoids such specifics. It evokes historically verifiable forms of violence, but history is overshadowed by the more pressing moral questions Goya's work poses. As we considered earlier, narrow conceptions of history can easily miss the larger sense of time that Goya's work engages. To pin the image down historically is, in many regards, to miss something important about what it aims to communicate.

As a moral commentary on executions, the print focuses on their particular cruelty, and it reminds viewers once more of the many different forms of brutality that routinely accompany armed conflict. Like rape, this kind of violence can go unnoticed when one imagines and represents war primarily in terms of combat. And yet, execution is a common form of wartime killing. It is also a kind of violence marked by its own particularities. To face execution during wartime is to be forced to hear the rationalizations of those doing the killing. In times of war and peace alike, executions often dress themselves in legal justification. Victims are judged and condemned according to the laws of the victors, even if as readers of the *Disasters* we have learned that there is in fact no reason, which is to say no law, which can justify the killing (see Prints 2 and 3).

In contrast to open combat, execution also implies a very different relationship to the killing and the dying. Soldiers on the field of battle can have generalized fears and anxieties about their prospects for survival, but a condemned man and his killers both know for certain when death will arrive. Death by execution has a scheduled time and place, and the knowledge of what lies ahead is often the most acute source of anguish for the condemned. It is no coincidence that only a few years after Goya made this print, Victor Hugo would launch perhaps the most famous nineteenth-century literary critique of capital punishment in his *The Last Day of a Condemned Man* (1829). Central to both artists' engagement with their subject is the devastating psychological torment that the knowledge of impending execution produces in the condemned. Such suffering is literally at the centre of this image in the form of the man who, hands bound in front of him, cannot move up the ladder to his death. His legs have buckled, and his body no longer moves on its own. The three men around him are trying to force his movement up the ladder while a priest prays by his side, presumably giving the man the last rites. The scene could not be further from the paradigm of heroic sacrifice. Rather than depicting uncommon resolve in the face of death, Goya portrays the devastating bodily effects produced by the knowledge that the end is mere moments away.

Composition reinforces the idea in several ways. To the right of the central group as we face them, we see another crumpled body in white. A man has fallen to his knees. His back is to us, and a figure in dark silhouette holds him. The kneeling figure is difficult to identify for certain, but there is reason to believe he is another of the condemned, the next in line after the man on the ladder. Whoever he is, he has turned away from the gallows, in contrast to the crowd that has assembled in the background behind him. Like the man on the ladder, he cannot look, even as others gather precisely in order to do so. On the left side of the image, under the gallows, things could not be more different. Against a bleak, unpopulated background, the bodies of two hanged men still swing, suggesting that only a brief moment has elapsed since they have dropped to their deaths. To move from right to left in the image is consequently to transit from life to death, and this spatial symbolism heightens the poignancy of the main victim's anguish. Collapsing precisely at the centre of the image, his position becomes a hopeless pause within the fatal right-to-left movement and everything it means.

For all that it delivers, however, there is also something striking about what the composition withholds. The strong, intersecting diagonals of ladder and ropes point upward, towards the place of execution proper, and one can almost imagine the platform, the support beam, and even the noose that presumably awaits the condemned man. Yet this place, the very source of the terror that has incapacitated him, remains out of sight, beyond the upper left border of the image. It could be that Goya wants to remind viewers once more that his image is merely a small swath of a much vaster world of violence beyond the frame, but the missing upper half of the gallows seems a more pointed kind of omission. By purposely leaving out the primary cause of the man's suffering, Goya's image in effect echoes the victim's desperate desire: where the man cannot go, the image does not go, at least in terms of depiction. In turn, the careful evocation of this fearful, deadly space beyond the image magnifies its terror. What we cannot see is often terrifying precisely because we cannot see it. Goya may also be signalling that there are limits to the kind of understanding we can develop while viewing the *Disasters*. It is not that what is above the upper frame defies representation, as some scholars claim about certain forms of violence, but rather that the nature of Goya's subject matter calls for reflection on the limits of seeing and understanding. "Look" – the image suggests – "but remember that you do not see the whole picture and cannot presume to understand fully." Goya will return to this visual strategy several times over the course of the series.

His concern with the meaning of looking at violence in an artwork takes on additional complexities as he turns to the subject of public killing. Among other things, executions are visual spectacles. Gallows are grim stages, and public hangings are inevitably theatrical. In contrast to other perpetrators of violence we confront in the series – rapists who do not want to be seen, for example – executioners deliberately exhibit the punishment they mete out, and as this image shows, crowds gather for the spectacle. Whenever onlookers appear within Goya's images, however, they raise the question of the relationship between their looking and our own. In this scene, for example, Goya appears to differentiate us from the crowd. They are gathered at a distance, while we are much closer to the gallows, slightly behind and below the main platform. In relation to the crowd, we are in fact looking behind the stage of this public theatre: the man's agony on the ladder, the workers pulling him up, and the priest, whose wooden expression, devoid of compassion, betrays his hypocrisy as minister to the condemned. Technically speaking, the crowd sees none of this. For them, the main event is not what we see in the image but what is staged above us, on the platform, beyond the frame. It slowly becomes apparent that Goya has depicted the literal and moral underside of the spectacle, and whatever compassion we feel for the man stems from the privileged access this perspective has afforded us.

As we have seen in earlier prints, however, Goya does not usually allow viewers to envision themselves as innocent moral witnesses for very long. While we might imagine our gaze to be more compassionate than the crowd's, the position Goya assigns us within the scene suggests that we are not mere onlookers. Within the world depicted, we stand in close proximity to the gallows, and we have unobstructed access to it. The most plausible explanation for our position is that we, who are not part of the crowd, are among those carrying out the execution. The illusion of witnessing this scene is consequently troubled by the suggestion that if we were there, we would in all likelihood be part of the apparatus of execution. Only on this side of the illusion, as viewers who know that we are looking at an image rather than witnessing a scene, does our compassionate response to the man's suffering – if that has been our response – seem less vexed. Still, the way Goya has subtly implicated the notional viewer in the violence cautions against superficial moral responses.

It is another example of the way Goya's prints prompt viewers to think as well as feel. The image spurs critical reflection, and it suggests that even as viewers of images, we may not always be who we think we are. At the same time, Goya's composition, which as we have noted plays masterfully with what we can and cannot see, underscores the differences between actually witnessing a scene and entertaining the illusion of doing so in an artwork. While it magnifies the terror by withholding its source, it also calls attention to the fact that we are not witnesses to the violence but rather viewers of images. If we truly were witnesses, there would be no frame to limit our gaze. Framing is a powerful expressive device that we will see Goya exploit to great effect in subsequent prints, but frames are simultaneously signs of artifice that can disrupt the fantasy of witnessing in order to prevent us from taking it too far.

A complex game is similarly afoot in the caption Goya has given the image, which most translations render as "Hard is the step!" or "Hard is the way!" In the most obvious sense the words refer to the man on the ladder, but they are not a simple or straightforward description of his plight. Given his situation, calling what we see "a hard step" is a pointed understatement, a minimizing that amplifies the pathos of the man's circumstances by way of contrast. The gap between the words we read and what we actually see, which for the man is far more than merely a difficult step, produces this effect. As in English, however, the Spanish idiom "to take a step" (*dar un paso*) is not always literal. It can also mean to proceed with a plan, to act on a decision, or to move forward with a course of action, and in this second sense the caption's reference extends beyond the man to the measures the authorities have taken in putting together the execution. "Hard" now takes on the meaning of harsh, inflexible, or uncaring rather than difficult, and in this reading the caption is no longer an understatement but rather an indictment of the cruelty. One of the meanings of the word *paso* in Spanish is in fact "a noteworthy event." "Hard is the step!" is also "Harsh is the event!"

For Spaniards at the mid-nineteenth century, however, the caption's key word would also have had strong associations with suffering and death. *Paso* is the word the Spanish traditionally used to describe the major events from the story of the Christian Passion. Each of the Catholic Stations of the Cross is a *paso*, and in this sense, the caption says that the image represents a harsh scene reminiscent of moments from the *Via Dolorosa*. Within such a framework, one can understand why scholars have seen echoes of the Crucifixion in the image (ascent towards a cross suggested by the intersection of ropes and ladder, for example, or possible visual citation of the tradition of the Descent from the Cross). Religious allusion, however, is once again deeply ironic, given Goya's treatment of the subject. The man on the ladder is neither Christ nor a Christian martyr. Nothing in the image suggests that redemption awaits him, and the only overt visual reference to religion is the priest, who, morally speaking, could scarcely be less attractive. The benediction he offers is entirely at odds with the sentiment conveyed by his facial expression.

In addition, the word *paso* itself had acquired an entirely secular meaning in the nineteenth century. Among the definitions gathered for the term in the 1852 *Dictionary of the Spanish Royal Academy* one finds "the moment of death or any other grave conflict." In addition to its previous meanings, then, the caption is also saying that this is a particularly harsh scene of impending death. In English one might call it a hard passing. Still another level of meaning draws on the fact that in its religious acceptation *paso* simultaneously designates both the event of suffering and the *representation* of that event. Jesus' first fall on the *Via Dolorosa*, for example, is a *paso*, but so are the various images and sculptures that depict the fall. The statues paraded through the streets of many Spanish cities during Holy Week each year are known as *pasos*, and believers will often have a preference for one *paso* over another in representing any given event. In this sense Goya's caption does not simply convey that the *scene* we see is especially harsh. It also intimates that what is before us is a difficult or harsh *image*.

Common to the meanings of *paso*, whether understood as step, measure, event, or death scene, is an underlying notion of movement in space and time. Belonging to the same word family as the verb *pasar*, "to happen," the word names events that take place or arrive, the way a step does. As we have seen in previous prints, however, when Goya engages questions of movement in the *Disasters*, his artistry often subtly encompasses more than the unfolding of events within the world he depicts. His sequence also plays knowingly with that other movement in which we are all engaged, the movement of our viewing as we turn from one print to the next. In this sense *paso* encompasses not only what we see in this image but also our own activity as readers who have in effect taken a further, hard "step" into the series by turning from the last print to this one. The caption anticipates and names the movement of our viewing and reading, and this gesture is itself only the first moment of Goya's reflection. "Hard is the step," it turns out once again, is the initial clause of a sentence that Goya does not complete until the next print.

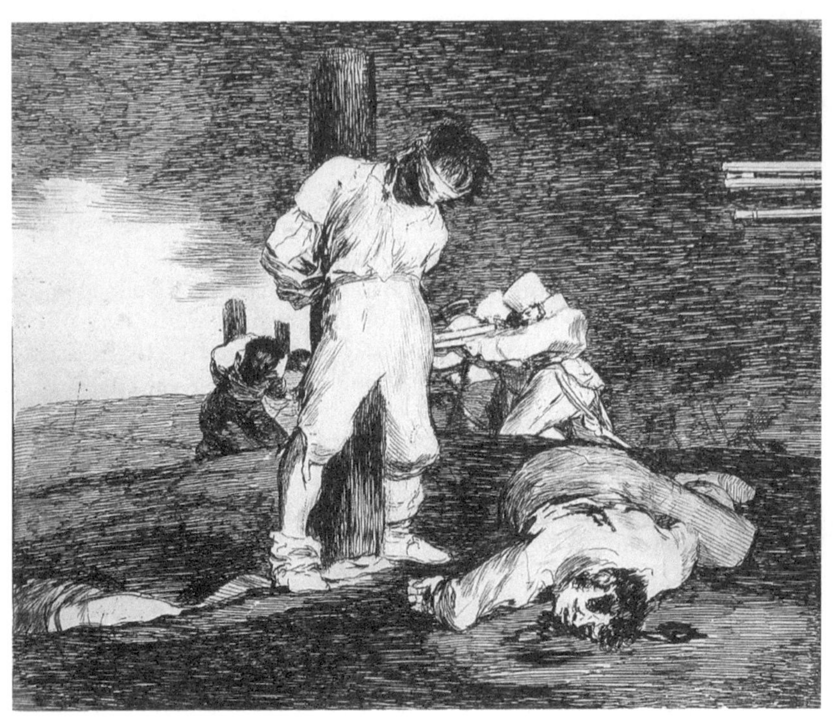

15

Y no hay remedio

"The step is hard, and" – we read as we come to a new image – "Nothing can be done." The expression Goya uses here, *Y no hay remedio*, literally means "There is no remedy." Often translated as "It can't be helped," it is what one says in Spanish when a situation is unavoidable, when it cannot be changed, or, as in this case, when things are hopeless. Once more we look at executions under way, but instead of a gallows we now contemplate killing by firing squad. The historical record is full of references to executions of this type, but again the scene is broadly representative rather than the depiction of a concrete historical event. In the foreground, just left of centre, a blindfolded man stands bound to a pole. In stark contrast to his predecessor in the previous print, he appears to retain his dignity, awaiting the inevitable. He stands, with head bowed, and as with many victims in the *Disasters*, strong tonal contrasts accentuate his presence in the darkness. Goya has spent considerable time on the details of his form: the billowing shirt sleeve of his right arm, the subtle volume of his pants, the fallen, bunched stocking that reveals his right calf. At his feet to the right, a corpse lies on the ground. Presumably this man once stood where the central figure now does, but, lifeless and unbound, his body has fallen in a mangled heap. One arm lies under his torso, the other is horribly twisted, and the cadaver's head turns awkwardly, showing us his face, which Goya has rendered in gruesome detail. His head rests on a slightly lightened patch of field that allows viewers to perceive black pools of blood on either side of it, and where his right eye would normally be we see only a dark stain. To the left and slightly below the central figure's feet, Goya suggests the presence of a second body that has fallen to lower ground, perhaps into a mass grave.

And then there are the weapons. The three rifle barrels that jut in from the right are among the most compelling details in the foreground. They evoke the presence of the soldiers who are about to use them, but strikingly, the men remain out of sight. Like the previous image, which withheld the gallows' main platform, Goya's composition here again plays dramatically with what we can and cannot see in order to produce a complex viewing experience. Given how close the rifle barrels are to us, for example, the fact that we do not see the soldiers is unsettling. Death is seconds away from arriving, but its agents remain out of sight. In some ways, however, we do see the men who are about to shoot, or more precisely, we see their analogues in the execution scene just behind this one, where not by coincidence three soldiers have just fired. In contrast to the foreground, the body at which they still aim has already slumped. As is often the case in Goya, the firing squad is depicted in ways that underscore the faceless, impersonal, modern machine-like efficiency of the killing. Presumably this is the very kind of formation that is just off to the right, about to dispatch the central victim. If keeping the soldiers outside the frame lends them a foreboding character, then, in this case it also depersonalizes them further, minimizing the human component of the killing machine. In an ominous part-for-whole logic, only the weapons signal the presence of the soldiers.

At the same time, our proximity to these unseen executioners once again raises questions about our own role as imagined witnesses to the scene. Where are we exactly, and what are we doing there? There are no definitive answers, but it seems highly unlikely that we are random bystanders or potential victims. The most plausible scenario, given the way we have been positioned, is that we are there with the soldiers. Goya has once again constructed an image that questions the innocence of our gaze, prompting us to reflect on our own activity as viewers and readers of the series. We often restrict moral judgments to what we see before us, with little or no self-examination. It is the familiar habit of thought that would have us believe atrocity is primarily the work of *other* people – in this image, the soldiers – rather than something in which we ourselves could become entangled. Goya pointedly challenges such assumptions by intimating our potential complicity with the violence. He suggests that, given the right circumstances, you and I could very well be one of those other people. He also tacitly raises the question of whether our looking – we are also outside the frame – is really so different from the soldiers'.

In this regard, while Goya's prints call for moral responses to the disasters he depicts, they also prompt viewers not to take moral witnessing for granted as something requiring little or no deliberation. This is particularly true when such witnessing unfolds within the illusion of an artistic image. In this print, for example, it is precisely because we are here, looking at an image, rather than actually witnessing a scene, that moral deliberation has been possible at all. If we were truly there, the image suggests, we would see the soldiers next to us, and things would be very different. As in the previous image, Goya's framing is thus both a powerful expressive device and a way of calling attention to the artifice with which the image has been constructed. The frame reminds us that we are playing art's game when we regard images as if they were actual scenes in the world, and it prompts us to reflect on the game's limits.

Awareness of artifice also helps to illuminate other facets of this image, like the foreboding sky looming over the executions. If this is the representation of a night scene, what is the brightness in the distance? The glow of distant fire, a cloud, perhaps daybreak? They are all possibilities, but what is distinctive about Goya's sky is precisely the way it resists such pinning down. Once again pictorial realism is not the primary objective of this background. Reminiscent of a vast cavern, the dark sky fatefully seems to enclose the figures, and if light in the darkness traditionally signals hope, the light at the end of this tunnel offers no solace. Equally ominous is the way Goya has emphasized the idea of repetition: the three posts receding into the distance, the three victims' upper bodies leaning at almost identical angles, the three soldiers, the three rifle barrels. Much of the power of this image stems from its suggestion that what we see immediately before us in the foreground is merely one instance of a scene that seems to repeat itself indefinitely. The executions extend to the horizon, and they could quite plausibly continue behind us as well. There is also a temporal dimension to Goya's line of executions. The man in the foreground is only seconds away from being shot, while the man behind him has already been killed, suggesting that the moment of death recedes in time as we move towards the horizon. If that is the case and the line does indeed continue behind us, what waits at our back is a future filled with more of the same. In short, Goya's composition suggests that the killing goes on endlessly, in space and time, and this idea is magnified by a caption that adds, "And nothing can be done."

In order to understand the meaning of the caption more fully, however, it must be read as the second moment of the reflection that began in the preceding print. There the victim had collapsed under the anguish of his approaching death on the gallows. Proximate as that death was, the last seconds of the man's life, his standing on the platform with the noose around his neck, nevertheless remained part of an impending and unrepresented future. Here, that future seems to have arrived. In this image, Goya depicts the very moment towards which the man on the ladder could no longer step, or, to be more precise, he depicts the equivalent of that moment within a different scene of execution. The central victim standing before the firing squad has arrived at those terrible, last seconds. "Nothing can be done" for him, but the caption's reference is not limited to the man we see in the foreground. By yoking the two prints together grammatically, Goya has effectively brought the narrative content of different scenes into dialogue with one another. As a consequence, this image becomes, among other things, the illustration of the fact that the "step" that so tortured the man on the gallows has indeed been taken. The two prints together thus convey the idea that regardless of what the condemned do – whether they lose bodily control or stand with more dignified stoicism – their last moment inevitably arrives, "and nothing can be done." The effect is similar to the one Goya achieved in the sequence of Prints 9, 10, and 11, where it slowly became clear that war rape happens, regardless of what its victims do.

It is not that Goya is a fatalist about war as such, but rather that his prints emphasize the ineluctable quality of war's violence once it has been unleashed. What, for example, can these victims possibly do? What could we do, realistically, if we were there, witnessing the executions? This sense of the fateful force of the violence is further intensified by the way Goya works with viewers' background awareness of the fact that they are looking at a series of prints. If *paso* in the previous print referred to both the content of the image and the image itself as one more "step" within Goya's series, this caption, which completes the sentence, continues the double reference. "And nothing can be done" refers not only to the inevitability of the violence within the scene but also, more subtly, to the inevitability of confronting this image as the next moment within Goya's sequence. In this second sense, nothing can be done because we have turned the page, and the image has happened. It is one more example of the way Goya's artistry plays with our viewing and reading.

Such playing often prompts viewers to reflect critically on the meaning of their looking, but Goya does not limit the exercise to viewers. He often practises the self-scrutiny he preaches by periodically creating prints that reflect in subtle ways on his own activity as an artist. In the previous print, where he depicts a spectacle deliberately constructed for public viewing, for example, Goya deftly raises the question of the relationship between the executioners' activities and his own. After all, he too has taken a "harsh step" in depicting the scene. He too has constructed and carefully "staged" the violence for public viewing, and while his print clearly aims to denounce what it depicts, it is nevertheless an exhibition of violence not entirely unlike the hanging. By making an image that, among other things, reflects on the subject of spectacle, Goya brings his own practices under scrutiny. Something similar can be found within his depiction of seemingly endless executions in this print. While the image clearly references the repeated use of capital punishment during the Peninsular War, Goya's composition also pointedly echoes the structure of *The Disasters of War* itself. Within this image, we see one scene of violence after another, presented sequentially, in a series that seems to move through time. The representation of serial executions is in this sense a *mise-en-abyme*, a moment in which Goya's art echoes its own serial nature, pointing to disquieting parallels between inflicting violence, on one hand, and representing it, on the other.

Like the viewers he so often implicates in his images, Goya's self-reflexive gestures convey his understanding that he himself, as a maker of images, is not above the fray. Something within the making of images of violence, he suggests, implicates the artist in the violence as well. More specifically, Goya seems to acknowledge in these prints that his *Disasters* may themselves be a form of violence, not only because of their content but also because of the power of images as images. Prints 14 and 15 set up provocative analogies between the killing that Goya depicts and his own activity as maker of the series. The point is not to blur the profound differences between actual executions and their representation, but rather to recognize the moral complexities of both viewing and making representations of violence. Critical reflection is a constant throughout the series, and as we will see in later prints, some of Goya's most gruesome images are also among the most markedly self-reflexive.

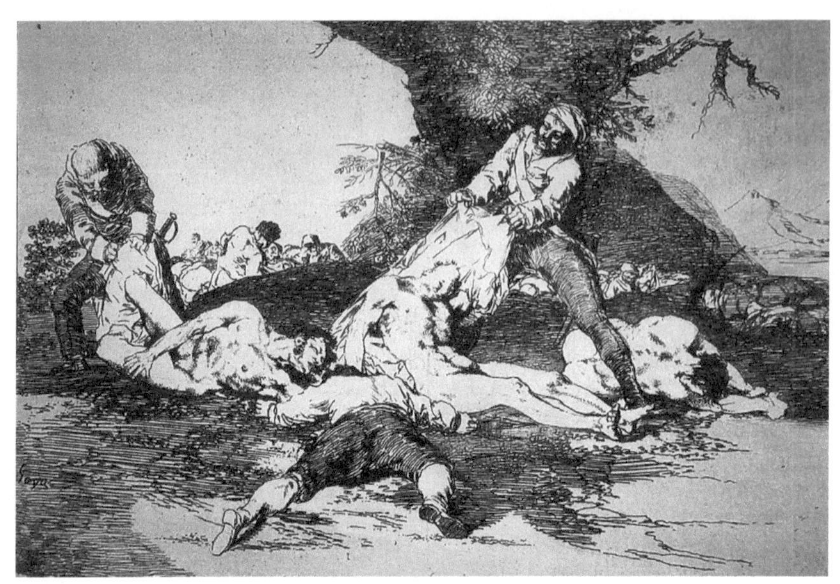

16
Se aprovechan

From the firing squads we turn again to the aftermath of battle. Four corpses lie across a field, and two soldiers are stripping them of their clothing. It is a common enough event in times of war. Reverence for the dead gives way to more pressing material demands, and the possessions of the fallen quickly become something for the taking. In this image it is difficult to know for certain if the living and the dead were friends or foes. In contrast to the soldiers, the victim closest to us appears to wear civilian clothing, but, given Goya's consistent dismantling of us-and-them narratives, such distinctions do not seem particularly important. Whether the soldiers are plundering the bodies of men they have defeated or stripping down their own dead matters little. Like Print 12, Goya's subject here is the treatment of the dead, regardless of who they were or how they died. More specifically, the image registers the callous handling of the dead by those who see them as a resource to be exploited.

Disregard for the dead appears not only in the matter-of-fact expressions of the soldiers but also, more pointedly, in their treatment of the bodies, in the awkward postures they impose on the cadavers as they strip them. Goya's composition, organized largely along intersecting diagonals, accentuates the force of such handling. The line that angles up and to the left, from the right foot and thigh of the corpse lying face down, through the neck and shoulder of the naked body on the left, to the upper arm and shoulder of the hunched fighter standing over it, for example, extends the tension of the tugging as the man tries to remove the cadaver's pants. More dramatic, and heightened by the tonal contrast, is the line that runs from the head of the corpse on the left to the right shoulder of the man pulling at the shirt. Secondary lines of composition – the right thigh of the body on the left, for example, or the left leg of the face-down cadaver – parallel the main diagonals and complete the compositional "x," which Goya has positioned low and to the left within the picture frame.

As if to encapsulate the drama of dead weight and its resistance to the pulling, the centre of the image has been reserved for the head of a corpse still caught in its shirt, and Goya's depiction of the soldier above it again emphasizes the force of the pulling. Particularly striking in this regard is the soldier's massive left leg, which is completely out of proportion with the rest of his body as it juts out in an exaggerated, physically expressive stance. Behind the leg another body, its back to us, appears to have already been stripped of its clothing. Together the four cadavers – from fully clothed to entirely stripped – thus represent the various stages of the activity under way. Like the two preceding prints, the victims in this image subtly register different moments within an ongoing process. At the same time, as we have also seen in earlier images, Goya knowingly reworks Christian iconography for ironic effect. Scholars have variously seen echoes of the Pietà or the Deposition in the depiction of the central body. Death in the *Disasters*, however, is almost without exception rendered as an entirely worldly affair. There are no hints of a metaphysical order that would redeem the dead, and in contrast to the religious iconography Goya cites, care for their bodies is precisely what is absent from this scene.

The caption, which is often rendered in English as "They take advantage," clearly addresses what the soldiers are doing, but once again Goya's words engage the image in ways that are more complex than they initially seem. To ask just what the soldiers are taking advantage of is to notice that the caption leaves the possibilities open by withholding verbal reference to a specific object. The soldiers could plausibly be taking advantage of the general situation, or – and this is the most common reading – the caption could refer to their taking advantage of the dead themselves. In this latter case, the words would refer to the way the soldiers unfairly avail themselves of their superiority over the deceased. In such a reading the caption names the morally reprehensible act of taking advantage of the defenceless, with the added irony that, technically speaking, the dead are no longer people in the philosophical or theological sense. "They take advantage" suggests that what the soldiers are doing is an affront to the remnants of personhood we habitually attach to the dead.

Along with this moral understanding of taking advantage, however, Goya's words also convey the more material, economic sense of taking advantage, as in "to make use of fully" or "to employ for optimum benefit." The Spanish verb *aprovechar* conveys more than its common English equivalent. "They take advantage" is simultaneously "They exploit fully," and much of the critical force of the image stems from its depiction of bodies that have in effect become material resources, with little or no distinction between them and other objects. This notion is heightened by a grammatical ambiguity in the original caption that is difficult to translate into English. Read as a sentence in the active voice, the subject of the caption *Se aprovechan* refers to the soldiers, but the very same words in Spanish can also be read as a passive voice construction whose grammatical subject is not the soldiers but the bodies. "They (the soldiers) take advantage" is simultaneously "They (the bodies) are used." The caption is a double entendre, and its grammatical play hinges on the very distinction between subjects and objects that Goya so dramatically depicts within the image. It is a fine example of the way verbal artistry – here, a sort of grammatical punning – augments the graphic dimensions of the prints, adding layers of meaning to the experience of their viewing. Without the caption this is an arresting image, to be sure, but coupled with Goya's words it becomes a far more complex reflection on "taking advantage," in both the moral and material sense.

Goya sets this scene of exploitation against a background that dialogues with the foreground figures in intriguing ways. The trunk of what seems to be an enormous tree, for example, looms behind the soldier who is pulling off the shirt. While it clearly provides necessary tonal contrast for what we see in front of it, Goya has also made the tree's shape subtly echo the compositional "x" in the foreground. If tonal and compositional considerations might help to account for the tree, however, its presence is nevertheless something of a novelty for those viewing the series in sequence. This is the first image of a tree to appear within the *Disasters*. The preceding fifteen prints are utterly devoid of plant life. It seems an odd omission, given the preponderance of outdoor scenes Goya depicts, but the absence speaks again to the way pictorial realism cedes to other concerns when Goya constructs backgrounds. Symbolic or conceptual considerations typically take precedence, and on this front the scant presence of plant life in the series is entirely consistent with the bleak world that Goya explores. Nature, growth, and flourishing life are the very antitheses of the desolation wrought by war's disasters. Their minimal appearance in the series is no coincidence, and more than one scholar has noted that when the natural world does enter the *Disasters*, as it does here, it typically appears like this tree, ravaged and truncated, with broken branches and withering foliage. War among humans, Goya intimates, is also in fundamental ways a war against nature.

Beyond its symbolism, however, this particular tree also poses something of a perceptual conundrum when it comes to questions of scale. If the soldier in front of the tree is standing relatively close to it, as the foliage above his left shoulder suggests, its proportions fall more or less within conventional bounds. The tree trunk in this case would be three to four times the width of the soldier's torso. Something very different happens to the tree's proportions, however, when one's attention turns to the crowds Goya has sketched in the background. Masses of people can be seen to the left of the tree, behind the soldier, and at the tree's right base. Their scale puts them at a considerable distance from the soldiers, but perplexingly, they are also in front of the tree trunk. In order to reconcile their proportions with the mass behind them, we would need to envision a truly colossal tree emerging from an enormous, mountain-like base. Goya's image in fact seems to suggest as much by linking the right side of the tree-base to mountains. The rounded contours of a mountain blur into the tree-base as it angles down and to the right, and further to the right still, a distant mountain echoes the slope of the tree's root ball. Simultaneously near and far away, natural and massively otherworldly, the tree thus creates the sense of a realm that is both familiar and at the same time disturbingly askew. Pictorial space echoes and magnifies the idea of a moral world gone astray. This will often be the case in the *Disasters*, where space, or more precisely the perception of space, appears to be subject to the violent and morally warped nature of the events unfolding within it. At the same time, as we have seen repeatedly in previous prints, Goya's background departures from realist illusion subtly remind readers that they are not witnesses to the stripping, but rather viewers of images.

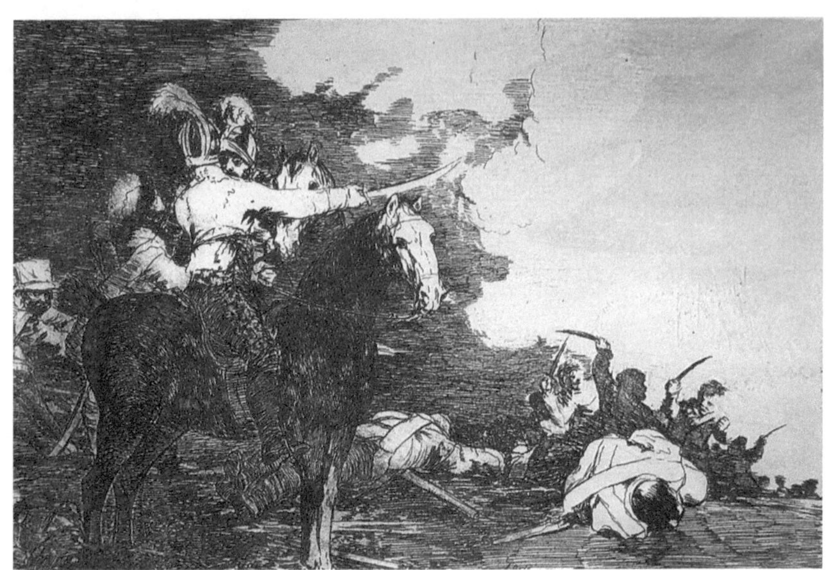

17

No se convienen

A new battlefield. On the left, two mounted officers confer with a soldier who has approached them. Behind this group additional infantrymen, perhaps reinforcements, enter the field from the left. Strewn before the officers to the right, the bodies of at least two dead soldiers suggest that things are not going well, and the mêlée, which is close at hand, threatens. With his back turned to us, the officer closest to our vantage point gestures with his sword towards the ongoing fighting that slopes down a hillside to the right. The position of the officers atop the slope is not arbitrary. Hilltops, promontories, and elevated positions of every sort have always held strategic military value, and they were indispensable to operations during the Napoleonic wars. Historians of the era note that across its many European theatres, the battlefield successes of Napoleon's armies were aided considerably by modern information systems, communications, and organization. A timely sense of the field of battle, whether through visual overviews or reports from the fighting lines, was essential to military command and control, and an advantage in this facet of warfare often determined the outcome of battle.

Strategy and tactics comprise an important part of Goya's subject matter here. More specifically, the image focuses on the difficulty of decision making in the midst of battle, as soldiers die and the enemy draws near. This is not the tactical planning of field maps and chess pieces, nor is it the celebratory depiction of heroic leaders. Urgent, life-and-death decisions are being made. In fact, the fighting is at such close range that firearms have been put aside. From the entering soldiers on the left, to the gesturing officer, to the fighters in silhouette on the right, swords appear everywhere. Conventional narratives of military tacticians vying with their counterparts give way here to something far less grand. This, the image signals, is what tactical decision making actually looks like. It is one more example of the way Goya's *Disasters* dismantle longstanding conceptions of wartime grandeur.

Given the stories of tactical and strategic supremacy that accompanied Napoleon's wartime propaganda, there is an additional edge to Goya's demystification. These are not just any officers under duress. They represent what was thought to be the most advanced military organization of its day. In previous prints Goya underscores the tightly disciplined, machine-like quality of imperial army units (see, for example, Prints 2 and 15). He is well aware of their status as the military face of an increasingly rationalized, modern world. Even the most modern nineteenth-century military thinking, however, assumed that the adversary would be an organized army, not the bands of guerrilla fighters that many imperial troops actually faced in Spain.

Drawing on this history, scholars of Goya have observed that guerrilla warfare is indeed the most likely form of fighting the officers face here, and in this regard Goya's subject is uncannily modern. It is an exploration of the challenges posed to military command by what is known today as asymmetrical warfare. The contrast between the uniformed combatants on the left and the shadow-like fighting men on the lower right seems to register such asymmetries by means of striking differences in technique. On the left, carefully delineated foreground figures, detailed attention to form, and the complex interposition of bodies. On the lower right, comparatively flattened, receding silhouettes in the distance. The strong tonal contrast between the two sides of the image and the dramatic diagonal that separates them heightens such differences. It is almost as if the officers and the silhouettes inhabit fundamentally different picture-worlds. As in earlier prints, differences in technique reinforce thematic contrasts.

At the same time, the figures on both sides of the image are set before enigmatic backgrounds that once again confound realist illusion. What is the darkness behind the officers? If it is the night, what is the white expanse on the right? Goya plays with the idea of a cloud in its lobed edges and the scalloped lines he has dawn in here and there, but as the whiteness extends further to the right, its transformation into a flat, bright sky-like backdrop suggests otherwise. The relatively abstract and symbolic quality of the backgrounds thus tempers realist perception once more. It subtly reminds viewers that, while we might momentarily indulge in seeing officers astride their horses, the world they inhabit is fundamentally different from our own, not only because they are in the midst of battle but also because they are figures within an image, and much as we might momentarily imagine otherwise, we are here, looking at a print.

While abstract backgrounds challenge the conventions of pictorial realism, the words attached to the image appear to be firmly grounded within the here and now of the scene. The caption reads, "They do not agree." In the midst of pitched battle against unanticipated adversaries, the officers are at odds about the proper course of action. It is a fine example of the way Goya's captions can delimit and specify the narrative content of his images. In this case, the words give the scene a meaning it would not necessarily carry independently. There are no obvious visual signs of disagreement between the officers, and without the caption one could legitimately assume that they are simply conferring with one another. At the same time, the caption brings into relief yet another facet of warfare rarely portrayed in European visual art before Goya: the divisions within military command during the heat of battle. It is an inherently antiheroic subject that counters romantic tales of unity, cohesion, and singleness of purpose typical of wartime myth making.

The caption, however, is not quite as narrowly focused as it initially seems. Goya's words are not circumscribed solely to the officers' conversation. "They do not agree" can also be an ironic, understated way of referring to the combat itself. By writing a caption that applies to the officers and to the fighting, Goya in effect turns the print into a wry reflection on the two very different forms of disagreement depicted in the image: the disagreement within a given side of the conflagration, and the violent disagreement of armed conflict itself. More generally, the print becomes a biting commentary on the difference between disagreement understood as contrasting opinions and its second meaning here as a sarcastic euphemism for the killing. Nuances in the original caption add further shades of meaning to Goya's word play. Among the numerous idioms one can use to express the idea of agreement in Spanish, Goya has chosen the verb *convenir*, a form of conceptualizing agreement spatially, as a kind of coming together. Etymologically then, the original caption, *No se convienen*, is "They do not come together."

There is consequently at least one more plausible reading of these words. As a commentary on the image itself, "They do not agree" also addresses the two, strikingly dissimilar sides of the composition. It names the radically different picture-worlds Goya has created on either side of the diagonal, worlds constructed with techniques and background tones so disparate that "they do not agree" or come together fully. The caption's reference thus simultaneously encompasses the officers, the combat, and the contrasting pictorial idioms with which Goya has constructed the image. It is one more example of the way Goya's seemingly testimonial depictions of war's disasters are, at the same time, subtle forms of artistic self-reflection.

Beyond the word play, one final detail has drawn the attention of many a viewer. In the midst of the chaos of ongoing battle, among the bodies of the fallen, and as the dissension between officers unfolds, two seemingly untroubled horses stand calmly, looking out in our direction. They have been rendered to look directly at the viewer, and they hold our gaze. It is one of the few times in the entire series that figures within the scene look out at us. If Goya has played with the illusion of our presence as implied witnesses in previous images, here that presence is pointedly acknowledged by the horses' stare. It is a calm, almost knowing gaze, and it comes from creatures that seem oblivious to their violent surroundings. Oblivious, that is, to everything except us. There is in this regard something disarming about their gaze. Then come the questions. What are we doing there, and why have we become the object of their attention? More importantly, what should our glance say as we meet the eyes of these creatures who do not plan battles or quarrel over tactics? What would this moment of eye contact mean if we were there, and how are we to understand it here, as we look at the image? It is difficult to know for certain, but in the worldly-wise gaze of these horses, Goya has made the meaning of our own looking a pressing question once again.

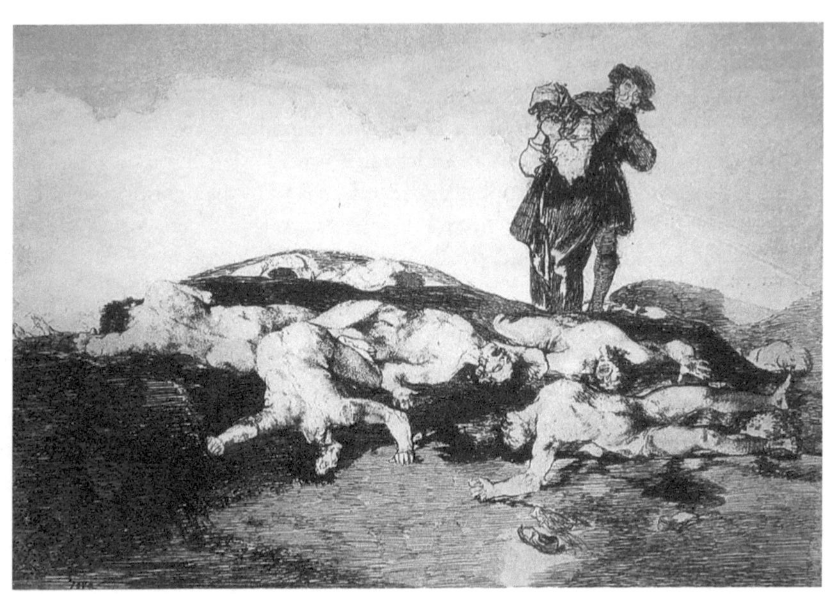

18
Enterrar y callar

Aftermath, again. Within Goya's sequence, this is the third print depicting dead bodies strewn across a field, and it confirms the subject as an important thematic cluster in the *Disasters*. In Print 12, a vomiting figure stood above a similar group of corpses, and in Print 16, soldiers stripped the dead of their clothing. Now, a man and a woman stand among yet another field of bodies. To turn to this image after looking at earlier, similar prints is consequently not an entirely novel experience. As was the case with Goya's images of rape, viewing this print in sequence involves recognizing the return of a subject that Goya had begun to explore earlier in the series. It is one more example of the way sequencing allows Goya to work with the idea of recurrence. It permits him to recreate within the movement of our viewing the experience of repeatedly seeing similar kinds of scenes during times of war. To see one killing field can be compelling. To come upon such fields time and again as we move through the *Disasters* is an experience of a different order.

Were we to extract this print from the series and consider it independently, the effect would be lost. The image's meaning would not be tinged, the way it is here, by the knowledge of what we have already seen. Memory informs the way we look, and, as we noted earlier, Goya's artistry in the series often exploits the effects of recollection as we turn to view new prints. When subjects recur in the series, however, they are by definition instances of repetition with a difference. While familiar, for example, the scene now before us also introduces new elements. The bodies of the dead appear entirely naked. In Print 12 they were clothed, and in Print 16 they were being stripped. Viewing the prints in order makes clear that somebody has already "taken advantage" of these dead men and their possessions, much as the soldiers took advantage in Print 16. It is an instructive example of the way images inform one another in subtle ways, even when they are not expressly linked together verbally.

Compositional and tonal contrasts in this image reinforce the differences between the living and the dead much as they did in Print 12. Roughly bisected along its horizontal axis by the line of sloping hills, the image assigns darker tones and strong vertical lines to the man and woman, who stand against a bright background. Depiction of the dead symbolically inverts those very terms, with mostly white, largely horizontal bodies set against the darkness of the hills. The attention to form with which Goya has rendered the five bodies in the foreground is particularly gripping, from the detailed musculature of the body on the left, to the ribcages and sunken abdomens of the figures at the centre and the lower right, to the awkward body postures everywhere: the arms and heads that no longer hold natural positions. Especially striking in this regard is the corpse that angles down towards the viewer, its head turned almost one hundred eighty degrees. Details like the shoes in the foreground add pathos to the scene, and the feet that break the horizon line on the far left, along with the portion of a cadaver on the far right, once again suggest the presence of additional bodies, out of sight, on the other side of the slope. Atop the knoll just left of centre, corpses seemingly blend into the landscape, as if they have become a sediment layer within the hill.

At the same time, however, something unusual about the bodies in the foreground has captured more than one viewer's attention, something that is in fact deeply unsettling, given Goya's subject matter. The white, largely unblemished male nudes that appear here and in other prints point to the tradition of classical and neoclassical sculpture. While the bodies are not statues – Goya's expressive treatment of heads and extremities makes this clear – one can perceive the echoes of classical statuary nonetheless, and they complicate the viewing experience considerably. What role does the memory of classical sculpture, along with the standard of male beauty it embodies, play in an image of dead men on a field of battle? More importantly, what place does it have in a print series dedicated to decrying the violence of war?

From the Italian Renaissance on, painting and sculpture had long competed with one another in a phenomenon known as the *paragone* or comparison of the arts, and it was not uncommon for painting to depict sculpture in an act of one-upmanship. Such motivation, however, seems highly unlikely here. Sculpture was also a common subject of drawing and engraving, whether as part of an artist's formal training or as a means of making images of famous statues commercially available, but again it is difficult to imagine that such practices have a thematic bearing here. More plausible in light of Goya's approach to violence is that the allusion to classical sculpture is meant precisely to raise the difficult question of the role of conventional notions of beauty in a world as dark and brutal as the one portrayed in the *Disasters*. Recalling the way Goya often plays with our viewing and reading, it can also be instructive to ask *for whom* these bodies look statuesque, sculptural, or even beautiful. Clearly, they are not so for the figures standing in the field, and it is difficult to imagine that they would be beautiful to us, were we witnesses to the scene. If there is beauty here, it is at the level of the image, on this side of its illusion, for a viewer who sees the echoes of classical sculpture as a form of visual citation. Once more, then, we confront the difference between the witnessing fantasy that accompanies most of the *Disasters* and the simultaneous knowledge that we are here, looking at an image.

Even at the level of the image, however, the question remains. What place if any does beauty have in the depiction of atrocity? References to classical beauty here and in other prints – the dead in Print 16 were similarly statuesque – suggest that for Goya the problem of beautiful violence was not a passing concern. Many viewers have suggested that allusions to the classical world may have been his way of signalling the insufficiency of the older art and its conventions, given his subject matter. There is, however, also a broader, more philosophical concern within such gestures. They signal an awareness of the connections between art understood as a particular kind of making, on one hand, and the violent unmaking – or perhaps remaking is a better word – of war on the other. Not unlike Prints 14 and 15, where the question of the artist's own practices began to come into view, there is in these statuesque bodies a subtle questioning of the relationship between art and the violence it seeks to understand. While earlier prints suggested that Goya was aware of the violence of representation itself (see, for example, Print 12), the bodies in this field bleakly intimate that wartime violence in effect "makes art" through its macabre transformation of living men into inanimate statue-like forms. Goya will return to this idea more than once in the series.

As if to remind us not to take the idea of statuary too far, however, Goya also plays a subtle trick on viewers in his depiction of the man and woman in the field. An initial glance suggests that they are weeping out of grief for the dead, but on closer inspection it becomes apparent that their hands are not raised to their faces in a gesture of mourning. They cover their faces because the stench is overwhelming. The man is pinching his nose shut, while the woman holds a kerchief over her face. Whatever ideas the image might have elicited concerning the statuesque qualities of the dead, Goya makes clear that the bodies could not be more different from their stone counterparts by evoking the smell of decomposing flesh. At the same time, the gesture towards a world of smells subtly distinguishes once more between the witnesses within the scene, who struggle with the olfactory assault of putrefying bodies, and the witnesses we imagine ourselves to be when we look at an image. The stench of the dead marks the limit of our witnessing fantasy.

The caption to the scene reads, "Bury and be quiet" or more colloquially, "Bury and shut up." It suggests that the bodies will soon find their place in a grave, and that the memory of these people and what happened to them will disappear. Historical accounts of the period confirm that anonymous, mass burials were part and parcel of the Peninsular War. The logical result of large-scale killing, mass graves were in fact a common sight in and around most fields of battle. Curiously, however, this caption does not accompany an image of burial. Instead it commands interment and silence in a near future that we do not see. In effect, the caption speaks to the way wartime casualties are fated to disappear from sight and mind. It addresses the way the dead, which we still see here, are destined to be forgotten, and it makes their impending disappearance the filter through which we take in the image. There is consequently an intriguing tension between what the caption says and what the print does. Goya clearly is not "quiet" about his subject. In fact he shines light, as it were, on both the bodies of the dead and the command that would have them disappear. The print is a commemorative act that aims precisely to defy the caption by testifying to the presence of the bodies.

But where, we might ask, does the imperative to bury the bodies and keep quiet come from to begin with? Who would issue such a command, and to whom? As is often the case, Goya leaves the question open. The caption could be his own commentary as artist on what is likely to happen in the near future. Alternatively, it could be an injunction directed at the couple by an unknown source. It could also be understood more narrowly as a representation of the thoughts of the man or woman as each contemplates the decaying bodies. There are no obvious or easy attributions, but one thing is for certain. Memory and forgetting are a central concern, and additional details in the original caption add revealing nuances to the call for silence. *Enterrar y callar* ("Bury and be quiet") is a modified version of a well-known Spanish proverb, *Comer y callar* ("Eat and be quiet" or "Eat and shut up"). Traditionally the saying conveys the idea that those who depend on others for their sustenance should maintain a prudent silence when it comes to the affairs of their benefactors. It is close to the English "Don't bite the hand that feeds you," although it literally instructs us not to speak to those who feed. Goya's rewriting of the proverb in this caption thus suggests that the silence and forgetting invoked here are not entirely voluntary. It hints that powerful interests have a stake in forgetting the bodies of the dead and that it is better for the less powerful not to say anything. While Goya does not specify those interests, it is no coincidence that they align themselves with the objective of continuing to wage war. The military, its hierarchies, and those who depend on them come to mind, but perhaps the caption gives voice to the larger logic of ongoing war itself as it calls on all those it touches to bury, forget, and move on to the next violent encounter.

Whatever the case, the caption transforms the print into a powerful statement on the role of memory and forgetting in the face of atrocity, and it speaks well beyond its most immediate historical context. It is also an example of the uncanny timeliness of many *Disasters*. "Bury and be silent" is an injunction that has accompanied all modern wars since the Napoleonic era, and the command remains with us to this day. Although rarely articulated publicly, it hovers over the countless, invisible deaths that routinely accompany armed conflict. It informs the way states habitually work to keep the dead out of sight in times of war. It describes what is happening at this very moment as the dead are being buried and forgotten in zones of conflict across the globe. What to do with the silenced memories of the dead remains one of the more pressing demands for historical thinking today. That Goya would have succinctly captured this phenomenon speaks to the prescience of his insights into modern warfare and the problem of its remembrance.

The print's timeliness, however, is not only a result of the historical recurrence of war, death, and the various injunctions to remain silent since Goya's time. As is often the case in the *Disasters*, the print also subtly addresses the question at the level of our own viewing. While "Bury and be silent" most clearly refers to the world represented in the image, the command also inevitably implicates us as viewers of the print. Like the man and woman, we too have seen the bodies. Unlike the couple in the field, however, we know ourselves to be looking at a print, and we know that sooner or later we will turn to the next one. Against this background awareness of our viewing, the command to "bury and be silent" becomes something of an open question, asking whether we too will consign these bodies to oblivion and speak no more of them, or whether they and the image that has brought them to us will linger within our memory.

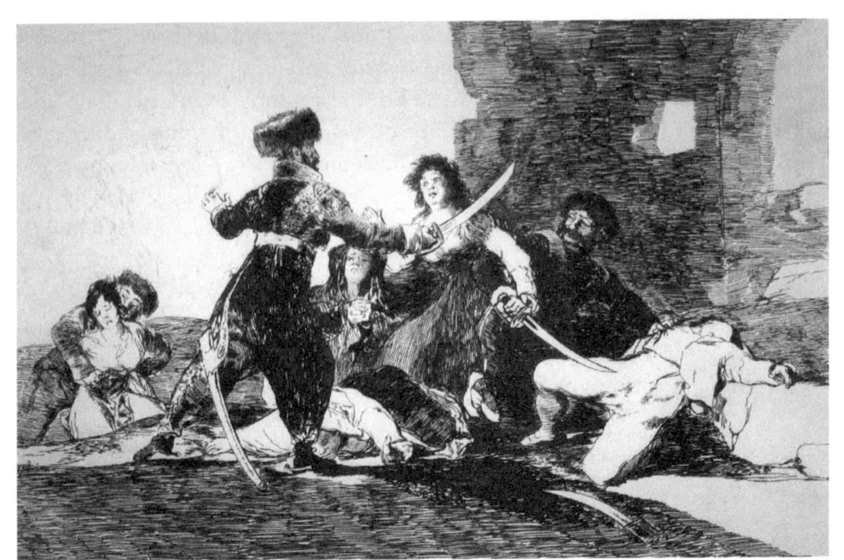

19
Ya no hay tiempo

Women are under assault again in an image that continues the line of inquiry pursued in Prints 4, 5, 9, 10, 11, and 13. Viewing this image thus again involves recognition of the return of a subject previously encountered, and the experience underscores how *common* violence against women is during wartime. When Goya plays with the boundaries of thematic clusters in the *Disasters*, it undermines the idea that one or two images within a given group adequately convey their subject. The series is striking in this regard not only because of its unprecedented exploration of the travails of everyday women during times of war but also because of the way it recreates for readers the experience of confronting this particular form of violence repeatedly as they turn from image to image.

Earlier prints also condition the way we are likely to interpret the narrative content of the scene depicted here. Viewed in isolation, for example, the sexual overtones of the assault in this scene are not as obvious as they become when the memory of prior images informs the viewing. It could be the case, as some scholars have suggested, that what awaits the woman at the centre of this image is simply to be slaughtered like the two figures who have already fallen. In light of previous depictions of women, however, the sexual tenor of the assault is far more evident. The soldier embracing his victim from behind on the left suggests more than mere physical restraint for viewers who have already looked at Print 9, where a woman struggled against an aggressor who also had her by the waist. Similarly, the pleading woman just to the left of the central victim is reminiscent of one of the victims in Print 11, who beseeched a would-be rapist in an almost identical gesture of prayer. For viewers who recall the rape scenes that took place under cover of archways, the arch that appears in the background here also takes on thematic significance.

While violence against women suggests links to earlier prints, the more obvious and immediate subject here is the central victim's terror. Her expression is the emotional centre of the image, and Goya has again made deft use of tonal contrast and the figure's position within the composition in order to highlight her visage in its moment of horrified panic. Earlier images in the series similarly depicted victims' expressions as they faced their final moments: the soldier who watched an axe coming down on him in Print 3, the women who confronted impending rape in Prints 11 and 13, and the man who could not step up to his execution in Print 14. The experience of victims as they face their end is a leitmotif in the *Disasters*, and Goya's steadfast exploration of this subject produces a powerful effect as viewers move through the series. Violence is consistently coupled with the anguished faces of its victims.

The phenomenon may seem common enough, but, historically speaking, it marks something new. Against the backdrop of centuries of European war art commissioned principally in order to celebrate victories, Goya's repeated emphasis on the subjective experience of the victims marks a modern turn. The everyday casualties of war emerge as new protagonists within the visual narrative of armed conflict. In the *Disasters* victims are neither tragic heroes, nor sacrificial martyrs, nor vanquished enemies meant to memorialize another's victory. They are people of every social class, who, like the woman in this image, are often portrayed in their terrified last moments. In this regard the series registers a profound shift within the history of European art when it comes to the question of *whose suffering matters*, which is to say whose suffering is worthy of both artistic representation and moral consideration. Throughout the *Disasters* the wartime torment of men and women, aristocrats and commoners, Spaniards and foreigners, soldiers and civilians alike all becomes equally worthy of attention in what amounts to an artistic democratization of the problem of suffering.

Through the faces of victims, Goya highlights the individualized, subjective experiences of these men and women. A consummate portraitist in painting, he is especially attuned to the expressive power of the face, the part of the human body traditionally understood to convey most strongly identity, interiority, and emotion. The *Disasters* gather together an extraordinarily wide array of faces and expressions, and their depiction at relatively close range is one of the primary ways Goya communicates the terribly intimate quality of the violence he explores. This image, for example, is a study in contrasting facial expressions: the look of the soldier on the left, the defeated face of the woman he has restrained, the face of the woman pleading for mercy, the terrified gaze of the central victim, the disquietingly serene face of the servant who has fallen dead at her mistress's feet, the businesslike glance of the soldier who has just finished off the man on the right, and of course the face in partial silhouette of the officer advancing towards the woman.

In contrast to the victims, when we see the faces of perpetrators they are often depicted like the soldier on the right, callous and largely unmoved by what they are doing. Rather than strong emotions, such faces typically register indifference to the anguish around them, and in their relatively dispassionate gazes – the calmness of rapists in Prints 11 and 13, the insouciance of soldiers stripping the dead in Print 16, or the glance of this soldier to his comrade – Goya suggests that one of the calamities of war is the way it deadens moral feeling within the minds of those it habituates to the violence. The cool, impassive faces of many of the fighters that populate Goya's images speak to war's radical undoing of the moral norms that aim to govern human comportment during peacetime.

The unfeeling faces of perpetrators, however, also implicitly raise the question of that other face that looks at the victims here, the face that both accompanies and eludes all pictorial representation because it is our own as we look at the image. What feelings does *that* face register? What sentiments, if any, does it express as it looks upon the woman's terror? While Goya has clearly rendered the scene in order to elicit feelings for the plight of the victims, he has also complicated such responses by once again placing the notional viewer in a morally ambiguous, if not compromising, position. Our vantage point in this image is disquietingly analogous to the advancing officer's. The ring of faces looking at *him* also offers itself up to *us*. Such positioning subtly suggests once more that if we were there we would in all likelihood be perpetrators of violence ourselves. Our faces would be the faces of fighters and, in this image, the faces of potential rapists. The point of such gestures is not to place a generalized kind of culpability on all viewers, but rather to remind viewers of the limits of the feelings, judgments, and understandings that we form when we contemplate violence in an image. It is a way of suggesting that sympathetic identification with the victims of violence often preempts the more difficult and uncomfortable task of moral self-scrutiny.

As with earlier *Disasters*, if we were there we would not be the sympathetic witnesses we believe ourselves to be when we are here, looking at an image. Perhaps because war unfolds within a radically altered moral universe that transforms those it touches, Goya's prints caution against presuming to understand fully as we look at semblances of that universe. The presumption of full understanding takes for granted that the space from which we look at images and the space in which the violence unfolds are, morally speaking, continuous. It mistakenly assumes that both spaces are governed by the same norms. Time and again, however, Goya's *Disasters* puncture this fantasy by finding ways to highlight the differences between actual witnessing and looking at an image. His prints beckon viewers to momentarily indulge in the witnessing fantasy, but he also reminds us not to confuse the images of violence he has created with the actual violence towards which they can in the end only gesture. It is one of the ways Goya's art reflects on the limits of the knowledge it attempts to convey.

The caption for this scene of desperation and terror reads, "There is no longer any time." It seems an uncomplicated thought, but, as earlier prints teach, when it comes to questions of voice and address, Goya's captions are rarely straightforward affairs. "There is no longer any time" could, for example, be a summary statement from Goya as the artist-chronicler, or from any viewer for that matter, concerning the victims. Little time seems to be left before they will be raped, killed, or both. Such a reading seems especially suited to the terrified woman, given her dramatic central role within the scene. She has presumably seen her servant die at her feet, and she appears to have struggled in vain to keep her male companion from being killed by the soldier on the right. (Her left hand still clutches at the cross-guard of the soldier's sword, even as her companion falls back lifeless.) If there is a figure for whom time running out seems most acute, it is this woman, and the caption appears to specify her particular anguish. The words could even be hers, the expression of her thoughts as her aggressor closes in. In such an account, "There is no longer any time" would be the verbal equivalent of the expression we see on her face. Her terror would be synonymous with the dreadful knowledge that time, which is to say life and hope, has run out.

Other readers, however, have pointed to a very different possibility, suggesting that the caption describes, not the desperation of the woman or her fellow victims, but rather the urgency with which the soldiers are proceeding. In contrast to similar, earlier scenes (Prints 9, 10, 11, and 13), the fighters here are not acting under cover of darkness. They are more exposed, and they are subject to the intervention of others. If this is a field of battle, active fighting could easily be taking place nearby, just beyond the frame, and the soldiers would not have the luxury of taking their time. "There is no longer any time" would in this account name their acknowledgment of the need to move quickly, and it would potentially explain both the sexual dimensions of the aggression and the reason for the killings. In this alternate reading of the caption, the image becomes a depiction of the moment in which intended rape shifts to outright slaughter, precisely because "there is no longer any time." It could also be that because "there is no longer any time," the soldiers will not be able to go through with their intended assault.

To hold such different interpretations together is to realize that the caption's ambiguity in effect turns the print into a meditation on the very different meanings of time for witnesses, perpetrators, and victims. By writing an open-ended caption that circulates among these various positions, Goya prompts viewers to inhabit multiple perspectives as they attempt to make sense of the words' relationship to the image. More broadly, the conceptual play of Goya's wording asks readers to couple their initial responses to the image, whatever they might be, with critical deliberation. To be horrified or moved by the content of the image is an important part of the experience, but Goya's captions consistently push readers further. Images that initially seem to grab us by the heart or the gut also speak to the head, with captions that foster critical reflection. There is, finally, an additional, relatively subtle irony in the caption's meditation on time. While time is running out for the women, or for the soldiers, or for both, at the level of the image time's depletion will never arrive. Victims and perpetrators have been suspended in a moment of terror that belongs to the "frozen time" of the image.

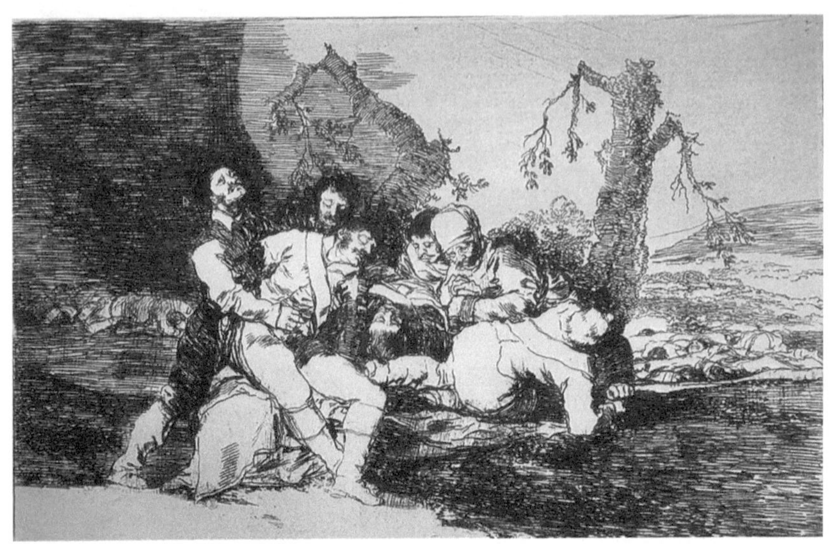

20
Curarlos y a otra

Active combat has ceased once more, and the wounded as well as those attending to them have gathered on a field. Behind them, to the left and to the right, the bodies of the dead testify to the scale of the carnage that has taken place. Like other prints, the image focuses on the consequences of armed violence after the fighting has abated. Ravaged plant life similarly registers the effects of battle, whether one approaches the trees that rise behind the men naturalistically – some have suggested they reflect the effects of artillery fire – or takes them as symbolic representations of the wartime withering of life more generally. In either case the trees offer a disquieting echo of the injured bodies before them, and each tree in effect presides over one of the two smaller groups into which Goya has subdivided the foreground figures: the three vertically oriented men on the left, and the four, more prone figures on the right.

In the first group, two men seem to work without much success to get a wounded officer to stand. His right arm has been severed or blown off. With legs spread and firmly planted, the attendant to the left of the officer bears much of the victim's weight as he holds him and looks skyward with a supplicant's gaze. A second man, who holds the officer under his left arm, looks down with eyes shut, while the officer's own closed eyes and slumping posture suggest that the prospects of standing are not very good. Within the second group of figures, things seem even more dire, as two men crouch over the bodies of fallen comrades. One of them holds the forearm and hand of a fallen soldier, while the other casts an additional mournful look downward. In the absence of further cues, it is difficult to know if the casualties before them are dead or alive.

While the image conveys the grave, possibly fatal nature of the wounds the victims have endured, Goya's caption takes things in a very different direction. It is a seemingly cold, efficient response to the scene, reading "Cure them, and on to another." The laconic sentiment is intentionally at odds with the pathos of the scene Goya has depicted. Although not obviously attributable to any of the figures portrayed, it is not difficult to imagine who might utter such words. The command form, the matter-of-fact response to the suffering, and the call for all to move "on to another" suggest a hardened, military point of view, perhaps the perspective of a commanding officer, or the expression of wartime thinking more generally. If we imagine the caption in Goya's voice, it is an ironic, critical citation of this form of thinking. By coupling the caption with an image of suffering, Goya makes a pointed comment on the act of calling for healing in the name of further killing. The print thus registers the violence of treating the wounded primarily as an asset or an instrument, something to be saved for further future use. In this sense it underscores a facet of wartime thinking that we have seen Goya critique in earlier prints: the way war fundamentally repurposes human activity – here, the activity of tending to the wounded – in order to continue the pursuit of its own destructive ends.

Once again, however, Goya's caption complicates quick or easy moral judgments by implicating the viewer in subtle ways. While we do not see the speaker of the caption's words, they have nevertheless been accorded a precise location within the image. Logically speaking, they must come from the place of the notional viewer, the very place we occupy as imagined witnesses to the scene. (Print 6 involved a similar gesture.) Goya has grafted the military perspective of the caption onto the place of our own viewing. In effect, the print has us "speak" these words to the men on the field as we read the caption, thus raising the question of our relationship to the wounded and to the words that address them. In addition, like other captions we have considered, this one suggests that if we were actually on the field we might not be the moral witnesses we imagine. Our gaze would be strongly conditioned by the demands of waging war, and we too might speak the caption's words in earnest. In fact, it is precisely because we are looking at a print rather than witnessing a scene that we can respond morally to the gap between the suffering of the wounded and the uncaring efficiency of the command. Once more then, Goya's caption plays with the differences between actual witnessing and the illusion of doing so as we look at an image.

The twofold nature of our viewing is also addressed by Goya's particular blend of pictorial naturalism and abstraction. While the bodies of the men here have been rendered with considerable naturalistic detail, for example, other elements of the composition are not strongly governed by such concerns. The dark swath of earth beneath the principal figures is resistant to an obvious naturalistic interpretation. Its contrast with other features of the landscape – the lighter foreground on the lower left, the equally light hills in the background on the upper right – is more easily grasped in terms of the need for tonal variation within the image than as an attempt to represent natural features of the terrain. Similarly, while the dark mass that fills the left quarter of the image might be imagined as the base of a nearby ravine or cliff, Goya has given so little attention to modelling its form that it remains largely abstract.

Its technical function in relation to the highlighted face of the attendant who looks to the heavens, however, is relatively clear. The slope that extends the gloom to the right of his head, along with the increased darkness around his figure, suggests that this backdrop is governed more by the urge to maximize the expressive potentials of tonal contrast than it is by the desire to represent a recognizable object in the background. Goya's rendering of the sky also complicates purely naturalistic perception with a visual puzzle we have seen elsewhere: Is the lightly shaded patch of firmament on the left behind the tree, for example, a cloud in a relatively bright sky, or is the brightness to the right of that patch the cloud, with its edges coming into view against a small swath of grey sky? Such gestures mark the limits of naturalist illusion, and among other things, they subtly remind viewers of the artifice with which the image has been constructed.

Goya's sequencing also informs the viewing experience here in subtle ways. To turn to this depiction of wounded men after pondering the terrified woman in the previous print is, among other things, to experience a relative diminishment in the dramatic force of the viewing experience. A scene of terror and impending death yields to the comparatively more muted drama of soldiers who have been injured. Goya often plays deliberately with such shifting dramatic intensities. Where there is sequence there is the potential for rhythm, and the artistry with which Goya sequences the *Disasters* reveals a complex understanding of the phenomenon: foreboding presentiments (Print 1) erupt into violence (Print 2); the ferocious intensity of hand-to-hand combat (Print 5) gives way to the more restful image of a wounded officer (Print 6); the excitement of ostensibly heroic cannon fire (Print 7) comes to a halt as viewers turn to a rider crushed under his horse (Print 8). Contrasts between one image and the next can accentuate meaning, while the repetition of very similar kinds of scenes (Prints 9, 10, and 11) often produces emphatic effects. Through sequence, Goya plays not only with the meaning of individual prints but also with the rhythm of our viewing.

In this image, the field of the wounded is both a turn away from the dramatic terror of the previous print and a return to a subject we have encountered before. The scene is reminiscent of Print 6, which also explored the pathos of injury, and the return of the subject here confirms the wounded as an important thematic cluster in the series. While repetition often signals such clusters, as we have seen, it also mimics the experience of repeated witnessing. It makes viewers confront the repetitive nature of wartime violence itself. The result once more is a complex viewing experience in which the memory of earlier *Disasters* and awareness of the twofold nature of our viewing are equally at work. In fact, as we prepare to turn the page it becomes apparent that while the command, "On to another one," has named the next violent encounter awaiting the men in the image, it has also described our activity as readers of the series who will move on to another *Disaster*. The caption has set up the context for the next three prints, and it will be useful to consider them together.

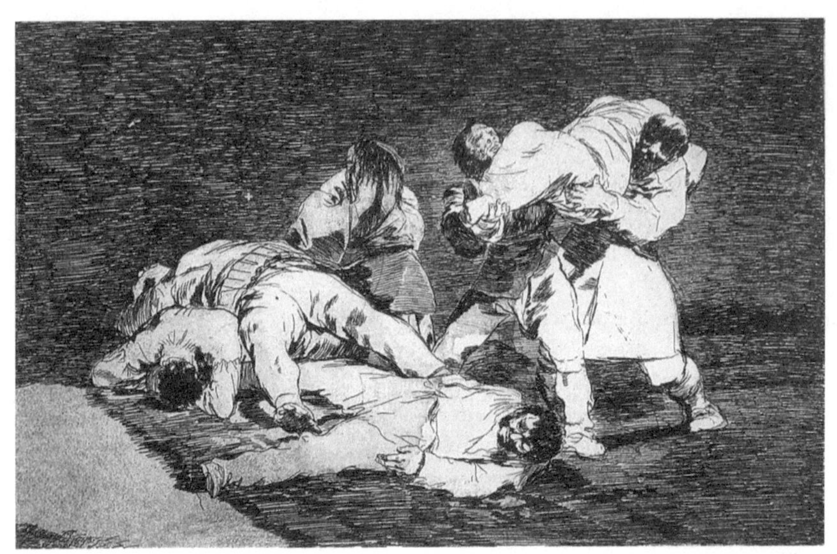

21
Será lo mismo

[See 23 for commentary.]

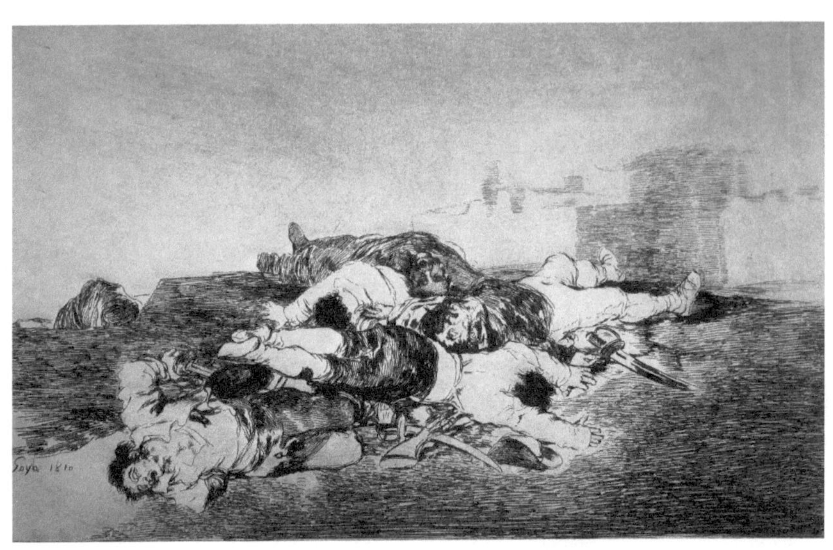
Goya 1810

22
Tanto y más

[See 23 for commentary.]

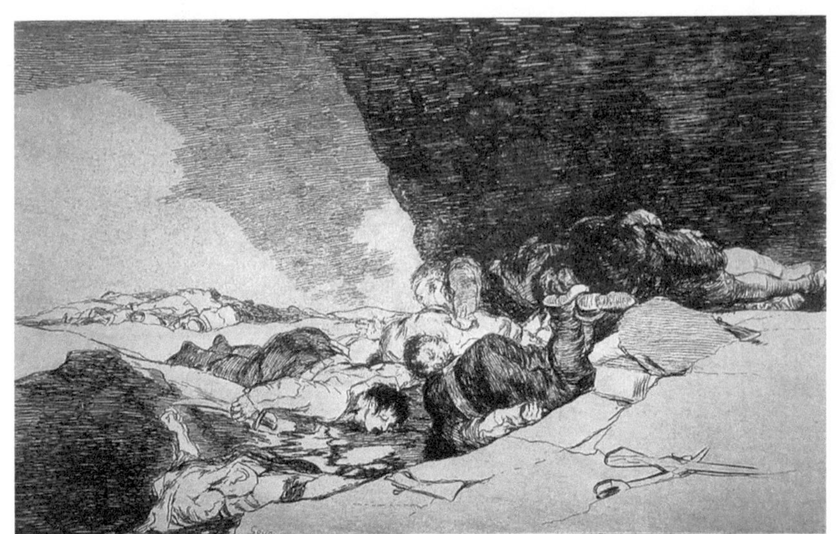

23
Lo mismo en otras partes

After wounded men, three successive images of the bodies of the dead. While the deceased appear throughout Goya's series, prints in which piles of dead bodies are the artist's primary subject are fewer in number, and their distribution in the *Disasters* is telling. Such images are entirely absent from the early pages of the series, for example, where the dead are typically ancillary figures or singular cases (the bodies under the cannon in Print 7, for example, or the crushed cavalier in Print 8). Only after roughly a quarter of the images on violence have elapsed do prints focusing on the heaped bodies of the dead begin to make their intermittent appearances (Prints 12, 16, and 18, as we have seen), and only after some twenty prints does Goya place one such image immediately after another. The resulting effect is subtle but forceful: the further one moves into the series, the stronger the visual claim of the bodies of the dead becomes. If death, rendered in its starkly material, biological sense, is one of the grand themes of the *Disasters* as a whole, in these prints, which approach the mathematical centre of Goya's meditations on the violence of war (forty-seven prints in all), it becomes the explicit subject. The bodies pile up here, not only within individual images but also within the movement of our viewing, which must confront heaped cadavers in three successive images.

In Print 21 the bodies gleaming in the darkness offer yet another striking example of the dramatic effects Goya achieves through tonal contrast. The setting could well be nocturnal, as many viewers have speculated, but in keeping with his approach to pictorial space more generally, the darkness has a strongly abstract quality as well. With the exception of the swath of lighter grey in the lower left corner – seemingly the face of a hillside – foreground and background provocatively dissolve into one another. It is difficult to locate a horizon line, and variations in the darkness itself complicate naturalist perception. Beyond symbolic or psychological meanings, in artistic terms the darkness is there primarily for the bodies. It is what makes them so starkly visible, a device whose artifice Goya has not gone out of his way to conceal within naturalist illusion. Look at the bodies, the image implicitly signals, but know too that they inhabit the space of an image. At the same time, the grieving woman that Goya has placed behind the bodies pointedly raises the question of looking once more. Seemingly overcome with grief, she cannot look, and there is strange tension between her not looking, and everything it means for her, and our own gaze as we take in the image.

Several intriguing compositional echoes link this image to the representation of the wounded men that precedes it. Once more seven figures have been subdivided into two groups. In one group two men hoist a cadaver to their shoulders. In the other, a grieving woman sits behind the bodies of three dead men. Right and left have been inverted with respect to the previous image, but the similarities are not difficult to grasp. Men stand and lift, and one of them again looks skyward, while next to them prone figures and those caring for them come together once more. Such parallels could be coincidental, the product of a consistent approach to composition, for example, but the very fact that one can readily see such equivalences is no accident. Goya has placed the images in immediate succession to one another, and he has also linked them verbally.

The caption to this image literally reads, "It will be the same thing." The words have puzzled many a viewer, and by itself the expression is indeed difficult to interpret. Within the sequence, however, the meaning is relatively clear. Colloquially, "It is the same thing" – *Es igual*, or *Es lo mismo* – indicates that something does not matter, that it makes no difference one way or the other. Its closest equivalent in informal English is "Same difference," and in this regard the expression clearly references what viewers have seen and read in the previous print. It conveys the idea that even if the men in the preceding image are cured in order to go "on to another one," "it will be the same" in the sense that death will arrive nonetheless. Bleak as the command to move "on to another one" was, it contained within it a faint promise of survival in the form of continued struggle. This print expressly extinguishes such promise. The caption turns the image into an illustration of what happens when one moves "on to another one." As with earlier pairs (Print 14 to 15, for example), the verbal links between two very different scenes thus brings their disparate narrative content – different bodies, in a different place – into dialogue with one another. Through the caption, the bodies of the dead in Print 21 become examples of the futility of the endeavours depicted in Print 20.

This idea of futility persists as readers turn from Print 21 to 22, where we confront a second pile of bodies. In contrast to the darkness, the new image returns us to a brighter sky over a field of battle, with city walls in the distance, and the weapons next to the dead make clear that they are fallen combatants. While the scene has no obvious connection to its predecessor – again these are different bodies, in a different time and place – the prints remain linked to one another, both thematically and by a new caption that also depends for its meaning on what has come before. It reads, "So much and more." The expression is typically used in

Spanish in order to agree with and amplify a prior statement or sentiment, and its immediate reference here is clearly "It will be the same." A fuller translation drawing on the preceding caption to which it refers would consequently be "So much and more *of the same*." The meaning of this implied "same," however, has begun to shift as we move from one print to the next. In Print 21, "It will be the same" was the equivalent of "It will make no difference," and it suggested that healing in order to continue waging war would, in the end, lead to death. In Print 22, "the same" that has become "so much and more" takes on additional nuances. It is in dialogue with the prior caption, but also with the prior image. It still registers futility with respect to the imperative to heal, but in light of the dead we have just seen it also acquires a quantitative meaning, signalling the many more *bodies* that have accumulated as viewers turn to this image, in what amounts to "so much and more *death*."

Print 23 extends the conceptual play further as viewers are once more taken to an ostensibly new time and place, but only to encounter more bodies. We now look at bodies piled up at what appears to be the entrance to a cavern. The caption reads "The same thing in other parts." Given the two preceding images of corpses and the repetition of piled bodies within this new image – they are in the foreground and on the horizon in the distance – "the same thing" now references the bodies even more clearly, but the caption also continues to dialogue with Prints 20 and 21 by repeating key terms from their respective captions. "The same thing in other parts" contains verbal echoes of "Heal them and on to an*other* one" (Print 20) and "It will be *the same thing*" (Print 21). Even as the accumulation of bodies builds from print to print, the word play in Prints 21, 22, and 23 thus continues to dialogue with the scene of healing and its caption. As a result, the sequence does something that no single image can achieve. The repetition of piled bodies mimics the experience of repeatedly coming upon such scenes, and it makes the repudiation of "Heal them and on to another" all the more emphatic. It is one more example of the subtle but powerful effects Goya achieves through sequential presentation.

The transition to Prints 22 and 23, however, also entails a subtle shift in terms of Goya's visual approach to his subject. In previous *Disasters*, living figures accompanied the piles of the dead (the man who retched over the deceased in Print 12, the soldiers plundering in Print 16, or the nauseated witnesses in Print 18), but now the deceased are left alone, or more precisely, the viewer is left alone in his or her encounter with them. There is as a result something more direct and arguably more disarming about the viewing experience, which includes looking at the gaping mouths and meticulously rendered faces of the dead. There are no other living figures, no other witnesses, only the piled bodies and the lifeless imprint of suffering on their faces. We are on our own as we attempt to make sense of what we see, knowing all the while, because the caption tells us so, that this is just one scene and that it is the same elsewhere.

The historical record substantiates that such scenes were a common sight during the Peninsular War, but to take these images primarily as attempts to represent specific historical events is again to risk overlooking the preponderantly moral – which is to say timeless – tenor of Goya's engagement with his subject. Dates and place names are conspicuously absent from the captions, as we have seen, and the settings depicted in these prints – abstract darkness, generic city walls, and the mouth of a cavern or overhang, respectively – resist precise historical location. It is not that historical context is altogether unimportant in the *Disasters*, but rather that the moral lens through which Goya engages the violence is far more pressing. At the same time, the artistry of such engagements – the way Goya constructs images, the way those images position the notional viewer, the conceptual play of the captions, the effects achieved through sequence – makes clear that his efforts in the series are informed far more by the pursuit of critical reflection than they are by the demands of historical representation. Such reflection continues in the next two images, which we will also consider together.

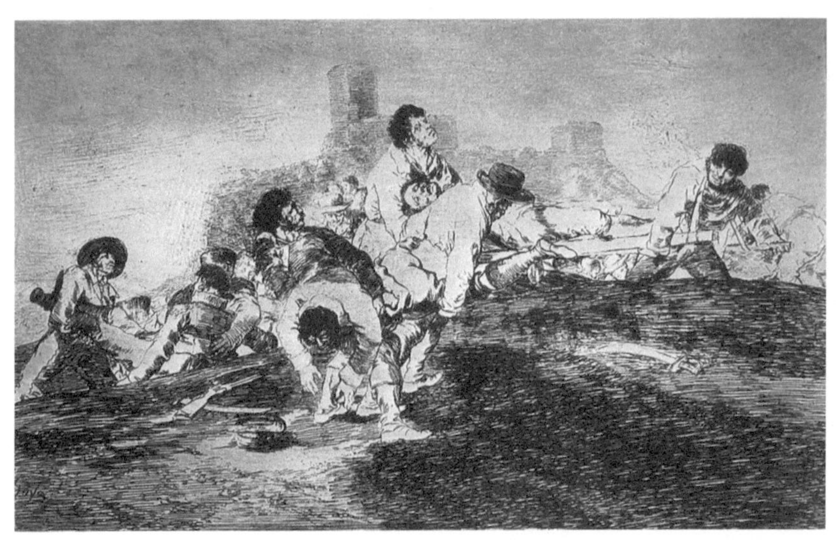

24

Aún podrán servir

[See 25 for commentary.]

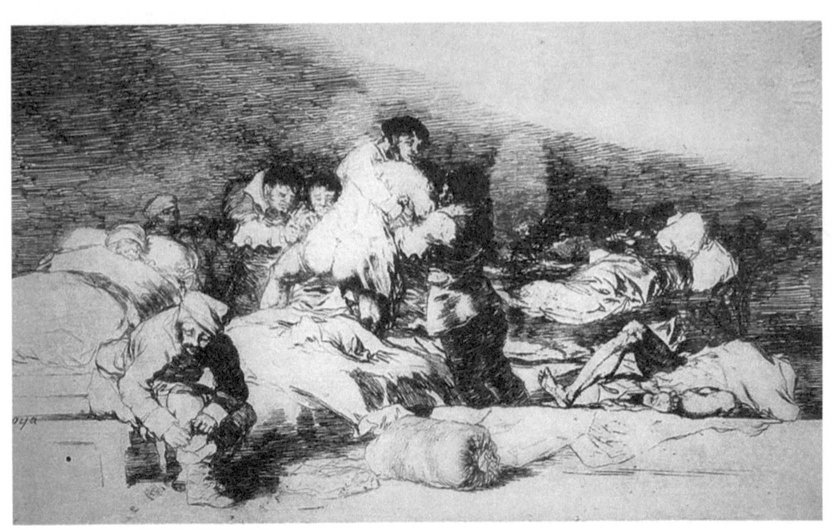

25
También éstos

Two more scenes of the wounded and those who tend to them. On their own, Prints 24 and 25 are fascinating examples of the persistence of Goya's interest in the aftermath of battle. More particularly, they testify to his repeated exploration of the various fates of casualties. Coming in the immediate wake of Prints 20 to 23, however, these scenes acquire additional meanings when the viewer turns to them. While Print 20 called for curing the wounded in order to move "on to another one," it was pointedly followed, as we have seen, by three successive images of mass death, in what amounted to a fundamental refutation of the idea of healing in the name of further fighting. Nevertheless, in these next two images viewers once again face the wounded and the prospect of their being cured for precisely such a purpose. By virtue of their position within the series, Prints 24 and 25 consequently become examples of the way the treatment of the wounded as an asset to be redeployed has not wavered, even as the bodies of the dead have piled up. Among other things, these two prints signal the unmodified persistence of the imperative to heal the wounded for further use. Print 24 reads, "They will still be able to serve," and Print 25 adds, "These too." In effect, the captions echo the basic sentiment of "Cure them and on to another one" (Print 20), despite the bodies that have accumulated in the interim (Prints 21, 22, 23). The six prints together thus subtly suggest the implacable nature of wartime imperatives. While the piles of the dead may have suggested to viewers the futility or hypocrisy of healing for future battle, these prints convey that no number of bodies will alter war's basic calculus.

This is not the first sequence that underscores the relentless nature of wartime violence and the thinking that sustains it. The rape sequence (Prints 9, 10, 11) and the transition from one scene of execution to another (Prints 14 and 15) produced similar effects. The unremitting nature of the logic of war is a recurrent theme in the series, and it is intimately related to the experience of viewing Goya's prints in succession. In addition to the meanings that sequence can bring to bear on any given print, the viewer's movement through the series acquires significance in its own right. Because we know ourselves to be looking at prints, we also know intuitively that, regardless of the horrors we contemplate in this or that image, more prints await us until we reach the end of *The Disasters of War*. The inescapable quality of what we see in the series is in this regard linked to the twofold nature of our viewing and reading. The knowledge that we are looking at successive *images* informs the illusion of witnessing successive *scenes*, and together both forms of perception create the sense of war's implacable nature. No single image prompts the experience. It is a function of our viewing, and it is easily lost when the series is approached in more fragmentary form.

In turning to these two prints, we also encounter variations on the theme of wounding. In Print 24, the drama centres on the physical challenges of moving the injured. Everywhere, the body postures of those attending to casualties signal arduous effort. Three groups, in each a wounded man and two men carrying him, struggle up an incline as part of a more general movement from left to right. On the far left, two men struggle to hold a slumped officer by the legs and shoulders. To the right and closer to the viewer, another two carry a second casualty more awkwardly. He hangs face down, with arms dangling, and the man holding him by the torso leans back, bearing much of the victim's weight on his hip and thigh, while a second carrier, his back to the wounded man, holds a leg under each arm and leans forward as he works his way up the slope. Just behind this group and to the right, a third wounded man lies on a stretcher. He is the only casualty whose face we see, and Goya has placed it – and the suffering it expresses – just above the centre of the composition. Diagonal lines from lower left to upper right accentuate the laborious nature of ascending the slope: the hill's horizon line on the left side of the image, the line of the torso and left leg of the second wounded man, the line of the carrier's back just below the face of the man on the stretcher, or, on the left side of the image, the line of three carriers' heads, each looking up and to the right.

As is often the case in the *Disasters*, the image also suggests that what we see in the foreground is part of a much vaster scene. Figures in the background, depicted between and behind the three principal groups, expand the scale of the activity under way. The field of the wounded, still strewn with weapons from the battle that has presumably taken place, could well extend behind the hill, as far back as the walls of the fortification in the distance. Other facets of the image heighten the drama. The main figures, for example, have been positioned on the threshold between the darkness of the lower half of the image and lighter tones of the upper half. Tonal contrast thus once again lends itself to symbolic interpretation as the wounded move between darkness and light. In both the immediate foreground and the background, however, it also becomes clear once more that naturalist illusion has not been a priority. The hill, the walls, and the sky lend themselves to naturalist perception in rudimentary ways, but the relatively cursory, quasi-abstract rendering of these parts of the image also discloses its constructed nature. Following the practice we have seen in many other prints, naturalistic depiction is coupled with the disclosure of artifice.

This same sense of space is even more notable in Print 25, which takes viewers from the field of battle to one of the few interior scenes in the series. The image is ostensibly the depiction of a hospital, as suggested by the bed on the left and the patient being treated just left of centre. Nevertheless, it is difficult to interpret the space in an exclusively naturalistic vein. While the contours of an archway appear on what could be a far wall, to the right of the central group, the abstract quality and shifting intensities of the darkness surrounding the main figures complicate any precise sense of place. Similarly, the diagonal that slopes across the upper right side of the image, defining a second, equally abstract swath of lighter grey, dispels whatever illusion of naturalist space has been created. The effect, once again, is to draw viewers into the scene while simultaneously reminding us that we are looking at an image.

In comparison to previous depictions of the wounded (Prints 6, 20, and 24), this hospital scene focuses on a wide range of differing states of injury. A man with head dressings convalesces in bed. At the foot of the bed another patient bends over his leg and appears to tend to a small wound on his calf. To the right and behind him, a group of five figures rises, offering the drama of an ongoing medical intervention. A patient, his head buried in his arms, crouches in pain as two men hold him up and another two work on his wounded thigh. With his back to viewers, the patient has propped himself up on his right knee, extending his left leg out from his bedding towards those working on him. A ligature around his thigh signals the attempt to regulate blood flow, and just above it a medic with instruments in hand probes into the patient's flesh, attempting perhaps to remove a bullet or shrapnel.

In an era before modern analgesics or anesthesia, the pain associated with the procedure depicted was excruciating, and Goya has masterfully rendered both the patient's suffering and his vulnerability as a patient. His subjection to the caretakers is echoed in his visual exposure to viewers. He is unclothed from the waist down, and his shirt has been pulled up and away from the operation site, exposing his naked buttocks. Just above the centre of the composition, the face of an attendant, his arm around the patient's back, manifests compassion in an expression that becomes a subtle measure of the wounded man's torment.

To the right of the group, on the floor and partially covered with a sheet, another patient lies, seemingly abandoned. It is difficult to know for certain whether he is dead or alive. The posture of his right leg suggests a body that is still living, and possibly writhing, but the sheet covering his torso and head intimate otherwise. Whatever his status, his dereliction on the ground offers a stark contrast to the other patients in the scene. Behind him, an attendant appears to lean over yet another patient who also lies bundled in a sheet, but the details of what is happening are lost in the darkness. Many viewers have noted the way this wide range of patients with varying states of injury creates a chaotic visual impression, and the image does indeed convey the disordered activity that might characterize a field hospital. At the same time, however, it is not difficult to see a symbolic progression in the image, from left to right. Tranquil repose and a minor wound give way to the dramatic suffering of surgery, which in turn yields to an abject body on the floor as the ambient darkness narrows and intensifies.

The captions to these two prints link them to the earlier question of healing, as we have seen, but they also engage their respective images in revealing ways. While Goya has underscored the pathos of each scene by placing an expressive face just above the centre of each image – the suffering face of the man on the stretcher (Print 24) and the face of compassion of the attendant (Print 25) – his captions are again pointedly at odds with such feelings. Whoever says "They will still be able to serve" and "These too" seems inured to the suffering, and the cold quality of the response is particularly strong in the original Spanish caption, where the verb *servir*, "to serve," not only refers to future military service but also means "to be of use," the way tools or other implements are of use. A reflection of the instrumental reasoning of wartime, the captions are a biting, ironic commentary if one attributes the voice to Goya. As was the case in Print 20, however, these captions also allow for another reading. Their most logical site of enunciation within each scene is again the place occupied by the notional viewer, and, however we may feel, we in effect "say" these words as we read the caption. In this sense, the words prompt us once more to consider our relationship both to the sentiment they express and to the viewing. Were we actually there, the prints suggest, we too might be saying such things. In a second moment, in fact, it becomes apparent that if we have been moved by the pathos of these scenes it is because we are here, looking at images, rather than witnessing actual scenes. Once again then, the difference between actual witnessing and viewing images subtly informs the viewing experience.

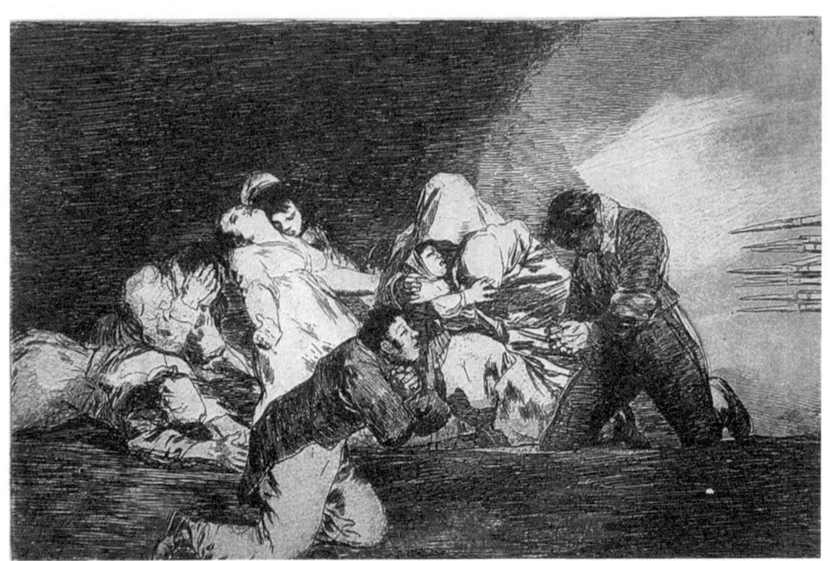

26

No se puede mirar

From images of healing we turn to a new scene of execution. The victims are clearly civilians, and their clothing indicates that they are of relatively high social standing. This could well be a family accompanied by household servants, although there is no way to know definitively. In a frock coat in the immediate foreground, a man kneels, pleading. Above him and to the left, with arms outstretched and head thrown back in anguish, a woman, perhaps his wife, prepares for the inevitable. Just behind her, the face of a female companion looks down woefully, while to the left two additional figures confront the end in different ways: one crouches with face in hands, while the other lies prostrate. (It could be that this second figure has already been shot, but his extended forearm and hand suggest otherwise.) To the right of the central figures, a nanny, her head and face covered, holds a crying child. Next to her another man turns his back to the firing squad, bowing his head as he clasps his hands in a gesture of prayer. Taken together, the group makes clear that the impending violence is indiscriminate, not only targeting civilians but also making no distinction between men, women, and children.

On the far right, halfway up the frame, the bayoneted muzzles of a firing squad jut in. The bundling of rifle barrels is not particularly realistic. It is difficult to imagine a firing formation that would lead to such an arrangement, but what the grouped rifles lose in verisimilitude they gain in terms of visual impact, and the absence of the soldiers themselves highlights the impersonal, faceless nature of the impending slaughter once more. In many ways, however, the firing squad and its weapons are not the point. Like earlier *Disasters*, the primary subject here is the victims' terror, their tormented understanding that they are moments away from dying. The image is in fact a study in the varied manners of confronting the end: pleading, despairing, turning one's back, covering one's face, etc. Goya individualizes the suffering and records its varied, deeply intimate forms.

Within the sequence, the print is also another thematic refutation of the healing that has preceded it, much like the bodies that followed Print 20. To turn to this scene from the hospital scene is to confront the pointlessness of healing, and it seems no coincidence that the killing here is reminiscent of earlier scenes of execution. Particularly striking in this regard are the truncated rifle barrels, which echo the rifles in Print 15, but earlier execution scenes also inform this one by way of contrast. Whereas previous prints depicted executions that were carefully planned and carried out, the scene depicted here has no such official trappings. There is no gallows, as in Print 14, and unlike Print 15 the victims have not been bound or prepared in any way. The execution is taking place out of sight, in a dark, enclosed space reminiscent of those places in which women faced rape (Prints 11 and 13). This is most likely an extra-official, summary execution.

The space in which Goya sets the scene appears to be the entry to a cave or grotto, much like the cavern in which we encountered a pile of bodies in Print 23, and the impending killing here illustrates how bodies might come to rest in such places. For nineteenth-century travellers, natural shelters provided a respite from the elements as well as protection from the open road, and they were often used as resting places. A family fleeing the fighting, for example, might plausibly stop in such a place. In addition to this possible socio-historical content, however, the setting is also strongly conditioned by the technical demands of the medium. The choice of settings such as this one serves a pragmatic purpose. It is a means of bringing together broad, contrasting tonal swaths – the blackness of the cave's interior, the lightness of the entrance – against which foreground figures can be differentiated. As we have seen, technical considerations regarding tone often help to explain the peculiarities of pictorial space in the *Disasters*, whether it be mysteriously abstract, "nocturnal" settings (Prints 1, 4, 10, 21), strange skies divided into darkness and light (Prints 6, 15, 17), enigmatic masses (the "mound" in Print 6, the gargantuan "tree" in Print 16, the "cliff" in Print 20), or the preponderance of domed structures such as arcades or caverns, which dramatically divide shadow from light (Prints 11, 13, 23, 26). Although frequently suffused with symbolic meanings as well – and life and death are the most common – such features of the *Disasters* speak to the way Goya does not go out of his way to conceal the artifice of image making, even as he captivates viewers with the horrors he brings into view.

In a similar vein, the strongly affective tenor of the image is modified in unexpected ways by a caption whose conceptual play transforms the viewing experience. It reads, "One cannot look," or more colloquially, "You cannot look." By itself the image is governed primarily by the pathos of the victims. With the caption, however, the print turns into a more complex meditation on looking and its relationship to the violence. To begin with, the words themselves can be read in any number of ways. "One cannot look" could be the description of a condition of visibility, or it could be a prohibition against looking. It could be a warning or exhortation not to look. It could also be what one says after one has looked and wishes one had not. More generally, "One cannot look" is clearly an expression of horror, a way of suggesting that one cannot bear to look – or perhaps that one should not bear to look – given the subject matter. The play of the caption's ambiguity becomes even more rich, and the ironies more serious, however, when we consider image and caption together and realize that we can only have come to "One cannot look" because we *are* looking, looking at an image whose caption tells us that it too is about looking and its limits.

Then there are the questions. Who does this caption describe, to whom is it addressed, and just what is it that one cannot look at? If it was not apparent initially, the caption draws attention to the fact that none of the figures within the scene look at the soldiers who are about to mow them down. The central figure pleads with his eyes shut, and every other victim has averted his or her gaze. In this sense the caption names the extraordinary difficulty – perhaps the philosophical impossibility – of looking at one's own death. Still within the illusion that would have us see people, bayonets, and impending death here, however, the caption also attaches itself to us as imagined witnesses to the scene. We are there, and we cannot look. It is unbearable. And yet if we *are* there, in the dark, witnessing this scene, should we not be doing more than failing to look? Then again, and this is a thought that our witnessing fantasy usually censors, perhaps we are with the soldiers, and still we cannot look. As is often the case in the *Disasters*, Goya positions the notional viewer in order to suggest that our gaze as imagined witness may be complicit with the violence.

"One cannot look," however, does not circumscribe itself solely to the scene depicted. If we step outside the illusion, it becomes clear that the words also speak to the image as an image, trading on the fact that we are *not* there, but rather here, looking at an image that has been deliberately composed so as to withhold the very source of the terror we do look at. What the caption now names is what is evoked by the bayonets but literally is not within the image and therefore cannot be looked at. In this regard, like the earlier depictions of execution (Prints 14 and 15), Goya's framing once again reminds the viewer of the artifice with which the image has been constructed. If the print at this level is about the limits of looking at violence in an image, it is consequently also very much about the limits of representing it, and about the limits of the illusion that would have us believe for a moment that we too are witnesses. What we cannot look at now in fact dispels the reverie of witnessing. We cannot look because we are *not* witnesses to violence but rather viewers of images. If we truly were witnesses, we would see the soldiers. At this level, then, the caption reminds us that we are looking at an image, and it highlights the differences between the victims' world and *their* not looking, with everything it means for them, and our own world, in which the fantasy of witnessing can no longer be entertained without some embarrassment. Sympathetic identification with the victims gives way to more complex moral reflection on the meaning of looking at others' suffering within an artistic image.

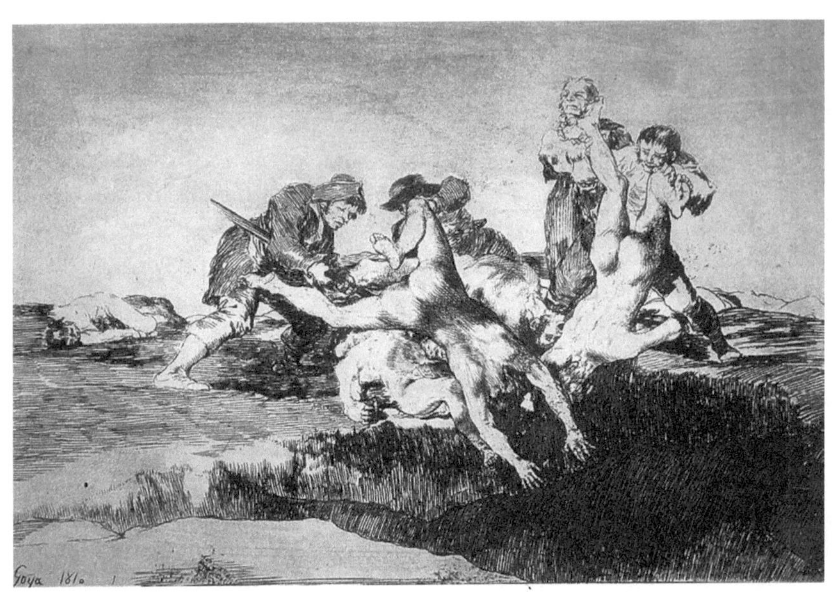
Goya 1810

27
Caridad

While the bodies of the dead manifest themselves with increasing insistence as readers move through the *Disasters* (Prints 12, 16, 18, 22, 23, 24), actual burials are a rare sight. This is the only image in the entire series to depict the moment of interment. Decomposing bodies were thought to be one of the primary sources of disease in the early nineteenth century, and military guidelines on both sides of the conflict in Spain stipulated that the deceased were to be buried quickly, usually in mass graves on or near the battlefield. This print clearly registers the practice, but the scarcity of such images within the series may also signal that, in a conflict that did not respect the traditional bounds of warfare, burial protocols were often not followed. The bodies we have already seen suggest as much. Beyond its documentary value, however, the print is also part of a broader reflection in the *Disasters* on the treatment, or, to be more precise, the mistreatment of the dead. By the time viewers turn to this image, they have seen a man vomit on the deceased, they have witnessed cadavers callously stripped of their clothing, and, in contrast to the burial under way here, they have repeatedly confronted piles of bodies rotting in the fields. Care for the dead, of the minimal type depicted in Print 21, where bodies were wrapped in shrouds and carried away, seems the exception to a rule of generalized neglect.

In the aggregate, Goya's images record a significant shift in the way the living relate to the dead during times of war. The forms through which cultures typically accord death meaning and value – respectful treatment of remains, religious ritual, commemoration, etc. – are almost entirely absent in the *Disasters*. More immediate demands eclipse any sense of care for those who have been killed: the nauseating revulsion of putrefying bodies, the imperative not to let anything go to waste, the necessities of hygiene, or more broadly, as was the case with the wounded, the need to move on to fight another day. Once again then, Goya's series addresses the moral as well as physical damage that accompanies wartime violence. The unfeeling treatment of the dead becomes a measure of the wartime coarsening of ethical life more generally.

In this image, what would normally be an act of final respect turns out to be one more scene of violence as workers harshly dispatch a pile of corpses. The central body that Goya depicts as it is tossed in an unseemly dive into the darkness encapsulates the unfolding drama. A hunched worker, behind and to the left of the body, shoves at it with a pole or pike in a gesture somewhat reminiscent of pitching hay, while a second worker manually pushes at the cadaver's left knee, helping to dislodge it from the pile of bodies behind it. The laborious, physical nature of the task is evident in the body postures of both workers. To the right, another worker lifts a second body by the legs as its shoulder perches on the edge of the pit and its head and right arm dangle into the burial site. Just behind them, a somewhat enigmatic older man stands. Two additional cadavers can be seen in the foreground. One lies between and slightly behind the two bodies going into the pit. Its head is thrown back, upside down, revealing the sunken eyes and gaping mouth of the only lifeless face we see in the image. Below the central figure, a fourth body on its back angles away from the pit. Its leg hangs over the edge, and its sunken abdomen brings its ribcage into stark relief. A lone corpse in the background on the left makes clear that some bodies have yet to be gathered from the field.

The strong contrast between the darkness with which Goya renders the pit and the comparatively lighter tones of the rest of the image makes the mass grave an arresting visual presence, and, with the exception of the horizon, virtually all of the composition's strongest lines, mostly diagonals, suggest movement into the blackness. The pole, the legs and arms of the central figure, the outlines of the second hanging body, the tilt of the bodies still lying in the foreground, and even the near edge of the pit, which angles down and to the right, all point into the grave. For its part, the darkness of the burial site, executed with little attention to geological detail, is symbolically charged insofar as the mostly white bodies are destined to disappear into it. A space of impending oblivion – particularly for readers who recall the command to "bury and forget" in Print 18 – the darkness is the void into which the dead will vanish from sight and memory. In this sense, the relatively abstract quality of the darkness – Goya makes no attempt to render the texture of the earth – makes it all the more disquieting.

Given what is taking place in the scene, the sarcastic caption, which simply reads "Charity," could not be more biting. The everyday meaning of charity in contemporary English, however, does not fully capture the depth of Goya's scorn. Beyond the act of giving aid to those in need, the word *charity* in nineteenth-century Spanish would have been understood as a more pointed reference to the Christian ethic of love. Within Catholic teaching, *caridad* (Lat. *caritas*) designated the greatest of the three theological virtues (now usually rendered in as faith, hope, and *love*). The word was a translation of the Greek *agape*, and it was synonymous with "love of God" and "love of neighbour." To evoke the term here thus carries an ironic charge that goes well beyond the mere absence of aid to those in need.

It speaks more trenchantly, and more deeply, to the fundamental suspension or abandonment of everyday Christian ethics during times of war.

This denunciation of cruelty also contains self-reflexive elements reminiscent of earlier prints. Like Print 18, to which it is thematically linked, the depiction of the white, unblemished bodies of the dead here again evokes the sculptural tradition of the male nude, and it raises the question of what role, if any, beauty should play within the world of the *Disasters*. More broadly, the statuesque bodies of the dead again raise the question of the relationship between the artistic act of form giving, on one hand, and the terrible violence that has made "statues" of these men within the scene on the other. Goya's print again probes the relationship between art and the violence it seeks to understand.

For viewers familiar with Goya's own semblance, self-reflection also takes a decidedly literal turn in this image. The older man standing behind the figures on the right is not simply one more anonymous bystander. His features correspond to the older Goya himself. Within this gruesome scene of heartless burial, Goya has included a self-portrait. Many have taken the gesture as a signal that the artist was an eyewitness to such scenes, and his biography makes clear that he may indeed have had occasion to see many of the kinds of events he depicts in the series. Given the way his prints so often reflect on the act of witnessing itself, however, the self-portrait here also lends itself to less biographical interpretations. For one thing, this Goya seems strangely disengaged. Though he is standing in the thick of things, his gaze is not fixed on what is happening before him, and he does nothing for dead. If the caption decries the harsh burial under way, there may well be a self-critical dimension to the seemingly passive stance of the artist within the scene, or perhaps it is a commentary on the limits of what an artist can do in such situations. Whatever the case, as earlier prints make clear, nobody is above moral scrutiny in the *Disasters*, be they Spaniards, Napoleonic soldiers, the viewer, or here, the artist himself.

Once again, however, things shift decidedly when we step outside the illusion. While we might question the Goya within the scene, the other Goya, the one who made this image, did *not* merely stand by idly. He created what we see, and in this sense artistic making seems to address some of those disquieting questions posed by the self-portrait. As was the case in Print 18, Goya's image making is a negation of the activity he has depicted. What at the level of the scene is a heartless dispatching of bodies becomes, at the level of the image, an act of remembrance. One might even say, noting the detailed pictorial attention with which Goya has rendered the bodies, that he has in some sense, artistically, furnished the care so singularly lacking within the scene. In this regard the caption has once again been playing with the twofold nature of our viewing. A sarcastic caption on one level has become a more subtle, straightforward commentary on image making as a form of care, perhaps even charity, at another. Goya's seemingly testimonial denunciation of the violence, it turns out, is also a complex meditation on art as a form of engagement and remembrance.

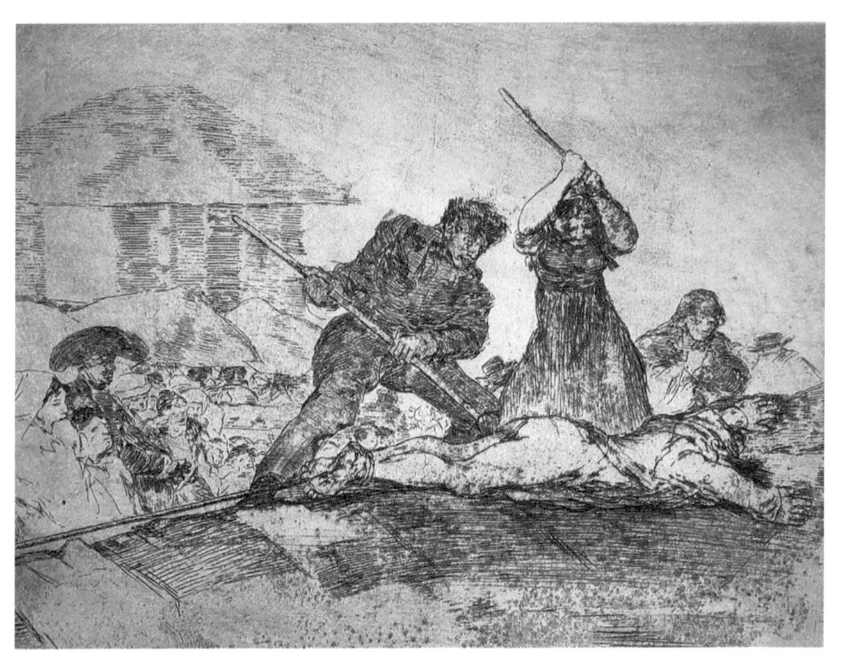

28

Populacho

[See 29 for commentary.]

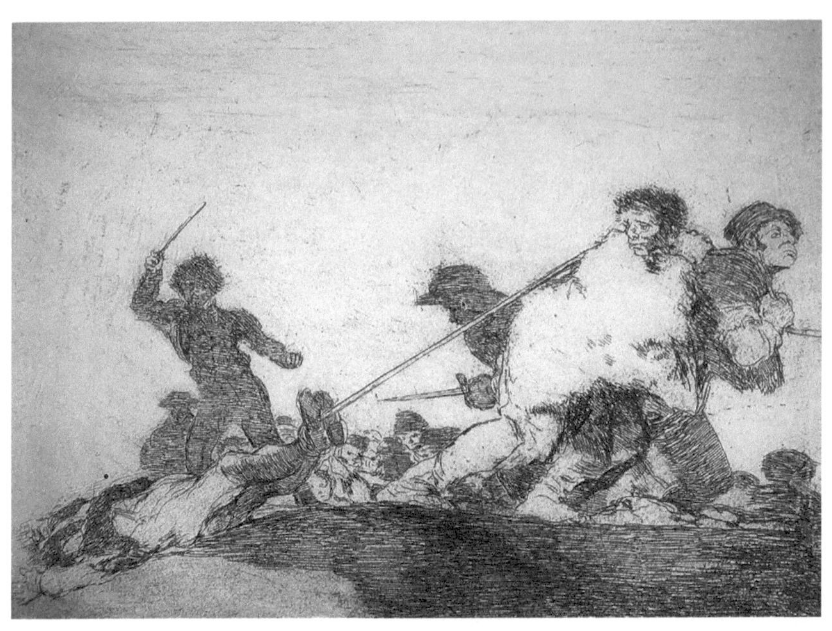

29
Lo merecía

The catalogue of violence expands once more with two prints that bring a new form of brutality into view. Historical records of the period are replete with tales of such mob violence, and many viewers have suggested that Print 28 in fact depicts the death of a historical personage, the Marquis of Perales, who was beaten and dragged through the streets of Madrid by a throng convinced that he had been collaborating with the French. It is clear once more, however, that these are not necessarily depictions of specific historical events. Goya has made no attempt to place either image in a recognizable setting, and the captions are similarly silent when it comes to historical details that might guide the viewing. In addition, as with earlier prints, the largely abstract backgrounds subtly remind viewers that the killing is taking place within the space of an image. Goya's approach to his subject here is moral before it is historical – the abstract pictorial space takes the violence into a more generic domain – and the two prints together pose disquieting moral questions.

In Print 28 a taut rope fastened around the victim's ankles angles down, exiting the frame at the lower left. The victim has been stripped of his trousers – a common form of humiliation during the war – and he lies face down. He is in all likelihood already dead. Above him a man and a woman, rendered in shadowed tones, assault the body as he is dragged. The man wields a pole with a half-moon blade on the end. The implement would be recognized by most Spaniards of the 1800s as a *desjarretadora*, a weapon that belonged to the world of bullfighting, where it was used to hamstring the bull prior to its final killing. Its presence here thus sets up an analogy between the ritualized slaughter of the bullring and the mob violence. At the same time, the way the man aims the weapon suggests further sexual humiliation in what amounts to a symbolic sodomizing of the body. Tellingly, Goya has repeated the weapon's angle throughout the image. It is paralleled by the stick the woman holds, the slope of the roof in the background, the angles of the tarp-like objects in front of the house, the outlines of the man's left thigh, and the numerous marks Goya makes to indicate the uneven quality of the ground over which the body is being dragged. It is as if the space itself is participating in the violence.

While the image does not differentiate many of the people in the crowd, several figures closer to the viewer convey a range of reactions to the violence. On the far left, a woman bites her fist in fear – or perhaps it is excitement – as she looks across at the victim, who is almost at eye level. On the far right, another woman looks down at the body with hands clasped in prayer. Together the two succinctly capture a gamut of feelings that runs from terrified fascination to compassion. Also in the crowd on the left, a priest wearing a distinctive long-winged clerical hat sits with seeming dispassion. He has been rendered in the same dark tones as the aggressors, perhaps suggesting his complicity in the violence, and his silhouette slants down at yet another angle reminiscent of the central weapon. That a cleric should sit by tranquilly as the scene unfolds is a particularly pointed moral indictment, insofar as priests were, officially at least, supposed to be representatives of Christian *caritas* (the charity so lacking in Print 27). In fact, historians have documented the Spanish Church's strong, active role in the fight against the French. Often priests were instrumental in inciting the kind of mob violence depicted here.

The caption reads *Populacho*, which is usually rendered as "Rabble." The pejorative term clearly conveys disapproval of the crowd, but by the time viewers come to this image they have seen so many other forms of equally reprehensible violence that it is difficult not to hear some irony in the judgment. If inflicting terrible harm on others qualifies the perpetrators as rabble, what perpetrators in the *Disasters* escape the qualification? It is one more example of the way sequence can subtly modify the meaning of individual prints. At the same time, questions of voice and address again complicate the viewing experience. One can imagine Goya speaking this caption, for example, but, as a judgment that comes from the place of viewing, it includes us as well. As with earlier prints, the caption raises the question of our relationship to it. Are we to identify with this judgment or take some distance from it and its speaker?

More intriguing still is the question of the caption's reference. The words are clearly directed at the two figures beating the body in the foreground, but logically speaking they must also encompass the crowd in its entirety. If that is the case, however, the vast majority of the "rabble" in this image is constituted not by perpetrators of violence but rather by those who have gathered to watch. Goya again brings the act of looking into relief, suggesting that to look at the spectacle is as worthy of scorn as the violence itself, and in this regard we ourselves come under scrutiny again. The position of the notional viewer reinforces the idea. If we were there, the print suggests, we would in all likelihood be part of the "rabble," on this side of the roadway, looking at the beating like the rest of them. As with earlier prints, our positioning suggests potential complicity with the violence, and it subtly plays with the difference between actual witnessing and viewing images.

If they are rabble and we are not, it is because we are on this side of the illusion, looking at an image. Even so, we would need to ask how different our gaze actually is from the crowd's. The point, once again, is to prompt self-scrutiny as we take in the violence.

The turn from Print 28 to 29 signals the frequency of such scenes. By making viewers confront two similar scenes sequentially, Goya conveys the recurrent nature of mob violence during wartime. Some viewers in fact take the image as a second moment of the same scene. It is literally something that one sees more than once, but this second image also subtly shifts focus with respect to its immediate predecessor. In Print 28 the assaults on the victim took centre stage, while those pulling the rope were out of the frame. Now the dragging itself comes to the fore. Two men haul a new victim. Like his predecessor, he is probably already dead, and shadow figures wielding weapons make clear that this body also faces mutilation. As the dramatic diagonal line conveys, however, the central drama here is the pulling, and Goya's approach to the faces of those depicted has also shifted. He no longer aims to portray individualized reactions within the crowd. His interest here is the emotional responses of the perpetrators themselves, the two men on the right whose facial expressions are rendered with more detail than any of the other figures in the scene.

Of the two men dragging the victim, the one on the right, confirms the pattern of indifference to suffering that we have encountered in earlier prints. Staring off into the distance, he does not seem to be moved by hatred or any other strong passion for that matter. His expression signals a matter-of-fact detachment, as if what he is doing is just one more form of labour. Judging by his visage alone, the man could be hauling anything. He offers viewers another example of the wartime deadening of moral feeling. The contrast offered by his companion, who casts a sorrowful glance down the rope towards the victim, however, could not be more pointed. There is sadness and pity in the man's gaze, and he is in many regards the emotional cornerstone of the image. The primary diagonal line traces both the rope and his sightline, and the fact that his compassionate glance travels down the very instrument by which he afflicts his victim is a measure of the moral complexity of the moment. The image offers a rare glimpse into the feelings of a victimizer. Among other things, it is an examination of the effects of the violence on perpetrators, particularly those like this man, whose moral conscience has not been anesthetized by the collective wartime sanctioning of brutality.

Such considerations, however, become more complex when one reads the caption, which surprisingly asserts, "He deserved it." As with earlier prints, it is a caption that is deliberately at odds with the emotional tenor of the image. In effect, the print presents viewers with an interpretive puzzle by coupling the depiction of a perpetrator's pity with a clichéd justification of the violence. But who would say such a thing? If the imagined speaker of the caption is Goya, "He deserved it" seems a strange and morally inconsistent departure from his consistent critique of violence throughout the series. As with other, similar captions – "It serves you right" (Print 6), "Bury them and be silent" (Print 18), "Cure them and on to another one" (Print 20), "They will still be able to serve" (Print 24) – the pronouncement here is more plausibly an ironic or sarcastic citation of wartime thinking than a straightforward expression from the artist. "He deserved it" is, in this reading, an expression of the justifications that often accompany brutal excess.

At the same time, the caption is an aggressive negation of the pity Goya has so carefully portrayed in the man's expression. "He deserved it" is what one might say in order to *minimize* compassion, and in this sense it is not difficult to imagine a bystander speaking the words in response to the man's pained expression, perhaps as a way of urging him on. "He deserved it" could also be what the man tells himself as he looks back with pity and regret, a way of dealing with his conflicted feelings, even as he continues to drag the victim. For that matter, the caption could represent the thoughts of his companion or anyone in the crowd. The ambiguity prompts viewers to explore the various possibilities. As in earlier cases, however, the caption is also a judgment that we all inevitably "speak" as we read the caption and look at the image, and the words once more raise the question of our relationship to what we see and read. Is our gaze like the man's? Is it coloured by the judgment of the caption? Or does it hover somewhere in between? However one answers such questions, the print has again induced viewers to reflect on their own activity as they take in the violence.

There is in addition one final facet of Prints 28 and 29 that only comes into view when they are viewed in succession. It comes from the experience of taking in two strikingly similar images that nevertheless bear radically different captions. In Print 28, "Rabble" judges the perpetrators. By contrast, in Print 29, "He deserved it" seems to judge the victim. In moving from one print to the next, then, viewers confront two fundamentally opposed modes of evaluation, two ways of appraising the violence that make little or no sense together. Markedly similar scenes of mob violence have been placed next to one another, coupled with contrasting and fundamentally incompatible pronouncements. It could be that Goya means to suggest the volatile nature of such appraisals during times of war, but one might also conclude that the point of the juxtaposition is to underscore the arbitrary nature of the judgments themselves in light of what unfolds in each scene.

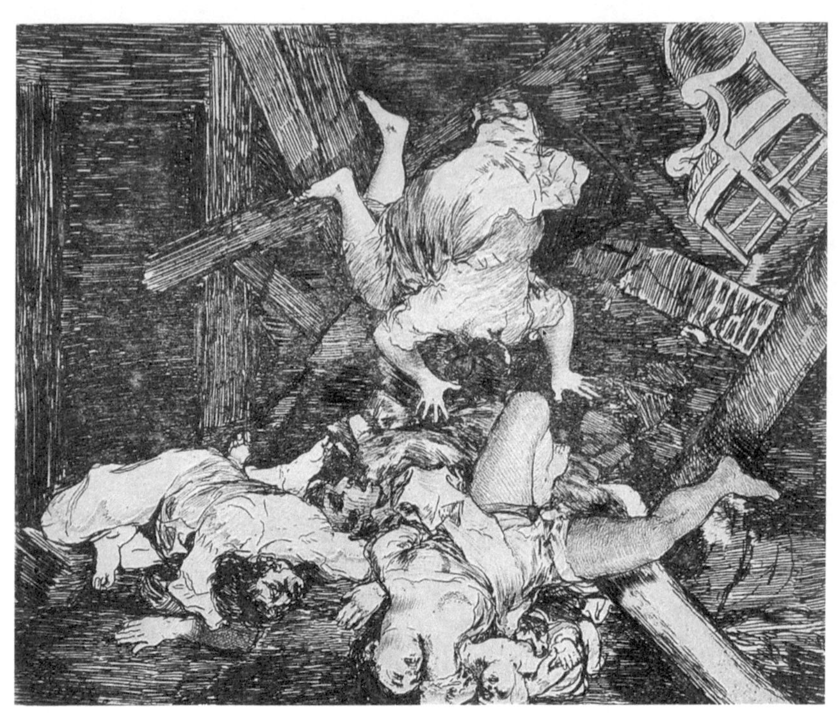

30
Estragos de la guerra

A new heap of bodies. In contrast to previous images, where the dead appear in exterior settings, they now come into view within the rubble of a collapsed building. Some thirty prints into the series, Goya registers yet another form of wartime violence. Scholars have noted that the scene most likely depicts the results of artillery fire. Bombardment was a common military tactic of the imperial army during the siege of Spanish cities, and Goya saw the destructive results of such attacks during his visit to Zaragoza in October of 1808. Military authorities of the day had called for artists to visit the city in order to commemorate its heroic defence against the French, and Goya travelled from Madrid in order to record what had happened. As we have seen repeatedly, however, heroic commemoration could not be further from the agenda Goya subsequently pursued. In this image we initially encounter a chaotic jumble of bodies, collapsed beams, some brickwork, and the remnants of household furniture. The armchair in the upper right and the civilian status of the victims suggest that the building was a private residence, and in this sense the image registers the impersonal, indiscriminate nature of the killing. It may in fact be the first image in the history of European art to depict the effects of bombardment on a civilian population. The casualties are what today's military culture would no doubt describe as "collateral damage." It is unlikely that they were expressly targeted by artillerymen. They are a byproduct of the warfare, and for viewers familiar with the history of bombardment of civilian centres in the wars of the twentieth and twenty-first centuries, there is something disturbingly prescient about what Goya has depicted here. It is yet another example of the uncannily contemporary reach of many of the *Disasters*.

Within the chaos, tonal contrast again plays an important role in bringing the victims into relief. As with so many of the dead in the *Disasters*, most of the bodies here are rendered in lighter tones that stand out within the gloom. At least five bodies are clearly distinguishable in the foreground, but the partial view of other body parts suggests that the number is higher. Particularly striking, because of the way her body has come to rest so unnaturally, is the woman perched upside-down in the middle upper half of the image. The pose could scarcely be more awkward, and the detail of her extended hands suggests that she died trying to break her fall. While her ungainly pose registers the effects of the violence, many have also seen in her the emblem of a world that, morally speaking, has been turned on its head. She is in this sense a token of the way war violently reorders bodies, places, and things.

Below her lie three adult bodies and the body of an infant. On the left, a man's mangled corpse rests on the ground. His lifeless countenance is reminiscent of other faces of the dead (see Prints 21, 22, and 23), and numerous limbs surround his body. Two feet jut out just above his waist, suggesting that another corpse lies behind him. Similarly, a single foot rests slightly behind and to the left of his head. Covered by what appears to be the hem of a dress, it signals the presence of an additional casualty. More disturbing, however, is the arm in the foreground, to the left of the man's head, which has been severed off entirely. It is in all likelihood the man's own – his right sleeve appears to be empty – but it is difficult to know for certain. Whatever the case, the image records the effects of a violence so potent that it can sunder limbs from bodies.

To the right of the man in the foreground lie a dead mother and child. This is not the first time in the *Disasters* that Goya has drawn on the maternal motif. In Print 5, a fiercely protective mother with babe in arms skewered a French soldier with her lance, and in Print 11, sexual aggressors tore a mother away from her baby, dragging her into the shadows to be raped. As these earlier images attest, when Goya draws on the motherhood archetype, its symbolism serves to heighten the emotional tenor of the image. Here, for example, the deaths become more moving precisely because they are a negation of the nurturing, life-giving role conventionally assigned to motherhood. The association is even more forceful if, as some viewers have proposed, the mother's exposed breast suggests that she was nursing her child in the moments immediately preceding death. At a more symbolic level, however, the dead mother and her infant are also an ironic inversion of the meanings of the Madonna and Child within Catholic iconography, where the pair traditionally signals not only the nurturing of life but also, more importantly, the nurturing of the promise of divine redemption. In this regard the image subtly conveys two ideas that we have encountered earlier in the series: the notion that during wartime nothing is set apart, revered, or otherwise exempted from the violence, and the view that a realm in which such horrors occur regularly is a world without redemption.

There is, however, an additional, deeply disquieting facet of Goya's portrayal of this mother. With exposed bosom, head thrown back, and legs spread apart, her body has been rendered in an overtly sensual if not sexual way. Some viewers have gone as far as to suggest that in this image the artist indulges in a necrophiliac fantasy by eroticizing the dead mother's body. Given the way Goya so consistently decries the violence of war and its terrible consequences throughout the series, however, there are reasons to believe that this depiction of the mother is not merely a sublimated expression of taboo desires. Her posture could, for example, be an attempt to record the way sudden, violent death can leave bodies in radically exposed, seemingly vulnerable positions, the way death rearranges bodies without care for the codes of decorum that govern the living. Within nineteenth-century Spanish middle-class culture, depicting a living woman this way would have provoked a scandal. The point of such a rendering here, however, may be precisely to prompt viewers to confront the absurdity of raising questions of sexual propriety when one is looking at a corpse. Taken together, the principal bodies in this image in fact register the utterly random way in which dead bodies come to rest. Some land in unnaturally rigid, inverted positions. Others lie on the ground twisted and mutilated, and still others come to repose in exposed, compromising postures.

It is also worth recalling that within the broader context of the *Disasters* this is not the first time that viewers have confronted the problem of attractive corpses. The echoes of classical statuary in Goya's depictions of nude male bodies raised similar issues (see Prints 16 and 18). Like her male counterparts then, the dead mother in this image may be a vehicle through which Goya poses the question of what role, if any, the pictorial conventions of female beauty should play within the world of the *Disasters*. It is another example of Goya's preoccupation with the problem of artistic form when violence and death are the primary subject. In addition, as with the male nudes, one must ask *for whom* this dead woman's body is attractive. Were we there, amid the rubble, such attraction would indeed be pathological. Arguably, it is only because we are here, looking at an image, that the question of her beauty even arises. Once more, then, we confront the difference between the witnessing fantasy that accompanies most representational art and the simultaneous knowledge of our position outside the illusion.

There is, finally, a fourth adult body within the rubble, and it too raises questions concerning our looking. Slightly behind and between the mother and the mangled man, the head of another corpse lies face up. Rendered in slightly darker tones than the other bodies, the man is easy to overlook. It is only as one attempts to make sense of the rubble that his face and head come into view more clearly, and there is something disquieting about the ease with which he could remain unseen. Goya has clearly made the image in order to draw more visual attention to the other three bodies, but the man's head awaits there nevertheless. Such variations are, of course, inherent to the creation of pictorial perspective. Some bodies are differentiated, while others get lost among their fellow dead. Some suffer spectacular forms of violence, while others remain in the shadows. Some make a strong claim to attention in the foreground, while others are absorbed into more generic forms of background violence. While such distinctions can be explained in terms of pictorial conventions, they take on a particularly charged significance within a print series whose primary aim is ostensibly to make war's horrors visible. Like the dead man here, who lies somewhat unseen within the triangle formed by the other three adult bodies, Goya's less visible victims raise questions about our habits and the way such habits can condition our attention. By coupling highly visible forms of violence with more hidden scenes of suffering and death, his images subtly prompt viewers to reflect on the conventions that shape the way we look. It is one more example of the way the *Disasters* gesture towards the limits of our witnessing by reminding us that all looking is partial and that every gaze is inevitably accompanied by some blindness.

In comparison to all prior captions, the text that accompanies this image is, on the surface at least, one of the most conventional. A straightforward descriptive commentary, it reads simply, "Ravages of war." The characteristic facets of Goya's verbal artistry – the ambiguities of voice and address, the ironic, critical tone, the subtle word play, and the complex interactions between text and image – appear to give way here to a more traditional labelling of the scene. For readers who have become accustomed to the more caustic tenor typical of the captions, there is consequently something disarming about the shift in tone. Some have also noted that the caption is closely related to the title of the series itself: the step from the "ravages of war" to the "disasters of war" is a relatively small one, and it could very well be that this caption influenced the Royal Academy's choice of the title for the first edition.

The caption's seemingly straightforward labelling of the scene, however, is not without its own conceptual complexities. To call what we see in the image "Ravages of war" has a strangely abstract, generalizing effect, given the pathos of what has taken place. "Ravages of war" names the disparate elements of the scene with a generic term for damage or harm, making no distinction, for example, between the rubble and those who have died in it. It may seem a small detail, but in an image that is precisely about the way wartime violence transforms people into inanimate things, the nuance takes on considerable significance. In its refusal to distinguish between the human and the inanimate, "ravages" verbally echoes the visual challenges of the image: the difficulty, beyond the most obvious victims, of making out bodies in the rubble, and the sense that the bodies, like the beams, the stonework, and the furniture, have become broken things.

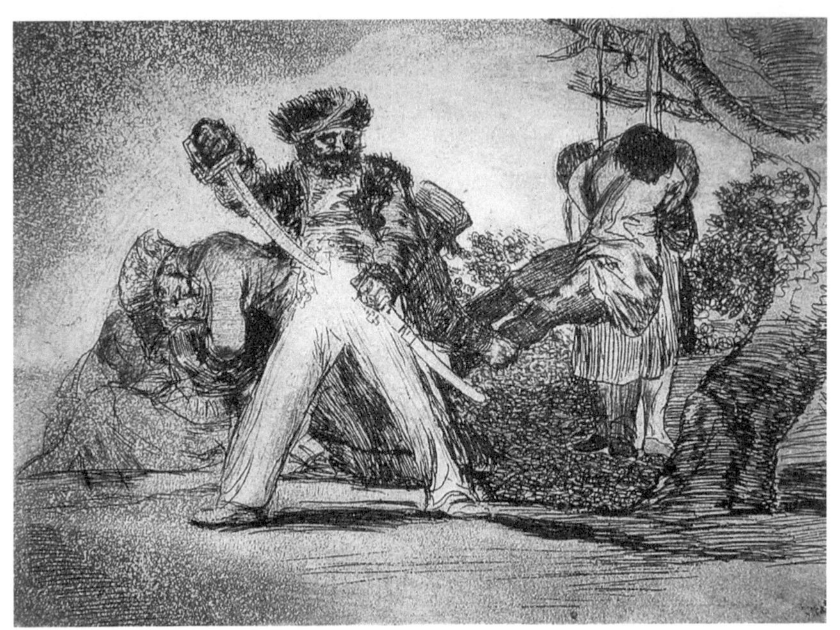

31

Fuerte cosa es!

From a setting of urban violence and destruction we return to another outdoor scene. Although place, as we have seen, is often difficult to determine with precision in the *Disasters*, movement through the series takes viewers through any number of environments. Constructed spaces – the world of archways, courtyards, and city rubble – alternate with settings of a sparse, ravaged natural world. The basic nineteenth-century categories of town and country find a macabre echo in such alternation, and natural cycles do the same: daylight scenes of violence alternate with seemingly more nocturnal settings. Settings similarly shift from the "anyplace" of abstract environs – here the strange "sky" in the background – to seemingly more naturalistic places. It is one more example of the way Goya's art of sequencing creates subtle effects that no single image conveys in quite the same way. To turn from print to print is to recognize slowly the idea that the violence of modern warfare is everywhere. As Goya suggests throughout the series, disasters unfold on battlefields, but also on city streets, in front of churches, in hidden corners, and in publicly staged spectacles. They are to be found in the extraordinarily wide variety of settings Goya gathers together. No place is beyond their scope, whether it be an interior bourgeois household, as in the previous print, or the field and trees before us now.

In this image viewers initially confront a familiar grouping of elements – soldiers and victims, hangings, the wielding of weapons – but the scene becomes less straightforward, and indeed enigmatic, as soon as one attempts to make sense of it in terms of narrative. Just what is under way here? The central soldier in the foreground either has just unsheathed his sword or is in the process of returning it to its scabbard. He is the most expressive of the figures in the image, and Goya has delineated him with swift, short, somewhat unruly strokes that accentuate the idea of his agitation and movement. His face, the only one we see fully, has a caricature-like wide-eyed expression that conveys intensity of feeling. It is difficult, however, to determine the emotional content of the intensity. What sentiments inform this soldier's frenzied gaze? In an artist as talented at conveying complex feeling through facial expression as Goya was, the soldier's intense but enigmatic feeling is telling, and it is part of a broader ambiguity that many viewers of this image have confronted, an ambiguity concerning the relationship between the soldiers in this scene and the victims.

Just behind the central figure, a second soldier grasps the legs of one of three hanged bodies strung up from a tree on the right, but to what end? And what exactly is the third soldier, hunched over a woman on the left side of the image, doing? The victims are clearly civilians. They include both men and women, and Goya's composition has framed them dramatically, within the "V" formed by the descending diagonal line of the central soldier's sword and left leg and the tree trunk that angles down from the right. This is not the first scene of hanging in the *Disasters*, and viewers who have moved through the series sequentially may well recall Print 14, where bodies swung below a gallows as a condemned man struggled to step up to his death. In contrast to that print, however, the dead here appear to have been the victims of a more impromptu form of killing. No spectacle of legality has accompanied their execution. They have simply been strung up in a tree, the victims of a summary execution or lynching, and Goya has left few cues about the reason. They could have been anti-French partisans or guerrillas executed by the occupiers; or they may have been collaborators with Bonaparte's regime, *afrancesados* who met their end at the hand of Spaniards. The political affiliation of the victims is not marked strongly.

In attempting to determine the soldiers' relationship to the hanged, viewers have consequently advanced one of two basic hypotheses. In one account the soldiers are understood to be the perpetrators of the violence. The central soldier, still caught in a frenzy of violent feeling, would have just participated in the slaughter of the civilians, and his comrade on the right would be tugging at the legs of the hanged body to assure himself that the victim is dead. The third soldier, crouched over a woman in a posture reminiscent of earlier prints, would in this version of things be an aggressor, and the scene would thus be one of open hostility. If the victims are understood as allies of the soldiers, Spanish collaborators or French citizens, however, a very different tale seems to explain what we see. Within such a framework, the central soldier would be drawing his sword to cut down the bodies, and his frenzied response would convey outrage at the sight of the lynching. The soldier to the right, rather than tugging at the corpse, would be holding its legs in order to soften the fall, and the soldier on the left would be leaning over a survivor, perhaps in order to aid her or offer some solace.

While viewers have usually opted for one version or the other, given the ease with which Goya could have signalled the allegiance of the victims, and in light of his routine indictment of both sides of the conflagration, it is worth considering whether ambiguity is not in fact the point. The difficulty of identifying one clear narrative context may contain within it a moral reflection, suggesting that in the end such questions are out of place in light of what has happened. Regardless of the side of the conflict to which they belonged – and it is worth recalling that as in most wars the majority of civilians often avoided partisanship – the victims have been hanged. As in previous prints, then, the experience of viewing this image may be an invitation to dismantle the wartime concepts – friend and enemy – that habitually organize our viewing.

The caption reads *Fuerte cosa es!* The literal translation is "A strong thing it is!" "Strong" in the Spanish idiom Goya uses, however, is understood emotionally, as a marker of shock or surprise. *¡Qué fuerte!* is an exclamation akin to the colloquial American English "Harsh!" or "Wow!" "A harsh thing it is" is a good approximation, and in this sense the caption underscores intensity of feeling. As we have seen in previous prints, however, its reference is not univocal. It potentially addresses more than one facet of the image. It could refer explicitly to the central soldier's frenzied response to what he sees, but the "thing" might also be the scene in its entirety. Given Goya's tendency to reflect on his own practice as an artist, it could also address the print itself, a strong or intense *Disaster* within the series. It is another caption that speaks to more than one dimension of the image, raising the question of just what "thing" has provoked such intensity. By prompting viewers to consider the various possibilities, the ambiguous voicing of the caption becomes a call to reflect on how different the "harsh thing" is for the victim, for the soldiers, for viewers, and for the artist himself.

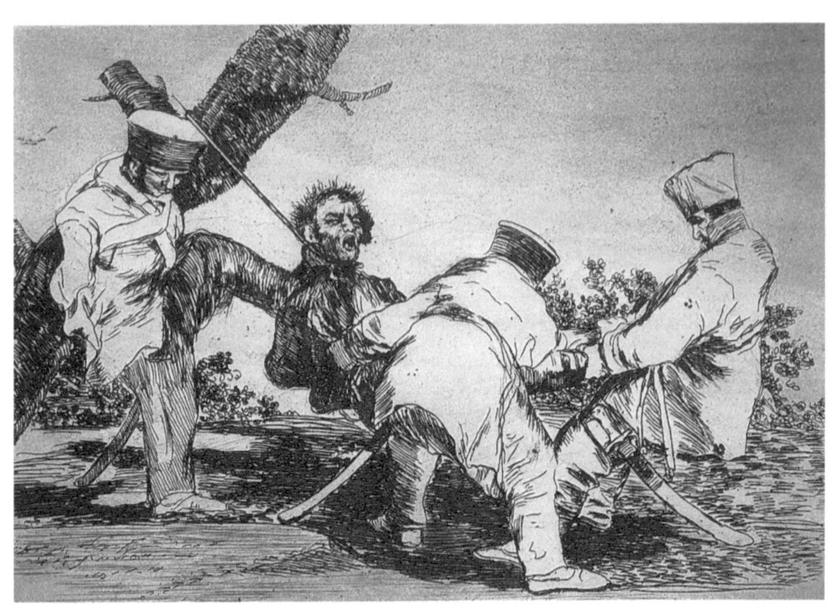

32

Por qué?

The cadavers of the hanged give way to an ongoing, brutal strangulation. Until now the majority of the *Disasters* depicting execution have avoided the actual act, tending to focus either on the excruciating moments just before death or, as in so many previous images, its immediate aftermath. Here, however, Goya takes as his subject a killing in progress, and he spares few details. If this is a hanging, it is not of the sort we have seen before. Whether it is because the tree's height and angle are inadequate to the task – the composition withholds the full shape of the tree – or because the soldiers in fact prefer the method they have chosen, the hanging has turned into a much more harrowing, intimate form of killing, a lynching driven by the bodily force of the soldiers, two of whom pull at the victim's legs from below as one steps down on his shoulder from above. The brutality has intensified with respect to the previous print, and unlike that scene, there is no narrative ambiguity here. Not only is this scene more violent in comparison to its immediate predecessor, but it is also excruciatingly clear in terms of narrative. The effect makes what we see all the more compelling, and it is another example of how sequence can subtly shape the viewing experience.

The dramatic diagonal descending from the stump of the tree branch on the upper left, through the rope, along the victim's body, across the waist line of the soldier in the centre, and down the sword of the soldier on the right amplifies the force of the strangulation across the composition. All figures are part of this macabre line of action, and just short of the half-way point down, the head and face of the victim have been rendered in full detail: a gasping mouth, closed eyes and furrowed brow, a head of hair standing on end. Many viewers have noted the meticulous care with which Goya has rendered this face, the suffering face of a life that is ending. Other faces, however, are worthy of notice as well: the face of a soldier in profile on the right, and on the left, the face of the soldier whose trunk-like leg, rendered with the same curves as the tree, presses down from above. Tonal contrast again takes on thematic significance – the dark clothing of the victim, the lighter cassocks of the soldiers – but the strongest contrast between victim and perpetrators is emotional, and it is recorded in the abyss that separates their expressions from his own.

The soldiers again register little or no emotion. Neither angry nor particularly moved, they seem to go about their business with a casual efficiency, as if the killing were simply one more of the day's tasks. That the killing has become routine, with little or no effect on them, is clear in their body postures and facial expressions, particularly those of the soldier on the left, whose hands remain in his pockets as he looks down with what appears to be a bemused smirk. Among other things, then, the image conveys something we have seen in earlier *Disasters*: the way war transforms extraordinary violence into something routine, the way it deadens the moral feeling of perpetrators, the way the violence has for them become an everyday affair. We have considered the phenomenon in the dispassionate gaze of the soldier dragging his victim towards her rape in Print 11, in the unperturbed stripping of the bodies of the dead in Print 16, and in the callous pitching of a cadaver into the mass grave in Print 27. Now we find the same detachment within the act of killing itself. Viewers who move through the *Disasters* in sequence slowly recognize that the fundamental dismantling and reordering of the basic moral codes that usually govern everyday life are an important, recurring theme in the series.

Precisely for this reason perhaps, the difference between actually witnessing such a scene and coming to it in an image becomes particularly charged. How are we to take in this scene of excruciating violence? As we have seen repeatedly, when Goya gives the gaze of others prominence in the *Disasters*, he also raises the question of our own looking. From here, for those viewing a print, judgments about the cruelty come quickly and unambiguously, but the position of the notional viewer within the scene once again tells a different, more complex story. If we were there and saw this, the place we occupy suggests that we would in all probability be allied to the soldiers. As witnesses, we would be implicated in the violence, standing at a short distance from extraordinary cruelty. Moreover, the impassive gaze of the soldiers, who are there, suggests that, if we were present, we too would find ourselves in a very different moral universe from the one from which we may have initially judged the scene. The point is not to nullify the viewer's moral discernment, but rather to complicate it, to prompt critical reflection on the fact that war fundamentally undoes the morality we might otherwise take for granted.

The caption is a straightforward and seemingly simple question, *Por qué?*, or "Why?," a search for reasons. A fundamental concern across the *Disasters*, it returns readers to the issue Goya took up early on, in Prints 2 (With reason or without it) and 3 (The same thing). In those early prints the artist raised the question of the relationship between the violence and the human capacity to reason, to understand, and to explain. Together, the two prints made clear that no reason or justification could adequately explain the violence. It is not that violence for Goya is somehow beyond human comprehension, but rather that, *morally speaking*, no explanation suffices. Deplorable as they might be, there are in fact any number of reasons one could summon to try to explain what is happening in this scene: the logic of war and its tendency to inure combatants to the pain of the enemy, the difficulty of maintaining "rules of war" once the fundamental moral stricture against killing has been suspended, the sadism that often ensues, etc. These are hard truths, and the *Disasters* do not shy away from them. As a rhetorical question, however, *Por qué?* is a comment before it is a search for answers. It asserts that no moral reasoning will do, precisely because such reasoning is itself one of war's primary casualties.

At the same time, the question of voice – who "says" the caption? – again remains an open one. Some readers have taken the caption as a representation of the victim's last thoughts. For others the soldiers themselves might ask the question, even as they proceed without really knowing why. The query can also be imagined in Goya's voice, as the maker of the image, and it certainly is a question that viewers are meant to ask themselves. As in earlier *Disasters*, the caption can be attributed to any number of positions – victim, soldiers, artist, and viewer – prompting reflection on the different shades of meaning this "Why?" takes on for each. It is good example of the way captions in the *Disasters* rarely let viewers remain satisfied with their initial reactions to what they see. Like the previous print, the words prompt readers towards conceptual as well as emotional engagement with the image, and they point to the various positions from which the violence and the image that depicts it can be experienced.

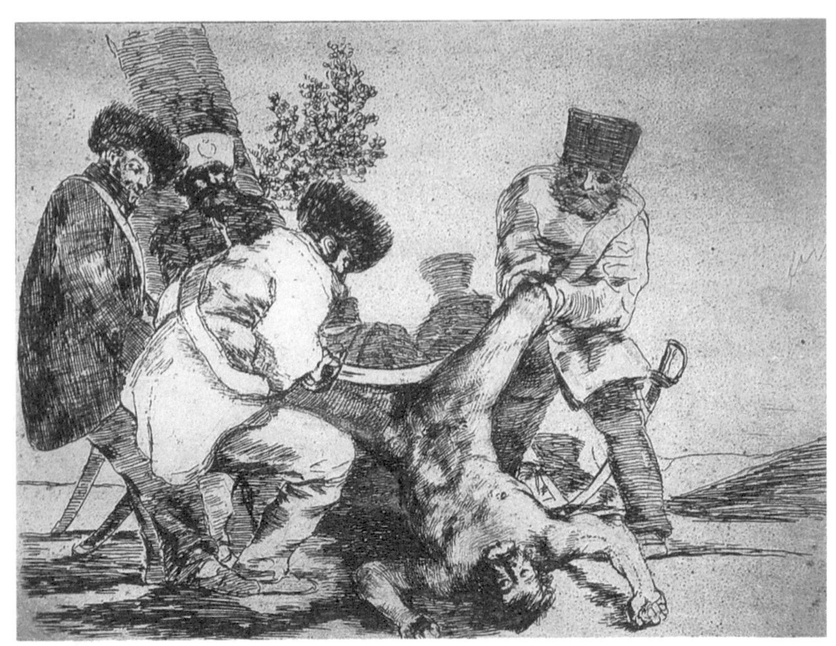

33

Qué hay que hacer más?

While the previous print broke new ground by rendering the extraordinarily brutal, intimate scene of a killing, in this *Disaster* viewers again confront a new subject, the violence of bodily mutilation. The fact that new forms of cruelty should continue to appear relatively late within the forty-seven prints on wartime killing is in itself telling, and it speaks to the extraordinary variety of horrific acts Goya brings together. Variation in the *Disasters* challenges the idea that one might "see it all" when it comes to the horrors of war. More always lies ahead, the series suggests. The forms of violence seem as varied as the imagination itself, and the *Disasters* together point to this apparently inexhaustible array of possibilities in a way that no single print or group of prints can. For viewers moving through the series in sequence, however, this print and its predecessor also subtly convey an additional idea. Simply put, the violence is becoming progressively more intense, grislier, and more difficult to take in. Gruesome as they have been, earlier *Disasters* seem less raw by comparison. No early prints in the series depict this kind of excess. While simulating movement through time, then, the series also organizes a voyage towards more gut-wrenching horrors, as if viewers were getting closer to the moral heart of darkness of the violence. This effect is lost in discussions of the *Disasters* that focus on a select handful of images.

The caption to this image, which one can translate as "What more is there to do?" or "What more must be done?," raises the issue of limits, suggesting that the emasculation under way is beyond the pale. As happens so often with Goya's captions, however, the words lend themselves to more than one reading. The print certainly poses a rhetorical question that we might imagine in the voice of the artist. In this sense the caption indicts the excess, much as the previous print's "Why?" decried the absence of any moral justification for the violence. There is, however, a more macabre way in which "What more is there to do?" is not entirely rhetorical, but rather a straightforward question. Because the victim has already died, the "more" in the caption takes on an additional, specific meaning, asking what remains to be done *beyond the killing*. The soldiers might very well have asked themselves the question, and what we see unfolding in the image is an answer. Death is not the limit to wartime atrocities. One can always inflict more harm on an enemy.

The historical record of the Peninsular War – and of warfare as such – is full of examples of bodily mutilation, and it is one more occasion to note the deeply antiheroic dimensions of warfare that Goya often takes up. While many warriors' deeds can be recounted in celebratory form, mutilation does not lend itself to such aggrandizing, and it poses a series of difficult questions. What prompts combatants not to stop at the death of their enemy? What does such additional violence accomplish? One might imagine the mutilation as a continuation of the rage of battle, but, as in earlier *Disasters*, Goya signals that excessive passion has not prompted the brutality depicted here. The expressions of the two soldiers pulling at the dead man's legs do not convey hatred or even anger. The men go about their business with little or no feeling. They could be butchering an animal, but their act is more than mere butchery. If they can inflict additional injury – the caption's "more" – it is because even in death the integrity of the human body conventionally retains some dignity as a vestige of the person who was.

The bodies of the dead are susceptible to additional violence because they are symbolic remnants of personhood, reminders of the living beings they once were. Mutilation injures the victim symbolically, by undoing the dignity of the body itself. It is an assault on the imagined person beyond their physical death, and this too intensifies the violence with respect to previous *Disasters*. Callous treatment of the dead (see Prints 16 and 27) progresses into active disfiguring as viewers advance through the series. Such violence makes visible the fact that wartime violence is never limited to killing. It aims to destroy more than the life of the enemy. In fundamental ways it strikes against the idea of the human as such.

Then there is the sexual nature of the mutilation, which Goya boldly emphasizes through the compositional "V" of the victim's legs, amplified by the angles of the tree on the left and the soldier's sash on the right. At their convergence, just below the centre of the image, the point of it all, the dark patch of the victim's groin and the bright sword that cuts into it, is one more example of Goya's mastery of the expressive potentials of the tonal contrasts inherent to his medium. The emasculation underscores the deeply sexualized patterns of struggle we have often seen on display in earlier *Disasters*. To vanquish the enemy is symbolically to feminize him. The genital mutilation literally takes away what was understood as the seat of manhood, and Goya's rendering of the victim's masculine, swarthy, muscled body and bearded head seems no accident. This is not the sculptural body Goya has presented earlier in order to question the relationship between art and the violence it seeks to depict. The corpse he renders here highlights conventional physical notions of masculinity because manhood, or more precisely its remnant, is precisely what the soldiers aim to destroy. Long before psychoanalysis would coin the term, the phallic nature of the violence – here one phallus, wielded waist-high, destroys the place of another – would not have escaped audiences for whom war and the performance of manhood were two sides of the same coin. In many ways, it is the flip side of the violence against women that Goya examined in earlier prints devoted to rape.

While this sort of act can be taken as a final, humiliating insult directed at the victim, however, within the context of the war in Spain it would also have been a message to the living. The mutilated dead were often made into objects of display. A deterrent against resistance, the disfiguring was meant to be seen by others. Historically speaking, it was aimed at a population of Spaniards hostile to the Napoleonic regime, an assertion that the same treatment would await any man who took up arms against the imperial army. A tension consequently arises again between our role as would-be witnesses, on one hand, and as viewers of images on the other. Because the violence here is intended to be seen, looking becomes an especially charged experience. If we were there, what kind of witnesses would we be? What would it mean to look? How would we respond? And if the soldiers are doing this precisely in order to display it, what is the relationship between what they are doing and Goya's artistic display in this image?

However we might approach such questions, they complicate the initial moral judgments we might have initially formed. In addition, even as the print asks us to indulge in the witnessing fantasy, it also signals the constructed, artificial nature of the image by surrounding the body with decidedly non-naturalistic details: the roughly rendered silhouettes of the soldiers behind the scene, the strange "extension" of the tree trunk's darkness into the space between the shoulders of the two soldiers standing on the left, the flatly enigmatic sky. It is one more example of the way illusion and artifice together point to the complexities of moral viewing.

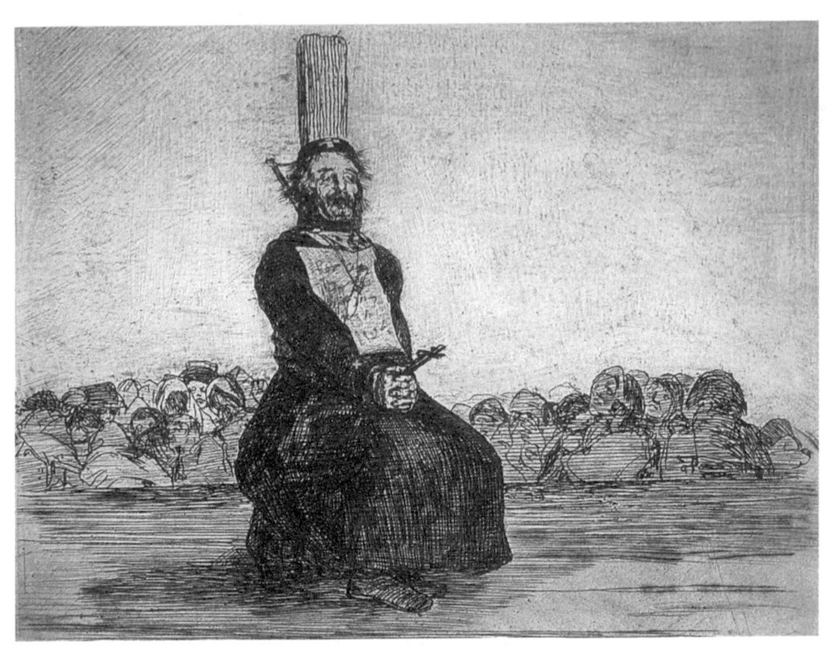

34
Por una navaja

[See 36 for commentary.]

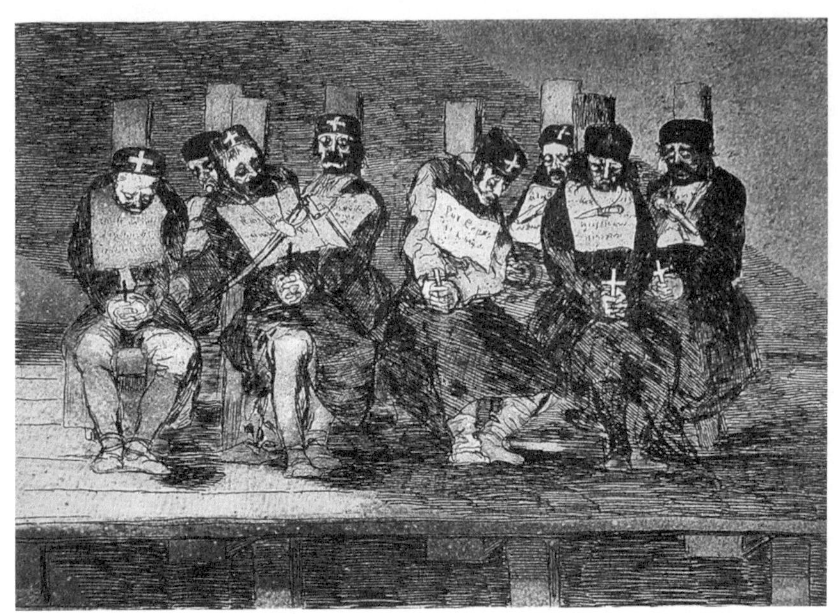

35
No se puede saber por qué

[See 36 for commentary.]

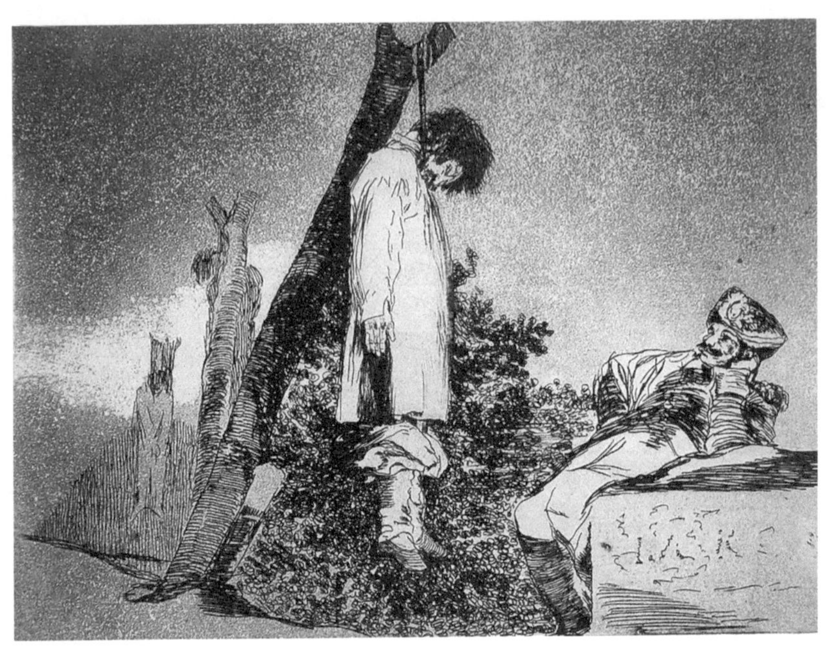

36
Tampoco

More spectacles of public execution, and again, a new form of killing. Although readily understood by nineteenth-century Spanish viewers, the method of execution depicted in the first two of these three prints is not always obvious to the present-day public. Garrotting was the common form of capital punishment in Spain throughout the nineteenth and early twentieth centuries. By French decree it was also the official, more dignified form of capital punishment during the Peninsular War. It consisted of a seat and post to which victims were bound with a metal collar fitted to the neck. The killing took place by a rapid tightening of the collar with a crank or wheel. In the first image we see part of the crank just behind and to the left of the victim's head. In the second, the cranks are hidden by the frontal view of the victims and posts. The procedure aimed to kill quickly, by breaking the victim's neck, but like botched hangings, slower deaths by asphyxiation often ensued. The religious paraphernalia – the crosses on skull-caps, the crucifixes in hand – were standard for the condemned.

In these prints, Goya takes up once more the subject of execution staged as spectacle for public consumption. In the first image the sole victim, elevated on a scaffold, sits lifeless before the crowd. Like earlier prints in which crowds appear (see Prints 14, 28, and 29), spectatorship is as much the subject here as the violence itself, and numerous compositional and tonal features of the image highlight the contrasts between the victim and those who have gathered to watch. A single, dark, vertical figure stands out against the greyness of a horizontally arranged multitude. If the print is among other things a commentary on the voyeurism that typically accompanies public killings, however, it also makes our own looking a problem once more by posing questions of the sort we have seen in other *Disasters*. How different is our gaze from the crowd's, and how should we look at a scene that has deliberately been staged for viewing? Goya's positioning of the notional viewer also complicates initial responses once more. The first of three images suggests that if we were there, we would be up on the scaffold, looking down on the crowd. If that is the case, in all probability we would be among the authorities doing the executing – Print 14 placed us in a similar way – which is to say that we would be accomplices to the violence. Like other *Disasters*, then, our position within the scene confounds easy moral judgments, drawing attention to the difference between being here as we look at an image and the place we would occupy if we truly were there.

The caption to this image reads "Because of a knife," or in some translations "On account of a knife." Like Prints 2 ("With reason or without it"), 3 ("The same thing"), and 32 ("Why?"), Goya's words return to the issue of reasons and justifications. As part of the occupation of Spain's major cities, French martial law forbade Spanish citizens to carry weapons under penalty of death, and the first of these three prints comments on the disproportionate nature of the punishment. The man on the scaffold has been executed because he was caught with a pocket knife. As part of the ritual of execution, the condemned were often forced to wear the evidence of their crime. That is the knife we see hanging around the man's neck, which Goya has depicted in fairly rudimentary form. In contrast to the knife, however, the artist has rendered the man's lifeless face in terrible detail, with closed eyes and an open mouth that still seems to gasp for air. This was no merciful snap of the neck but rather the slow death of a strangulation.

The condemned also commonly carried a verbal announcement of their crime. That is the sign under the knife, and a closer look at it reveals the first word to be *Por* – i.e., "because of" or "on account of" – the very word with which Goya's own caption begins. The print's caption, we are led to believe, is a quotation of the announcement on the man's chest. The words within the image are reproduced outside it for ironic effect, and again the irony depends on the difference between being there, where the words would have been part of the ritual of execution, and being here, looking at a print in which Goya has made those words an object of critical reflection by reproducing them as a caption. There is an additional wrinkle. If we were there, we would be able to read the words on the man's chest. The reason we cannot is because we are looking at an image constructed in order to make only the first word legible. If we can reconstruct the content of the sign on the man's chest, it is only because we have access to Goya's caption, one more reminder that we are looking at an image.

When we turn to the next print, the bodies have multiplied, from one to eight. Like the piles of the dead earlier in the series (Prints 21, 22, and 23), repetition amplifies, reminding viewers that what we see in any given image is but a small portion of what is taking place within a larger theatre of war that remains out of sight. As we have seen elsewhere, repetition also simulates the experience of witnessing similar atrocities more than once during times of war. Executions of this sort often took place one after another, and movement from print to print mimics the repetition. Like the man in the preceding print, several of the victims in this second image wear the weapons for which they have been condemned. Knives and even a sword hang around the necks of the dead, but there are also men who simply bear the written announcements of their respective infractions. In contrast to the previous image, however, the caption to this one no longer reproduces official reasons for the killing. Instead, we read, "One cannot know why."

Attached to an image in which each victim is made to announce the reason for his execution, the caption is a pointed refutation of official rationales, and it raises the issue of how to reconcile our moral understanding with what we see in the image. In the literal, legal, and historical sense, viewers can most certainly understand why several of the men have been executed, but the caption signals that such reasons are not sufficient. Official rationales can explain what has led to the deaths in terms of immediate causes – i.e., the crimes under martial law – but they do not speak to the moral dimensions of the killings. Again, the print does not suggest that the violence is itself somehow beyond any form of comprehension. Rather, it exhibits how the terms of conventional moral reasoning fall short within the world depicted. If wartime suspends the basic moral prohibition against killing, it also creates its own, new regimes of justification, regimes in which one can be killed, for example, for carrying a pocket knife. As we saw in Print 32, the very kind of moral reflection that would ask "Why?" is often one of war's first casualties. It belongs to the world of our viewing more than to the world of the disasters themselves.

Viewers consequently face once more the difference between actually being there and being in front of an image, where the moral sensibility that would find the executions abhorrent is presumably still intact. The print suggests that if we were actually there, our judgments might be different. In the last image we had been placed on the scaffold, suggesting that we were perhaps accomplices to the execution. Now, in the very next image, we have been positioned within the crowd, the very crowd we may have judged for a moment in the previous print. Then comes the question. How is our looking fundamentally different from that of others who might also be in the crowd? Whatever the answers, the place we have been assigned entangles us in the spectacle in ways that trouble the judgments we might have initially formed. Careful attention to the image and its caption teaches that if we were there we might not be moral witnesses at all.

When the exhibition of violence becomes the subject in the *Disasters*, however, Goya often extends this sort of moral self-scrutiny to his own activity as a maker of images. In Print 33, part of the viewing experience involved recognizing that the violence of castration was driven by the soldiers' desire for others to look at the mutilation, as a message to the living. In that case, disturbing parallels between Goya and the soldiers came to the surface. Similar parallels emerge in Prints 34 and 35, where the relationship between the spectacles staged by the authorities and the spectacles created by the artist becomes an open question. Despite the differences between the two kinds of spectacle – one aims to display and legitimate the violence, while Goya's is fundamentally critical – the unsettling similarities between them are difficult to overlook. Not only have the authorities and Goya both created a violent spectacle, but the very form of the violence depicted here also echoes the form of the *Disasters* themselves. The dead men each wear a "caption" that aims to explain their death, and the first print expressly draws an analogy between the words within the scene and the words of the artist. Similarly, in the second print, the dead bodies, lined up in a series, each with its own verbal text, echo what Goya has been doing within the print series as a whole. Like Prints 14 and 15, in these prints we again find Goya's art reflecting on itself critically in order to highlight the moral quandaries posed by pictorial representation when it takes terrible violence as its subject.

Turning to Print 36, we confront another dead body, the result of a hanging. In terms of narrative content there is no obvious relationship to the previous two *Disasters* beyond the theme of killing. Both the method and place of execution in the print take viewers elsewhere, but Goya links this image to its immediate predecessors with the caption. It is the word *Tampoco*, the negative form of "also" in Spanish. The word first appeared as a caption in Print 10, with the image of women who "also" did not want to be raped. Here, it conveys the same sense of "Not in this case either," and it refers again to the problem of moral understanding. Although the scene has changed in fundamental ways – we no longer see scaffolds, crowds, or garrottes – the words inform readers that here too "One cannot know why." The image thus becomes a third moment of reflection on the problem of knowing why, but now in a seemingly very different context.

Whereas the previous two prints were expressly focused on the official explanations that appeared as part of the executions, in this print we move well beyond the world of legal justifications. Viewers are taken to a quasi-natural, outdoor setting in one more scene of a battlefield hanging. Such deaths were the common fate of captured guerrilla fighters, whose bodies were often left to hang by roadsides as a warning to other potential insurgents. The print, however, is doing much more than referencing this history. Bisected by the vertical line of the hanged man in the foreground, the image is organized around two ideas to which Goya often returns. On the left, the line of receding victims conveys the notion of seemingly endless repetition, much like Print 15, and again there is a self-reflexive dimension to this. We encounter a series within an image that is itself part of a series. On the right, by way of the sitting officer who stares at the body, Goya poses the question that haunts so many of his prints, the question of looking and its meaning. Together the two sides of the pyramid with which Goya has organized the composition thus couple artistic self-scrutiny with an invitation for viewers to do the same.

At the centre, the victim has been rendered in the image's lightest tones once again. For some viewers, the trousers bunched below the man's knees indicate that he too may have been castrated, an idea informed by the historical record but also by the viewing of earlier images. Without the castration in Print 33, the suggestion might not be as strong. Others have proposed that the trousers have fallen because the man has been hanged with his own belt, the cord countrymen commonly used to cinch their pants at the waist. In either case, humiliation has been part and parcel of the killing. The primary centre of interest for most viewers of this image, however, is not the victim. Despite the pathos of his death – the tilt of his lifeless head, the long shirt that seems to accentuate his hanging, the trousers – viewers' attention tends to focus far more often on the officer, and more specifically on the enigmatic expression of his face.

Clearly untroubled by the spectacle before him, he sits calmly at what might be taken for a desk, a shape more symbolic of his ease than plausible in any realistic sense. He leans back with bent right arm resting at his hip, while his left arm supports his head in a posture reminiscent of the classic melancholy pose. But hovering somewhere between distracted attention, reverie, bemusement, and even satisfaction, this is not the visage of a melancholy man. Many have suggested that he is reclining to contemplate his work, the way one might step back, for example, to view an artwork. With the "desk" at his side, he would be at home in a drawing room, and if that is the case, art making and the violence it seeks to understand have come into intimate contact with one another once more. Both Goya and the officer have "created" a hanged man, and both the officer and we ourselves, as viewers of the *Disasters*, are engaged in disquietingly similar activities, looking at a dead man as art. Again, the point is not to blur the difference between an actual hanged man and the artistic representation of one, but rather to raise the moral question of what it means to make and view scenes of terrible violence in artistic form.

Returning to the caption, which asserts that here too "One cannot know why," it becomes apparent that the move from the previous prints to this one has entailed a considerable expansion of the framework to which the problem of understanding applies. No longer simply a critique of official rationales, "One cannot know why" now addresses the seemingly endless killing on the left, the death of the man in the foreground, and the gaze of the officer on the right. In effect, Goya has amplified his reflection on the limits of moral understanding to a much grander field, as if war itself, beyond specific forms of killing and their rationales, can never be fully reconciled with the moral reasoning that governs our thinking during peacetime. To move from print to print in this grouping is to experience such an expansion, which no single print conveys on its own.

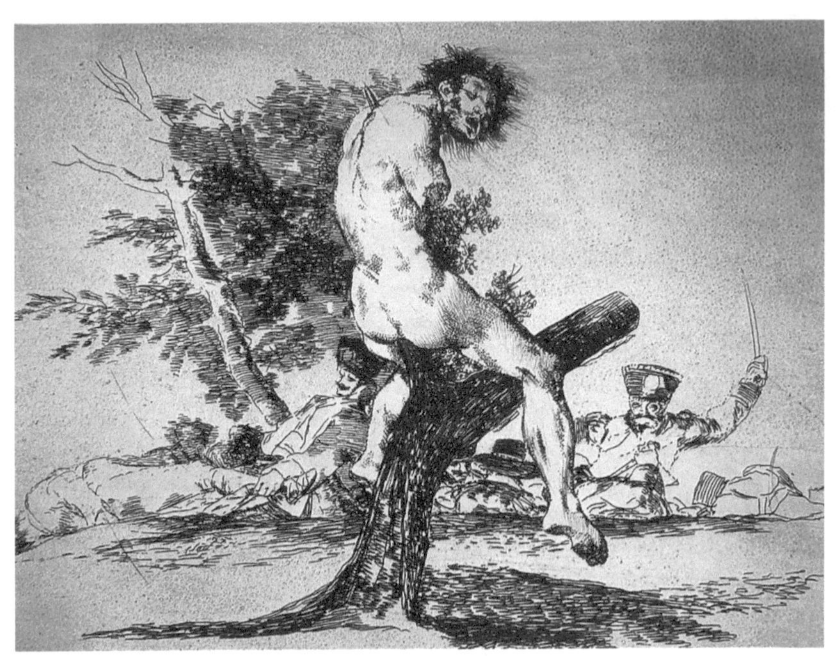

37
Esto es peor

"This is worse," reads the caption as we turn to one of the grisliest images in the series. For viewers moving through the *Disasters* in sequence, the brutality against the dead has intensified once more. From the indifferent or disrespectful treatment of bodies, to the castration of the deceased, to active lynching, to this scene of mutilation and impalement, the cruelty continues to escalate. Within the context of the war, the impaled body in the foreground is another deliberate, horrific display aimed at the living. The perpetrators have done this in order for it to be seen, and the sexual nature of the violence – the anal penetration of the lifeless body – is of a piece with the broader, sexualized aggressions we considered earlier. In the distance, rendered with far less attention, ongoing fighting again links the single central figure to a wider theatre of conflict, from the soldier dragging the fallen body on the left to the officer brandishing a sword on the right. Also within the fighting, to the left of the central victim's right calf, the broad-brimmed hat typically worn by Spanish partisans makes clear that the confrontation is between guerrilla fighters and the professionals of the imperial army. The kind of violence depicted in the foreground was reserved precisely for guerrillas, as a warning.

Naturalism and abstraction once again make for a curious background. While the setting is clearly outdoors, the darkness to the right of the tree extends oddly for foliage, unless one also understands it as a shaded swath required to provide the tonal contrast for the body in the foreground. The strangely mottled "sky" similarly straddles the line between pictorial realism and more abstract tonal variation. Viewers familiar with earlier *Disasters* will in addition recognize the ravaged flora, a sign of the natural world gone awry. While trees in previous prints have often served as makeshift gallows or posts for firing squads, however, this image presents a new variation. The tree stump traversing the victim's body has been transformed into an instrument of violence in its own right. It takes some time to shape a stump into the impaling stake it has become, and awareness of the deliberation with which the perpetrators must have proceeded contributes to the scene's horror.

In pictorial terms, the body itself, however gruesome, seems an odd assemblage. Viewers have noted the strange angle and twist of the head, the excessively long neck, and the way the lower body is out of proportion with the torso. It is almost as if the body parts were three separate ideas that never came together. Still, the overall effect remains arresting, and it may subtly suggest that the violence this body has suffered has altered the natural proportions of the human form. At the same time, the image returns us to an idea we have seen Goya insinuate before. In Prints 16 and 18, the white, largely unblemished bodies of the dead were rendered in ways that recalled the artistic norms of classical statuary. In this print, Goya takes the idea further. Not only does he render the torso to highlight its sculptural qualities, but scholars have noted that he also alludes to a specific, famous statue.

Known as the Belvedere Torso, the sculpture was widely considered the epitome of classical male beauty in the eighteenth and nineteenth centuries, and it was routinely reproduced in drawings and engravings. Evoking this figure within one of the more harrowing images of the series raises again the question of the relationship between art and the violence it represents. It asks what role notions of beauty can or should come into play in the depiction of horrible brutality. For some viewers, the visual citation of the torso signals the inadequacy of classical artistic norms within the world Goya explores in the *Disasters*. If that is the case, the gesture is deeply ironic, and it depends on the difference between the witnessing fantasy we bring to our viewing and the understanding that we are looking at in image. Within the world depicted, the impaled cadaver would not be reminiscent of the Belvedere Torso, and any appreciation of its form would verge on the obscene. Only at the level of the image, where we understand what we see to be a particular kind of rendering, does the famous sculpture appear as a visual citation. The stump of the arm, for example, has been depicted in order to evoke the idea of broken statuary, a detail that presents itself at the level of the image rather than the scene. To reflect on the artistic problem Goya poses through the torso thus requires that viewers take some distance from the immediacy of the horror.

At the same time, as with Prints 16 and 18, there is a macabre reflection here on the "making" of sculpture. The perpetrators have transformed a living human being into an inanimate, statue-like object for the purposes of display. They have, as it were, engaged in their own form of art, and Goya's print is an extraordinarily acerbic commentary on the kind of "making" that wartime violence unleashes. Here too, however, the artist lets neither himself nor viewers off the critical hook. Like the imagined perpetrators, the artist has also made a violent spectacle, and we ourselves have been looking at an impaled corpse as art, the way one might take in classical sculpture. Again, the point is not to suggest simple equivalences, but rather to pose difficult questions about the making and viewing of art when the subject is disastrous violence.

Returning to the caption, which tells us that "This is worse," we face a series of disturbing questions. What is worse and why? If the words suggest that the

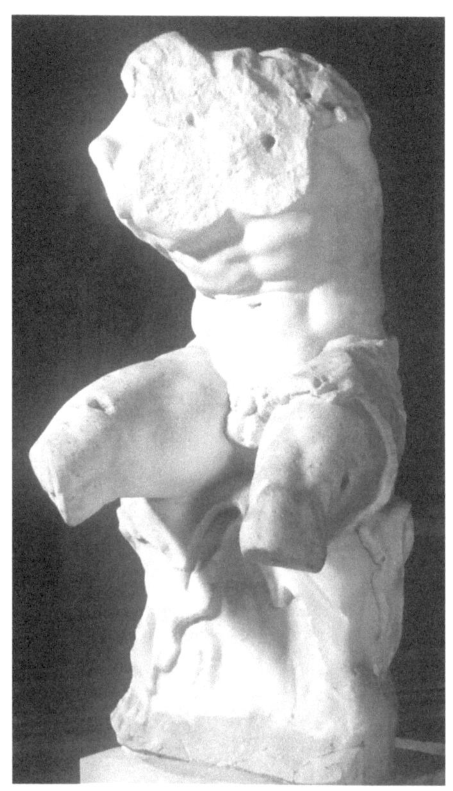

violence is worse, it could be a reference to the assault on the human form, which seems to have reached a new level of intensity here. The very notion of comparison, however, seems somehow out of place. For the dead man, things are neither better nor worse – he remains dead – and it is difficult to imagine that those living and fighting within this world engaged in such questions. Where comparison does seem a more natural activity is within our own viewing experience of the prints, as we turn the pages of the *Disasters*. If we imagine the caption in Goya's voice, it says that this image is worse, in the sense of "more difficult to look at."

Perhaps it is worse because, as with the preceding prints, we still cannot know why, or it could be that it is worse because we have discovered echoes of classical beauty within a scene of impalement. The neutral pronoun "esto" ("this") leaves open a rich range of interpretive options. It could be that the *violence* is worse or that the *image* is more trying, and it is an additional example of the conceptual richness and ambiguity of Goya's captions. If the caption is saying that the image is indeed worse for the viewer, however, we would have to acknowledge something deeply self-absorbed and even narcissistic within our horror, which takes the image of a man who has been killed, mutilated, and impaled as an experience that is worse for *us*. Whatever the case, neither Goya nor the viewer is allowed to remain at an innocent remove from the violence on display.

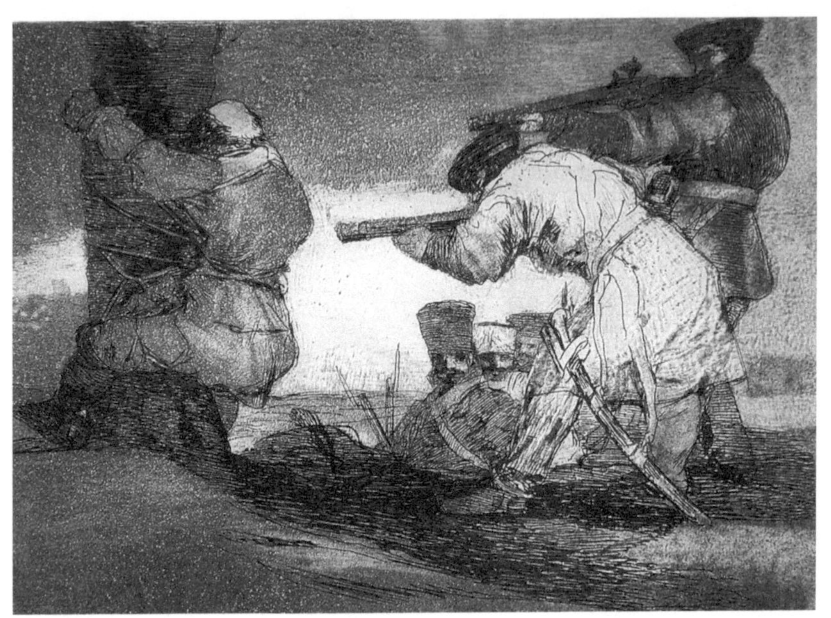

38
Bárbaros!

One more firing squad. By itself the image is compelling enough, but in the wake of what we have already seen, recognition is also an important part of the viewing experience. The soldiers' position is reminiscent of those firing in Print 2. It is the kind of squad we saw in Print 15, and it is the presumed formation of the soldiers beyond the frame in Print 26. An additional example of effects that build as viewers move through the *Disasters*, the visual echoes of previous prints subtly shape the way we look. While repetition often mimics the experience of repeated witnessing, however, it can also do something else. Repeated encounters with similar kinds of violence can make the killing seem more routine, less difficult to take in. We can become inured. In comparison to the brutality of the previous print, for example, this image seems to make less of a claim on our horror. It is, in many regards, "less bad." The man tied to the tree is about to lose his life, yet firing squads have become a commonplace. The image does not impart the shock of the new, the way its predecessor does, and this phenomenon casts light on the extraordinary variety and novelty that generally characterize the *Disasters*. In part, their power to affect depends on variation. Goya knows intuitively that even when violence and suffering are the subject, we respond more fully to the new than we do to the familiar.

Today viewers often acknowledge the "compassion fatigue" that accompanies repeated encounters with media representations of suffering and tragedy, and in this sense repetition in the *Disasters* poses a thoroughly modern dilemma. It is a particularly disturbing problem given the series' reliance on our moral sensibilities as a point of departure. To the extent that viewing the *Disasters* is meant to convey war's uncomfortable truths, however, desensitization may be no accident. Indifference to the suffering of others has been one of Goya's subjects throughout. We have found it in the uncaring faces of perpetrators, as signs of the moral damage that accompanies wartime violence. Now, in an image that immediately follows a print that was "worse," our own ability to feel is put to the test by a scene that recalls others, a scene that might be "better" in the sense of "easier to look at." If previous encounters with similar disasters do in fact diminish our ability to feel, however, then we and the uncaring perpetrators we have been judging would again share more than we might initially confess. We may even begin to understand how it is that soldiers can come to feel little or nothing in the midst of repeated atrocity. It is another way in which the *Disasters* routinely short-circuit easy moral judgments, not only within individual prints but also as viewers move from one print to the next.

Judged through the lens of pictorial naturalism, a number of elements seem out of place in this image. The deliberate aiming stance of the soldiers, for example, is at odds with the short distance between them and the victim, but it heightens the drama of the impending execution. While the tonal contrast between the two soldiers individualizes them, it also dispels any idea one might have of natural lighting. Similarly, the dark orbs of the officers' eyes as they look at the execution from the background veer towards caricature, but the blank quality of their gaze adds an additional chill to the scene. Behind them, the typically mixed, grainy "sky" could be an exercise in abstraction. Together these various elements suggest that if the impending violence might be imagined on a field, Goya has not tried to hide the fact that it is also taking place within the artificial space and time of a carefully constructed dramatic composition.

The victim, who has been bound so as to straddle the tree with his back to the firing squad, is something of a conundrum to contemporary viewers. Why reverse the traditional face-forward positioning of the condemned? Why bind him so thoroughly? While it is difficult to know for certain, one of the more plausible explanations is that the victim can no longer stand. It was common practice for the imperial army to execute captured prisoners who because of age, disease, or exhaustion could not keep up with their captors on forced marches. If that is the case, the victim is a straggler, and the tying signals his physical exhaustion. Still, the ligatures, the staring officers, the close range of the squad, and the fact that they are about to shoot a man in the back together convey a sense of excess, and there is an additional, important detail. The victim's head, gleaming in the grey, is tonsured. The soldiers are about to dispatch a clergyman.

Church officials were routinely killed during the war. To the occupying army they were representatives of the obscurantist, reactionary order that Napoleon hoped to replace. They were also often important actors within the war, prompting the illiterate Spanish masses from the pulpit to wage holy war against the invaders. It is noteworthy, then, that the print does not give the victim special treatment in pictorial terms. Keenly aware of the institutional power of the Church in Spain and of its role during the war, Goya decries the violence, but he does not invite special sympathy for the clergy. In fact, the print reverses the common pattern in the *Disasters*. It is usually the perpetrators who are faceless, while the faces of victims abound.

The caption reads "Barbarians!" A simple, forceful denunciation of the violence, the term would have been particularly salient for nineteenth-century viewers. At the time that Goya penned it, the term *bárbaro* meant "fierce" or "cruel" and also "uncivilized" (Latin *rusticus* and *incivilis*). With classical roots in Greek and Roman culture, claims of barbarism almost always imply a civilized "we" who names and judges a foreign, less civilized "other." For much of the eighteenth and nineteenth centuries, modern European nations had routinely justified their imperial ventures, for example, by imagining that they were "civilizing" barbarians. Alongside this tradition, however, there has also often been an acknowledgment that "we" can in fact be as barbarous as "they" seem. Renaissance thinkers like Las Casas and Montaigne had made the point in the sixteenth century, and in the eighteenth century, Rousseau famously suggested that civilization was what made humans barbarous. Goya's caption seems to draw on this legacy of humanist commentary. In this image the French imperial army, which was purportedly fighting for a new civilization based on the enlightened values of post-revolutionary France, have become barbarians in their own right. The idea recurs throughout the *Disasters* as Goya suggests that, whatever the ideals that motivate war, the violence unleashed in the name of such ideals thoroughly discredits them.

The context of our viewing and reading is central to this understanding of the caption. Taken by itself, "Barbarians!" could be read as a typical patriotic insult hurled at the enemy, and many scholars have suggested as much. Within a series that has repeatedly dismantled the distinction between "us" and "them," however, "Barbarians!" is not simply one more instance of denigrating the enemy. It decries the violence, but it does not easily lend itself to facile nationalist interpretations. We have seen Spanish partisans inflict similar or more "barbaric" acts of violence in preceding prints, and from the outset (Prints 2 and 3) Goya has made clear that both sides of the conflagration are equally unjustified. "Barbarians!" in the context of the series is a cry against the violence as such, and it aims at the myth of "civilized" warfare. In addition, attentive viewers will have learned by this point to question the innocence of the "we" who might utter such words. Only in light of what has come before does this obvious truth emerge, and it a good example of what can be lost when the *Disasters* are fragmented or only partially reproduced.

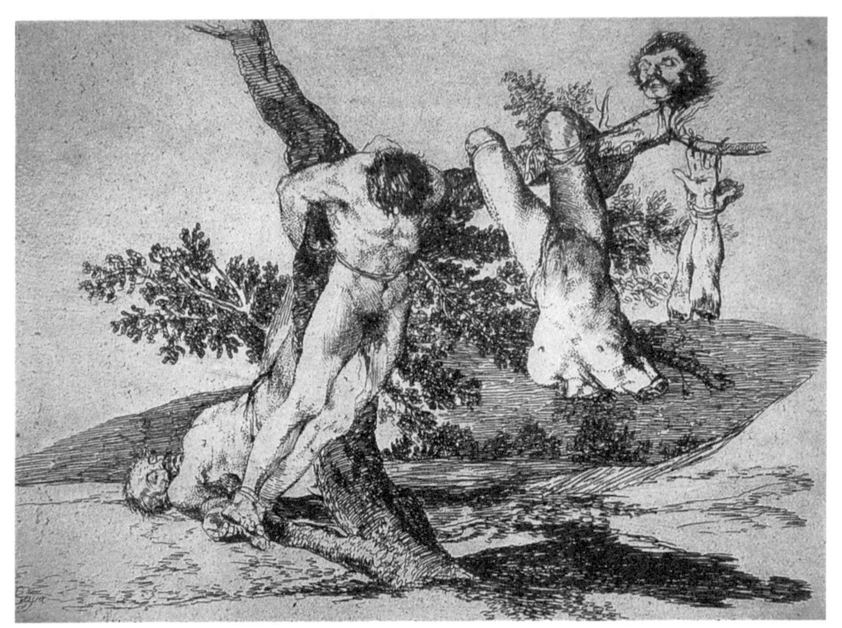

39

Grande hazaña! Con muertos!

[See 40 for commentary.]

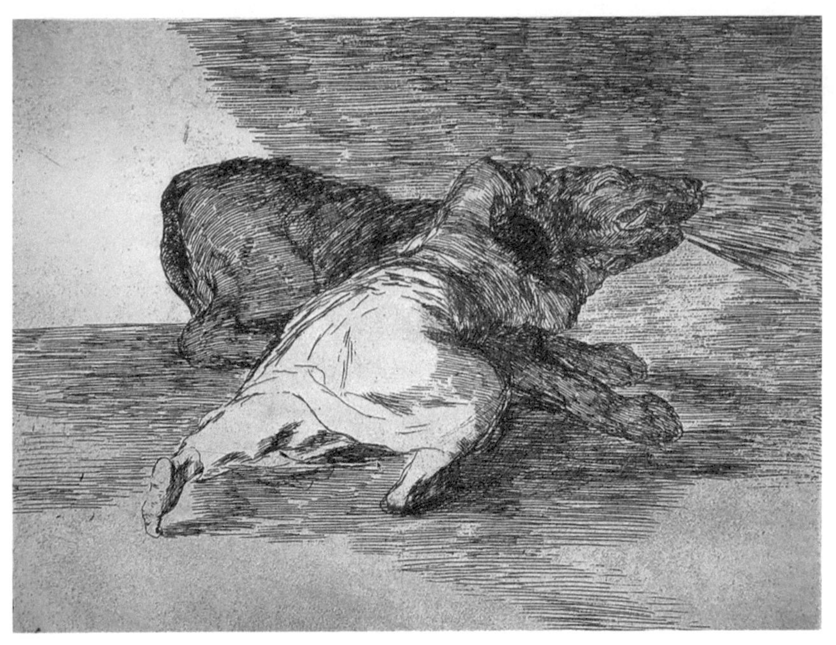

40
Algún partido saca

In the next two prints, Goya's critique of the brutality comes to a head, and the series pivots in a new and unexpected direction as his meditations on wartime violence begin to come to a close. We encounter a final display of extraordinarily brutality, followed by an enigmatic image of a man struggling with a beast. In the first scene, three bodies have been bound to a tree. On the left, a corpse hangs upside-down with head and shoulders resting on the ground, its legs presumably tied to the back of the tree trunk. The second body, bound at the feet, abdomen, and hands, slumps forward with head bowed. The posture initially suggests standing, but the pose has been forced by the way the perpetrators have tied him, and he and his companion to the right appear to have been emasculated. The third corpse hangs inverted from a branch, with the ligatures visible around the knees. This body has been decapitated and partially dismembered, and the dark patch of earth beneath it suggests bloodstained soil. If there has been an increasing assault on the human form in the *Disasters*, this print is in many ways its culmination.

Because display is again part of the story – the perpetrators have done this precisely in order for others to see it – looking remains especially charged. How to take in this excess, knowing that it has been carried out in part for us in our role as would-be witnesses to the violence? Within the terrible world Goya depicts, such display would be a warning to passersby – "This could happen to you" – but this time there are no obvious markers of the side of the conflict to which these bodies belong. As in earlier *Disasters*, by leaving open the question of who these victims were, the image offers them up as representatives of the human as such. In the face of what has been done to them, the question of their affiliation matters little.

At the same time, the difference between actual witnessing and looking at an artwork comes to the fore once more. Among the most gruesome of the *Disasters*, this image depends for its power on our seeing the mutilated bodies of three dead men and imagining what such a real-life encounter would mean. The testimonial force of the image, however, yields to a different kind of perception when we recognize the upright man as a visual citation of St. Sebastian, now without arrows, and, more significantly, without the redemptive narrative of martyrdom through which the figure was habitually understood. Something similar happens with the mutilated bodies, which in a second moment again betray their proximity to the standards of beauty governing the male nude in neoclassical sculpture. The gesture is particularly powerful because we have seen it before. Earlier *Disasters* – Prints 16, 18, and 27 – have in some sense prepared the way. While these kinds of perceptual shifts are common within the archive of pictorial realism, they take on very particular meanings within an artwork that, among other things, aims to bear witness to war's violence. Such changes in perception draw attention away from the here and now of the scene. They belong to the world of images, and in effect they remind us that we are looking at violence within an artwork.

An even stronger shift of a different order takes place when readers attempt to make sense of Goya's caption, "A great deed! With dead men!" At the level of the scene depicted, the scene we momentarily imagine ourselves witnessing, the deed is no doubt the killing and dismembering of these people, but it is also what the killers have done with the body parts, the way they have arranged them, artistically, as "ornaments" on a tree. And still at the level of the scene, there is the difficult knowledge that they have not done this for just any reason. Somebody has done this in order to horrify and intimidate through this macabre "art." Goya's caption, however, does not restrict itself to the scene depicted, where the "deed" would most logically refer to the perpetrators. The words also address the image, where they name a different deed, which is Goya's feat as an artist. He too has composed with body parts, arranging them into an image. He too wants us to look. He too has made something with dead men, a making that is in the etymological roots of words such as deed or feat, a making that we can hear in the original, *hazaña*, where the traces of the Spanish verb *hacer*, to make, still echo.

One of the most violent images in the series, it turns out, is another moment of self-scrutiny in which making and viewing images of violence – as viewers we have also been doing things with the dead – come under critical examination. As we have seen in previous prints, the kind of self-examination that Goya prompts proposes that art should be aware of the ways it gives form to violence. It suggests that the perspective proper to viewing violent images involves simultaneously indulging in illusion and recognizing artifice, and it intimates that critique not only should move outward, towards the violence, but also must turn inward, to both the maker and viewer of the image. It is a powerful synthesis of the self-reflection that informs much of the series, and it is no coincidence that it comes in the last gruesome print to explore the subject of post-mortem mutilation. In many ways, the print is the climactic moment of Goya's reflections on violence and its representation in artistic form.

The few remaining images on the subject of violence will turn elsewhere, in what amounts to a kind of narrative afterword, and Goya marks that things are coming to a close by shifting abruptly from the quasi-naturalistic pictorial mode that has predominated to something very different in the next image. As viewers turn to a new depiction of struggle, they also transition into a new kind of visual code. Print 40 departs from the sorts of pictures we have encountered until now. The two principal figures do not lend themselves easily to a literal interpretation, and what we see no longer offers itself as something we might imagine on the field of battle or elsewhere during times of war. Most viewers initially wonder what they are looking at, and the enigma becomes more challenging if we attempt to couple the image with the caption, which reads "He (or it) gets something out of it." The only print reminiscent of this kind of representation thus far is Print 1, "Sad presentiments of what is to come to pass," which had a strong allegorical component. Rather than presenting the illusion of actual violence unfolding before our eyes, this image is an attempt to give form to a more abstract set of ideas.

Much of the scholarly work on the print has suggested a specific decoding of the allegory. The beast has recently been taken to be a bulldog, for example, and as symbol of Great Britain, the print is then understood as a commentary on British involvement in the Peninsular War. In this reading the caption would be an assertion that British participation was neither altruistic nor particularly kind to the Spanish people. Historians have documented incidents of pillaging, rape, and abuse within the British army at levels equal to the excesses of the French and the Spanish themselves. "He (or it) gets something out of it" would in this sense emphasize that Britain stood to gain much from the Peninsular War. Spain was a nearby, proxy theatre in which to wage war against Napoleon, and the conflagration precipitated a crisis of Spanish sovereignty in colonial Spanish America, where Britain was able to advance its own interests to the detriment of its old imperial rival. After the conflagration, the Spanish monarchy's South American empire would quickly unravel, and Spain would become a second-tier power within European politics. In this reading of the caption, the print would be a reminder that the British alliance with Spain against Napoleon was at all times guided by anglo-imperial self-interest.

While the interpretation offers viewers stable footing for an otherwise baffling image, there are reasons to explore other possibilities as well. To begin with, the beast has none of the telltale signs of a bulldog. There are no hanging jowls or characteristic folds on the head. If the animal resembles a dog in some ways, it does not clearly belong to any recognizably specific breed, and its proportions in comparison to the man are enormous. One would have to conclude either that Goya fell flat in attempting to render the emblem of Britain, or that he did not conceive of the animal in terms of national provenance. In addition, if the animal is a representation of Great Britain, how are we to understand the human figure? Logically speaking, one would expect the man to be identified as a member of the French imperial army, Britain's rival on the peninsula, but he is clearly not a soldier. He is barefoot and dressed in what is more likely the garb of a Spanish countryman. He also seems to be holding his own in the struggle. The angled lines emanating from the beast's mouth suggest laboured breathing or perhaps even wounded braying, and the man has landed a painful blow with his dagger. What might initially be mistaken for a large tooth in the animal's mouth is in fact the blade of the man's knife, which has pierced its lower jaw. If there is a national allegory here and the man is a representation of the Spanish people, it makes little sense that he would be attacking an ally.

In light of Goya's consistent tendency to challenge patriotic identifications, it seems more likely that the dog or beast in this image is an allegory of war as such, a way of giving form to the concept after some forty prints have rendered specific forms of violence in excruciating detail. The series opened with an allegorical print, and now as Goya's reflections on violence begin to wind down – at almost the exact mid-point of the series as a whole – allegory returns, as if zooming out again to the general phenomenon that loomed as we began. Again, it is an effect that is lost when the print is viewed by itself. The human figure would in this sense be a representative of people more generally, or humanity at large, in times of war. If that is the case, however, the caption then becomes a particularly pointed and disheartening observation. After everything we have seen, after repeatedly looking at the morally catastrophic dimensions of war, we read a caption that asserts that something is nevertheless to be gained from it.

The words suggest that however deplorable the violence, however abhorrent it may seem through the lens of peacetime moral sensibilities, war would not happen unless those involved believed that something was to be gained. The Spanish idiom Goya uses here, *sacar partido*, literally means to derive advantage or benefit, and one can imagine it in the voice of the artist, as a critical commentary. It is significant, however, that Goya does not specify whether the words apply to the human figure or to the beast itself. Both the man and the creature could be the subject of the sentence, suggesting that the calculation that "something is to be gained," in the strategic, material sense, pervades all sides of wartime conflict. In effect, it is a summation of the logic we have seen at work elsewhere. It is the frame of mind that justifies killing, rape, torture, pillaging, and mutilation, precisely because something is to be gained.

As we leave this image, it is also worth noting the way the turn to allegory at this point in the series takes viewers away from the eyewitness immediacy typical of the majority of the prints on violence. Allegory points elsewhere. It challenges strictly realistic modes of perception. In effect, the tension between naturalism and artifice that we have seen within so many of the preceding *Disasters* plays out here in the movement from one print to the next. Allegory makes clear that Goya's images do more than merely record what we might have seen had we been there. It calls attention to the way images draw on convention in order to convey content. The fact that Goya turns to it is in this sense another way of reminding viewers that the picture-world of the *Disasters* is just that, a world that can point to terrible realities but nevertheless remains at some degree of remove from them as well. Within the sequence, it also works like a form of punctuation. We began with allegory (Print 1), and now, as the section on violence begins to close, it reappears. Significantly, in the few prints that follow, Goya will turn to a new final subtheme.

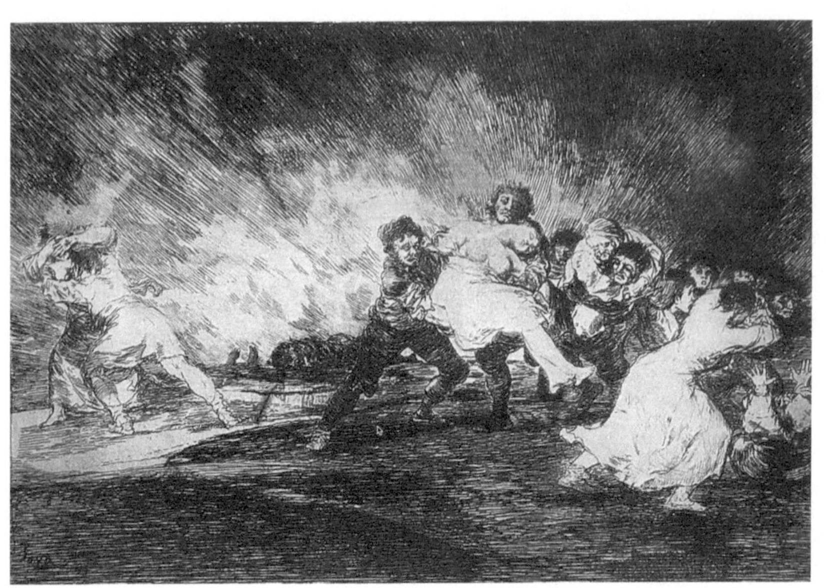

41

Escapan entre llamas

[See 43 for commentary.]

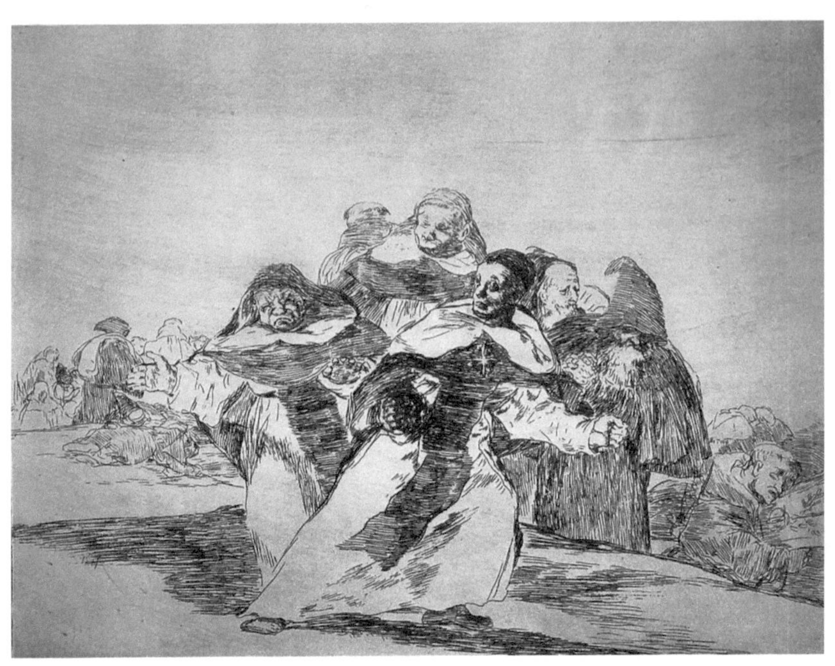

42
Todo va revuelto

[See 43 for commentary.]

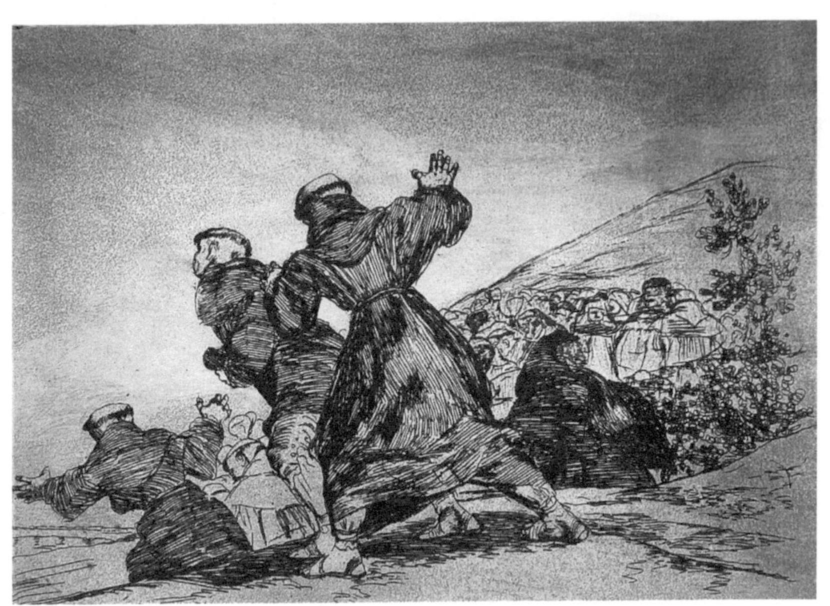

43
También esto

After so much violence we turn to images of people in flight, as if the only thing to do in the face of all that has come before is to run. The prints' position within the sequence is in this sense central to their meaning. Had images of people fleeing appeared earlier, they would not carry the weight they do here, where the reasons for the running have accumulated, print by print. At the same time, flight takes on symbolic as well as literal meanings. The figures in these prints are each fleeing their situation, but the theme of escape also marks the way Goya's reflections on the violence of war are themselves coming to a close. It is one more example of the analogies Goya often sets up between movement within the world he depicts and the viewer's movement through the series. We see people running as we ourselves begin to take leave of the war section of the series.

While the subject of flight links the prints together thematically, each one explores a different subset of people. In the first (Print 41), whose caption reads, "They escape among flames," civilians have been surprised in the night by fire. Goya manipulates tonal contrast to great effect in order to convey the terror of those who in the darkness must run for their lives. The lines of darkness and light that swirl out of the background brightness not only convey the movement of the fire but also suggest the idea of engulfment. The diagonals that define many of the foreground bodies echo the background angles of darkness and light, emphasizing the centrifugal movement of all. The victims are running out and away, towards us, and as we take in their plight we might again notice the difference between actual witnessing and witnessing by means of artistic images. Were we there, what would we be doing? What would it mean to be witnessing as others help? And then the realization: if we can see but cannot help, it is because we are not there but only indulging the illusion for a moment.

The fact that these people are escaping "among" flames, as the caption informs us, is also apparent in the body language of many of the victims. Women on the far left and right of the image hold their hands to their faces in gestures that signal the panicked experience of feeling the heat and breathing the smoke. On the right, the outstretched arms of a victim signal desperation, and just right of centre, the collapsed body of a woman who has lost consciousness, perhaps from smoke inhalation, emerges from the background in the arms of men. Like her counterpart in Print 30, her breast is uncovered, raising the issues that nudes often evoke in the *Disasters*. Given earlier, similar depictions, it seems likely that Goya is suggesting at least two things with this figure. Within the world depicted, her partial nudity signals the way bodies become subject to exposure as a consequence of the violence. At the level of the image, however, the depiction of the woman also raises the kinds of questions we have considered elsewhere. Is this beautiful or merely titillating, and if so for whom? How would it be if the viewer were actually there rather than looking at an image?

The crowd behind the foreground figures on the right suggests that there are many more people in the darkness, and at the base of the brightness, to the left of the man at the centre, dark masses and the silhouette of two feet make clear that others have already succumbed to the flames. The numerous figures who risk their own lives to aid those in trouble lend the image additional drama, from the man on the left, to the two men who support the unconscious woman, to the man to the right behind them who carries an elderly woman on his back. The fire has clearly caught everybody off guard, and they flee with only the clothes they happened to be wearing. A powerful depiction of the catastrophe as it unfolds, the print also documents one of the more easily overlooked facets of war's disasters: the violent uprooting and displacement of civilian populations. Before us are war refugees in the making.

In the next two images of flight, Goya turns more specifically to the impact of the war on Spain's religious communities. Although not obvious to many present-day readers, the two prints have commonly been understood to address the wartime dismantling of the Spanish Inquisition (Print 42) and the suppression of the monastic orders (Print 43) respectively. In addressing these broader historical phenomena, they allow for both literal, naturalistic viewing and more allegorical interpretations. Print 42, with the caption, "It all goes a jumble," depicts high-ranking clerics in a state of panic, and to make their office clear, in the bottom right-hand corner Goya has rendered a priest carrying a sword and an olive branch, a well-known emblem of the Spanish Inquisition. Historically, by the late eighteenth century the Inquisition was a pale shadow of what it had been, but internationally it remained an important symbol of religious oppression. Napoleon had abolished the institution as part of his secularizing agenda, and here Goya depicts a clergy that no longer wields its traditional power.

Within the scene, the reasons for the running need little explanation. As earlier *Disasters* make clear, there was no love lost between the French imperial army and the Spanish clergy. Although we do not see the immediate threat, these men could very well be running for their lives. In a more allegorical key, however, the print speaks broadly to the topsy-turvy world of shifting ecclesiastic power and privilege during the war years. The "jumble" names not only the movement of figures on a field somewhere, but also the chaos that followed the dismantling of a longstanding institution within the Spanish Church. Particularly telling in this sense is the every-man-for-himself quality of the movement conveyed. The position of the two central figures, angling away from one another in the foreground, suggests that they are parting company, and the clerics in the background on the left, whose backs are turned to us, appear to be running away from the position of the viewer.

Together these elements not only communicate a sense of chaos, as the caption specifies, but also the idea that what is unfolding before us is a panicked disbanding of the group. By itself the image would be a powerful enough statement, but following the previous image, in which civilians were risking their lives in order to help others in need, the self-interest of those fleeing here offers a stark contrast. The fear in the central figure's face seems combined with calculation, and the faces of the figures behind him have been rendered as grotesque caricatures. While Goya's matter-of-fact observation that "Everything is a jumble" seems neutral enough, neither the image nor the caption elicits much sympathy. For many, the print is reminiscent of the anticlerical stance the artist had taken years earlier in his satirical *Caprichos.*

In contrast, the next image is marked by a more urgent sense of flight, as monks appear to run, hands in the air. The downward sloping lines that organize much of the composition, from the mountain in the background, to the incline of the foreground, to the angle of several arms and shoulders, heighten the sense of movement. A crowd of religious in the background also makes clear that what we see here is again part of a larger process. Viewers have noticed, however, that there is something odd about these monks. The physical appearance of the three is almost identical, and they are visually linked to one another through posture. Some have suggested that the arrangement of the foreground figures may be an attempt to depict not three different monks but rather one figure at three moments in time. This is especially true of the figure closest to the viewer and the one immediately behind him. Their proximity to one another and the position of their lower bodies suggest that they are the same person depicted at different moments.

If that is the case, the image is an attempt to depict movement by delivering three distinct versions of the same monk as he runs. Goya has even made the bottom portion of the first figure's cassock transparent so that the relationship between the positions of the legs can be seen more clearly. We thus confront the tension between naturalist illusion and the artifice of the image once more. If we were there, perceiving movement would not be the problem it is here, as we look at an image. The illusion of witnessing is troubled by Goya's experiment, and his ingenuity as an artist in attempting to suggest movement comes to the fore. At the same time there is another curious visual echo of the series as a whole within this image. Goya has constructed a series – i.e., the monk in movement – within an image that is itself part of a series. Even as we approach the end of the prints on the violence of war, then, the kind of self-reflection we have seen across many other *Disasters* persists. The fleeing monk is, among other things, a way of posing questions about the relationship between what we see within Goya's images, on one hand, and the making, sequencing, and viewing of the series as a whole on the other.

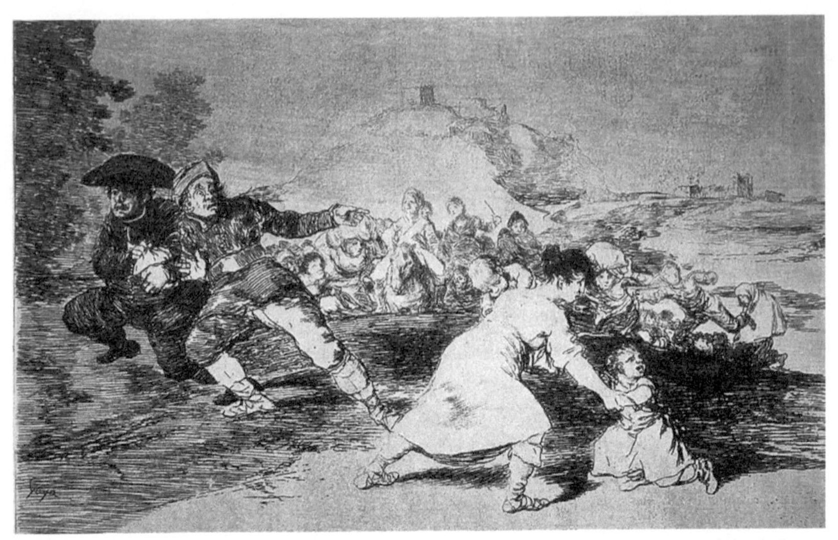

44
Yo lo vi

[See 45 for commentary.]

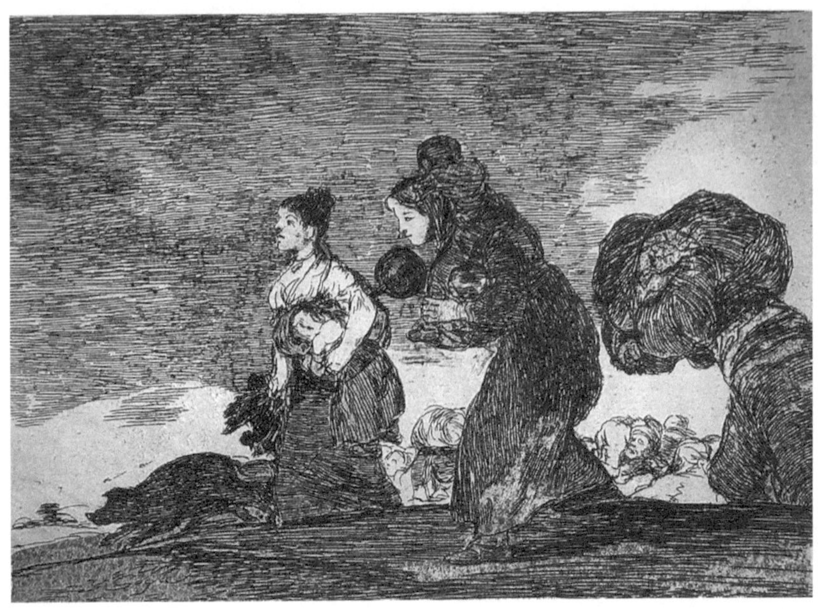

45
Y esto también

The fleeing continues in two more images of civilians on the move. In the first, townspeople run from impending violence. As in previous *Disasters*, individualized foreground figures appear in front of crowds in order to signal the collective dimensions of what is underway. The masses, led by a mounted partisan, march forward, towards us, while figures closer in the foreground run from right to left. In the far background, the contours of a village provide additional context. A town is being abandoned, presumably as enemy forces approach. Spaniards had been instructed to defend larger cities when possible, but to evacuate and destroy smaller towns if resistance was pointless. This, however, is no orderly evacuation. The enemy is close, and the primary subject is the terror of those fleeing.

On the left a priest, recognizable by the long-winged hat, makes away with a sack of money, while his companion points back in fear towards the approaching threat. In the foreground on the right, a panicked mother with an infant in tow and a toddler at her feet heighten the sense of terror as they too glance back at what is approaching. While both groups face the same danger, there is a difference between them, and it is emphasized once again through tonal contrast. On the left, men of some authority, in darker tones, escaping with money. On the right, in the lighter shades Goya so often reserves for victims, a mother with children. It is not difficult to see a critical commentary here on the way ecclesiastic and civil authorities often took care of themselves to the exclusion of others during the conflict. The priest makes off with a sack of coins, while the mother's care for her children – she turns towards the menace as she gathers the toddler – provides a telling contrast.

Much of the force of this image, however, has to do with the fact that Goya has again kept the cause of it all – the thing that has caught the gaze of the man, the mother, and the child – out of sight. Like earlier prints (14, 15, 26), the composition places the source of the panic beyond the frame, even as its presence somewhere off to the right cannot be ignored. The threat is more ominous precisely because we cannot see it. Our primary access to it comes through the terrified faces of those who do. Had Goya depicted an army approaching on the right, it would have diminished the effect. It is no coincidence, then, that Goya's caption is expressly about the question of seeing. It reads "I saw it." Many scholars have suggested that the words are an assertion that Goya himself saw scenes such as this one, and this print has frequently been evoked in order to argue that what Goya records throughout the *Disasters* is based on his own eyewitnessing of events. While this may be the case for some images, it is clearly not the case in others, but to dwell on what Goya might actually have seen misses the mark in many ways.

In an image deliberately composed to call attention to what we can and cannot see, "I saw it" is something of a conceptual game. Aside from Goya himself, each of the terrified foreground figures might retrospectively say the words, and we ourselves literally say them as we look at the print and read the caption. For us, however, "I saw it" highlights the difference between our seeing and theirs. By deliberately withholding their "it" from us, the caption subtly reminds us once more of the way pictorial conventions – the composition and framing – shape our own seeing. Had we actually been there, we would have seen it too. We cannot see their "it" because we are looking at an image. In this sense, if we understand "I saw it" as a motto for the series as a whole, as some suggest, its lesson is precisely *not* to take Goya's prints as straightforward forms of testimony, but rather to notice that the challenges and limits of looking are as much his subject as the violence itself.

The print following "I saw it" seems more direct by contrast. Its caption reads, "And this too," which is to say, "I saw this too." While the words link the two prints together, however, this image takes us in a new direction. The preceding four *Disasters* depicted people fleeing from imminent danger. Now we turn to the slow and steady march of refugees, with their possessions in tow. Goya does not convey the reasons for their march, but there is no need. The many prints preceding this one provide the narrative context. Like earlier images of women combatants, Goya exploits conventional notions of the feminine to great effect. Through their association with domestic space and children, these women encapsulate war's violent disruption of households, its undoing of the idea of home. A group of male refugees on the march would not have the same effect, and the absence of a male head of household here may also point to the way war often leaves women and children to fend for themselves. Some viewers have suggested that the three foreground figures represent a single household. The central figure with a child on her shoulders would be the lady of the house, while her stout companion to the left and the man behind her to the right can be understood as household servants.

Unlike in so many other *Disasters*, there is no immediate threat, and perhaps for this reason the emotions Goya renders in the faces of the women convey neither urgency nor panic nor terror. The central figure hunches under the weight of the child she carries, but her expression seems calm, or perhaps resigned, in its forward-looking gaze. Her companion, rendered to suggest the strength of a working-class woman, stares forward with determination. Together they express the feelings of many civilians who abandon their homes in search of safety, the war-weary but determined search for something better. At the same time, these women pose those questions that have often accompanied our viewing. Who would we be if we were there, and what would we do? What does it mean to witness as people slowly march by? As viewers of images who are looking from a place of relative comfort, what does it mean to be here, looking at the dispossessed? Such questions become more pressing, and perhaps more uncomfortable, when we recall that while these women belong to their time, they belong to ours as well. We routinely see them or their contemporary sisters on the various screens that deliver the news, and Goya's questions remain. What does it mean to look, and what does looking ask of us?

While the previous print played with what we could and could not see, this one seems not to depend so strongly on the framing for its effects. Even so, the caption conveys a similar idea, "(I saw) this too," and precisely because of the verbal link to the previous print, we might ask ourselves what if anything has been withheld here. It then becomes clear that although it is not emphasized in quite the same way, the central figures are also looking towards something we cannot see. This time, however, what is beyond the frame is their destination, the future and the questions it poses to all refugees. Where will they go? How will they be received? What will become of them? In addition, the difference between their looking and our own comes to the fore once more, perhaps troubling our identification with them and the pity it may have raised. The point, again, is not to dismantle empathy altogether but to suggest that the difference between our situation as would-be witnesses and theirs as refugees makes such responses more complex than they might initially seem.

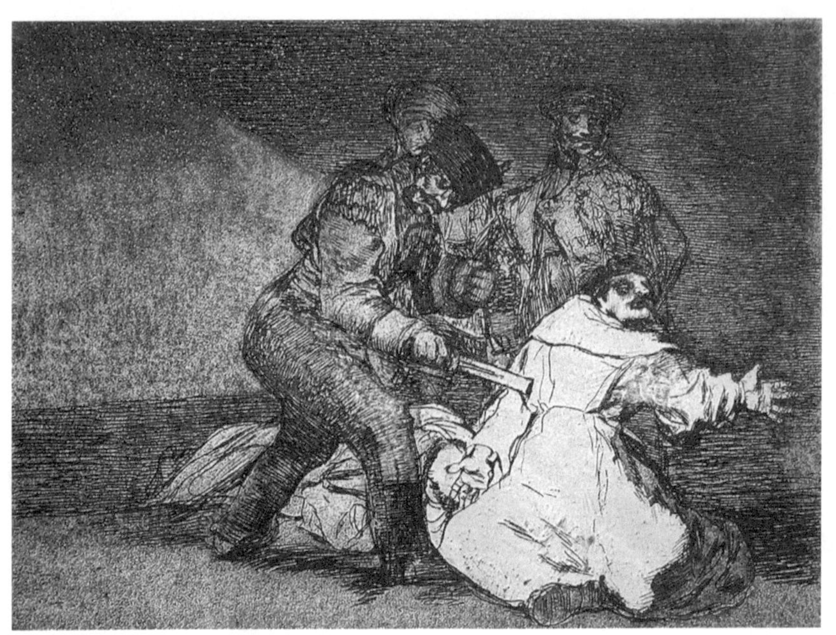

46
Esto es malo

[See 47 for commentary.]

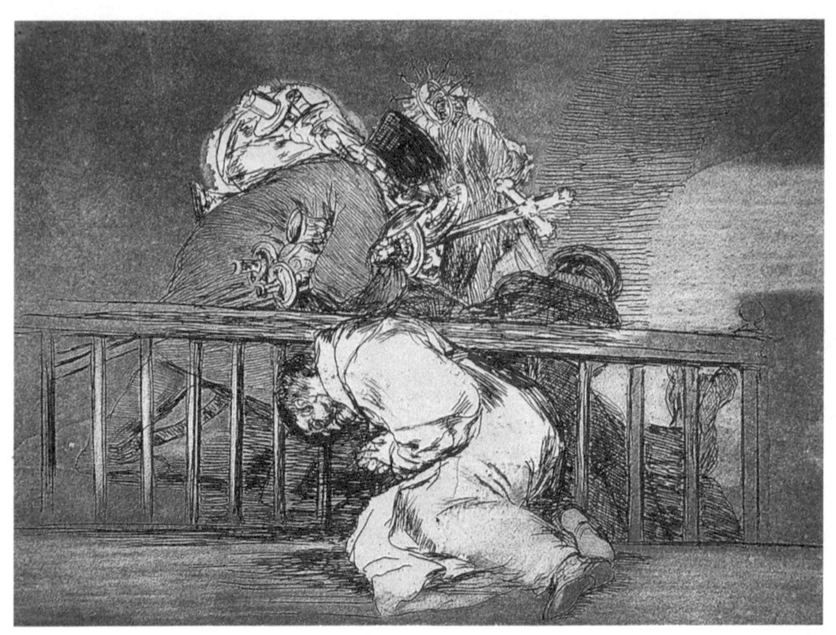

47
Así sucedió

Turning from images of flight, Goya closes his reflections on war's violence with two final prints on murder and plunder. The outdoor settings of Prints 41 to 45 yield to the enclosed darkness of these last images, and whatever notions of escape the previous prints conveyed dissipate as we again face a killing in progress. In Print 46, a friar slumps as a soldier thrusts his sword into his torso. As if illuminated, the victim's white cassock is one more example of Goya's deft use of tonal contrast to highlight the suffering of victims, and again this friar is not the only casualty. Behind his murderer's legs to the left, the body of at least one other clergyman has already sprawled across the floor. Of the three soldiers, rendered in darker greys, the two in the background stand impassively, signalling once more the kind of desensitization to suffering we have encountered in other prints (see Prints 11, 16, 27, and 32).

The darkness in which the violence unfolds is a by now familiar, relatively undefined pictorial space. The grainy sense of a ground or floor in the foreground gives way to a band of horizontal darkness that crosses behind the solders' legs, and in the upper half of the image the lighter left quadrant contrasts with the darkness on the right, behind the soldiers' heads. The compositional diagonal, from upper left to lower right, runs from what might be the silhouette of an archway, through the central figures and down the victim's left leg, heightening the general movement and force of the sword thrust. We might conclude from the presence of the friar that we are somewhere in a monastery or church, but as in so many of the *Disasters*, such particulars are not the priority. The killing overrides such concerns. As for the victim, there is something decidedly off about the way he has been rendered. The head seems a ghoulish caricature in comparison to the soldiers, and its proportion – compare the head with the hands and arms – is scarcely natural. It could be that, as in other *Disasters*, this kind of departure from a more naturalistic rendering is meant to be understood expressively, as if to convey the difference between victims and killers at the level of the body. It could also be that the way the victim has been rendered is meant to suggest that all killing is a form of disfiguring, but it is difficult to know for certain.

The original caption reads "This is bad" or "This is wrong," or even "This is evil." A straightforward moral evaluation of what is taking place, the words assert precisely the sense of right and wrong that has consistently been absent throughout the world of the *Disasters*. As we have seen repeatedly, Goya often signals that one of war's more profound calamities, beyond the gruesome physical details of the violence, is the way it obliterates commonplace morality, the way it undoes any claim to the values we usually name with words like good, evil, right, and wrong. Goya shows that in suspending the fundamental peacetime prohibition against killing, war in effect turns the everyday moral universe on its head. It is for this reason perhaps that his prints prompt us so often to reflect on the difference between the moral here and now from which we look and the very different universe in which the violence unfolds. Coming at the end of these many prior reflections, the affirmation that "This is wrong" is a more powerful gesture than it might seem if we were to encounter the print by itself. Within the series, the caption is a closing insistence that we understand war itself as a moral disaster ("bad," "wrong," "evil"), and Goya's characteristic irony and sarcasm are absent here. Instead we read the earnest expression of a basic moral judgment, a final affirmation of moral clarity in the face of everything we have seen.

Those who have viewed Goya's prints from the beginning may also notice an additional, intriguing detail. While the artist generally decries all forms of violence regardless of who the victims are, there has been one group with whom Goya has not seemed to have been entirely impartial. Whether one considers the morally suspect priest in Print 14, the faceless victim in Print 38, or the less than favourable depictions of clergy in Prints 42, 43, and 44, the critical stance Goya adopts in rendering Spain's men of the cloth is not difficult to detect. Against this backdrop, Goya's unambiguous assertion in this print that what we see "is wrong" takes on additional nuance. Even when the victim belongs to a group for whom Goya has shown little sympathy in previous *Disasters*, what is happening is nevertheless wrong. By virtue of their position at the end of Goya's meditations on the violence of war, the words convey the idea that in the end no killing, not even the killing of those for whom the artist himself has shown some animus, is morally justifiable. It is one more example of the way Goya does not let himself off of the hook as he reflects critically on war's disasters.

In the last of the forty-seven prints, another friar sinks against a balustrade, while behind him soldiers make off with their plunder. Again, we seem to be in the interior of a church or monastery, and for a moment one might imagine some sort of narrative continuity between this image and its predecessor. Comparison of the central figures in the images, however, reveals little resemblance between the two victims, and the balustrade, along with the suggestion of a barrel vault on the right, signals a different space. Still, in one image a friar was being killed, and in the next a dying clergyman is abandoned as soldiers take away their loot. The link is thematic, and it suggests that the killing we have just witnessed in Print 46 and the looting we now see are bound to one another in a relationship of effect and cause. The plunder makes visible the reason for the killing in the previous print.

The caption reads, "That's how it happened" or "It happened that way," and in Spanish the words echo the traditional ending of folk narratives. The caption is in this sense a verbal marker of the end of this particular story, but Goya has again chosen a Spanish verb for happening that is difficult to translate fully. As in Print 8, he has used the verb *suceder*. "That's how it happened" is also, more subtly, "That's how it followed." Throughout the series what follows the violence – its aftermath and consequences – has been as important to Goya as the violence itself, so it seems a fitting end that plundering follows the "evil" of killing. We have seen Goya focus on the economic dimensions of war elsewhere in the *Disasters*: the plundering of the dead in Print 16, or the priest running with money in Print 44. Here, in the last print of the section on war's violence, the theme of plundering returns with the additional force of a conclusion, as if to say that in the end such plundering is what war is fundamentally about. God and country, the traditional ideals for which soldiers continue to fight and die today, could not be further from this final pile of loot, and perhaps that too is one of war's recurrent disasters.

At the same time, it is no coincidence that the soldiers are plundering religious objects. Historically speaking, such thefts were routine during the Peninsular War, but beyond the historical circumstances we might imagine there is something symbolic at work in this last image as well. It is a final expression of the fact that, as we have seen across the series, within the world of war's disasters nothing is sacred, set apart, revered, or protected. Not religious relics, not the integrity of the human body, not the sick or the injured, not civilians, not friars, not mothers, not children, not the dead. Nothing belongs to the moral "out of bounds" that most of us who view and read Goya's prints take for granted, and the fact that the plunder here is a form of desecration underscores the idea. The image is also a closing reminder of the material interests – territory, natural resources, the control of populations, or, in this case, straightforward theft – that often lie just below the surface of the stories that states tell in order to justify their actions.

Along with this last indictment, however, viewers who have become accustomed to the way Goya plays with the position of the notional viewer will also find the questions that accompany so many of his prints. Who are we in these scenes, and what are we doing there? What does it mean to imagine oneself in the darkness witnessing murder and plunder, and how does momentarily occupying that position alter whatever ideas we might have about our compassion – and indeed our morality – as we look at images of violence? We might ask similar questions of Goya. What does it mean to make art out of murder and plunder? If the forty-seven prints that Goya dedicated to the violence of war teach anything, it is that that bearing witness through art is never the straightforward affair it might seem, and that when violence is the subject, self-scrutiny on the part of artists and viewers is as important as the horrors being displayed.

Afterword

As the forty-seven prints we have considered here make clear, *The Disasters of War* rewards slow, sequential viewing and reading. It is one thing to come to the series, as many viewers do, through a selection of prints, but it is another entirely to move through Goya's images sequentially, while giving his captions their full due. Those who have traversed the prints reproduced in this volume will be well prepared for subsequent parts of the series, which take up Goya's two additional grand themes: famine (Prints 48–64), and his allegorical images on the depressing political aftermath of the war (Prints 65–82). My goal in this book has been to comment on the more limited corpus on wartime violence in order to revisit several commonplaces about Goya's print series and to draw attention to facets of his artistry that have not always been as central to discussions of his work as they might be.

One of those commonplaces has been the story of Goya's purported realism. Within the critical literature on the *Disasters*, it is not uncommon to read that Goya was the first great European realist on the subject of war, and in contrast to prior art, his approach was indeed a radical departure. It broke with the traditions of pictorial idealization that preceded him, both in earlier war art and in the long history of depictions of religious martyrdom. Profound changes of this sort often produce the "realism of the new," and after experiencing Goya's prints we may feel that earlier war art was in fundamental ways deceiving us by suggesting that terrible violence is ultimately redeemed by a higher, providential purpose. The new truth of war that Goya's work conveys is the worldly, secular truth of warfare; the fact that, despite the grand ideals of God and country that routinely accompany armed conflict, there is nothing to be redeemed about the violence it unleashes. What the *Disasters* do, time and again, is to show how war renders our moral and metaphysical categories meaningless. No prior artist comes close in taking on the longstanding myth in which "we," the just or the good, fight against an evil enemy. Goya's prints relentlessly assault this myth and show that in many ways war is the undoing of the basic moral distinction between good and evil. This is not to say that the difference between worthy and less worthy causes disappears entirely. It is that after the *Disasters*, it is difficult to accept that any end can justify war as a means.

This moral realism, which lays bare war's fundamentally amoral power, however, should not be confused with what is conventionally known as pictorial realism. In comparison with the common visual conventions – the academic style – of printmaking in the late eighteenth and early nineteenth centuries, Goya's *Disasters* are decidedly *unrealistic*. His art often flouts the rules of perspective that had developed since the Renaissance, and despite his historical subject, Goya's prints do not aim to represent actual events, situated in historical time. His approach to figure similarly ranges from carefully rendered three-dimensional forms, to grotesque caricatures, to unapologetically sketch-like simplifications, to flat silhouettes. Any glance at more conventional prints of the period confirms that Goya's visual idiom departs considerably from what were understood to be the conventions of pictorial naturalism.

For some, Goya deforms realist visual codes in order to tell us something about the way war warps or undoes the perception of those caught up in its violence. Others have suggested that his visual style – particularly, the presentation of violent details against abstract backgrounds – conveys the traumatic nature of witnessing and remembering terrible violence. Scholars have also drawn parallels between Goya's prints and the way photographers would later experiment with depth of field for emphasis or expressive effect, and others have suggested that his prints replicate the subjective experience of seeing, where what you look at is in focus while the surrounding visual field is not. Biographical approaches to Goya's work often link the *Disasters* with the nightmarish seeing of his so-called Black Paintings. Common to these various attempts to understand Goya's prints is an emphasis on the subjective dimensions of his art, an attempt to interpret his departures from visual naturalism expressively, as signs of the artist's temper or disposition. Perhaps because of their late, posthumous publication in 1863, the reception of the print series has been coloured with a nineteenth-century romantic sensibility that in many regards remains with us today. It is the sensibility that, like the Preface that accompanied the first edition, approaches Goya's art in terms of the artist's inner vision, and the approach has yielded wonderfully suggestive insights.

While Goya's life (1746–1828) did indeed extend into the first third of the nineteenth century, however, emphasis on the seemingly romantic dimensions of his work runs the risk of missing the mark when it comes to the kind of scathing criticism Goya mounts in the *Disasters*. The artist came of age in the eighteenth century, and he was steeped in the courtly culture of the Spanish Enlightenment. He was sixty years old – an old man by the standards of the day – when Napoleon's war came to Spain in 1808, and much of the force of his later work can be understood in light of his disappointment and at times despair over the failure of the ideals of the Age of Enlightenment. A century that had dreamed of universal peace ended in the worst wars Europe had seen since its wars of religion of the 1600s. Belief in the possibility of a rational, reform-oriented cosmopolitanism committed to the idea of progress came crashing down as revolution and reactionary nationalism tore much of Europe apart. The shortcomings of enlightened monarchy in Spain, the devastation of war and famine, and the restoration of a reactionary regime in the person of Ferdinand VII were front and centre for Goya as a court painter. In many ways he witnessed first-hand the violent end of the eighteenth-century culture of enlightenment in Spain.

Goya's basic coordinates for addressing such drastic events, however, came precisely from that very culture, and the *Disasters* as a whole belong more squarely within the tradition of eighteenth-century critique than they do within the framework of romantic vision. In fact, many of the seemingly striking, modern features of Goya's prints can be understood more fully in light of the eighteenth-century tradition of visual satire. The ahistorical "anyplace" typical of Goya's images is consistent with satire's minimal interest in place in comparison to the human vices it aims to criticize. Goya's depiction of representative forms of violence rather than actual events similarly coincides with satire's aim to criticize common behaviours and dispositions rather than specific happenings. The visual idiom of the prints, in which detailed naturalism coexists in the same image with visual simplification and caricature, was common within satirical prints of the day, and the verbal component of the *Disasters* is marked by irony, sarcasm, word play, and wit, hallmarks of the genre. The conceptual play we frequently find between text and image is also characteristic of the satirical tradition. This is not to say that the richness of the print series is exhausted by satirical conventions, but much of what has puzzled modern-day viewers and readers of the *Disasters* finds plausible explanation within such conventions.

One need only turn to Goya's openly satirical 1799 print series, the *Caprichos*, in order to note immediately that we are in an almost identical visual and verbal world to the *Disasters*. In the earlier series, composed of a similar number of prints, Goya's subjects were the more traditional targets of eighteenth-century satire: superstition, poor education, prostitution, social hypocrisy, the ignorance of the clergy, etc. In the case of the *Disasters*, however, war afforded Goya a new theatre in which to explore in detail far more virulent forms of human vice. If there is a documentary quality to the prints, it has more to do with the satirist's documentation of vice in all of its violent variety than with the photojournalist's recordings of actual atrocity. Satire also helps to explain the uncanny timelessness of the prints, their ability to speak well beyond the time of their making. In depicting the moral failings of human comportment as displayed during wartime, Goya took on a subject destined to remain with us as long as warfare itself does. Satire has the ability to reach into our present precisely because the genre is at home in the time of human folly, which is to say in every age.

The particular kind of satire we find in the *Disasters*, however, has also made this dimension of the work easy to overlook. Humour is traditionally part of the satirist's tool-kit, and we are accustomed to experiencing satire with a chuckle. In the *Disasters*, however, what Goya puts before us is a profound and macabre catalogue of human failings, and his tone changes accordingly. His ironies are caustic. Behind his sarcasm there is often despair, and the consequences of the behaviours depicted could not be more harrowing. Goya's is a bleak, dark satire. Educated viewers of his day would have been aware of two very different strains of satire as it developed out of classical Roman culture: the relatively gentle, humorous forms of social ridicule that take Horace as their primary reference, and the more bitter, aggressive variant as exemplified by Juvenal. The *Disasters* participate in the Juvenalian tradition, a harsh, morally indignant and pessimistic form of satire which can go unrecognized by those accustomed to its more lighthearted and humorous Horatian cousin.

The satirical tradition also sheds light on the importance of moral self-reflection that we have found throughout *The Disasters of War*. It is not uncommon for satire to ridicule the vices of others only to then envelop us, its public, in its critique. Goya's prints repeatedly invite us along a similar path, from our initial horror or moral condemnation of what we see to the more difficult, self-scrutinizing questions we have encountered. To his credit, Goya asks similar questions of himself in prints that reflect on and trouble the act of making art out of war's horrors. Both in the making and the viewing of such art, his prints dismantle the idea of an innocent gaze by suggesting once and again that we may be more complicit with the violence we look at than we like to imagine. In this regard, *The Disasters of War* is as much about the moral and ethical quandaries of making and looking at images of wartime atrocity as it is an exposé of such atrocity. It is no surprise that more recent thinkers like Susan Sontag, who wrote searchingly on the moral complexities of representing suffering, saw in Goya an early fellow traveller. He is modern not only for his depiction of the horrors but also for the complex moral meditations his prints elicit.

The series also carries out a prescient, and to my knowledge unprecedented, reflection on the difference between experiencing war, on one hand, and viewing images that depict war's violence on the other. As I mentioned at the outset, Goya would have been keenly aware of that fundamental difference and its moral implications, and in the little he wrote about his art he routinely underscored invention and caprice. At the same time, as optics developed into an empirical science and new visual technologies began to proliferate, late eighteenth- and early nineteenth-century artistic images had increasingly come to be understood as well-crafted illusions. For this reason, perhaps, the *Disasters* pointedly invite us into their illusions and at the same time remind us of their artifice. If Magritte's *Ceci n'est pas une pipe* has become a placeholder in European art for discussions of the twofold nature of pictorial representation, we would do well to recall that there is a longer history to which such double consciousness belongs, and that in the *Disasters* the twofold quality of pictorial representation becomes especially charged.

Goya's art underscores both the promise and the limits of pictures as forms of understanding. His images are deliberately constructed to beckon us in, but they also deliberately do not let us linger in the fantasy of witnessing for too long. One of the more profound truths the *Disasters* convey is what combat veterans of virtually all wars repeatedly signal to the uninitiated when they return home: you may have some idea of what war is like by looking at pictures, but if you haven't been there, you cannot fully understand. Goya was much more than the first major European artist to deliver the unvarnished truth of war in his images. He was also the first to explore in sustained fashion the ethical stakes of making and viewing images of atrocity. Before the two World Wars, before the Holocaust, before the many wars and genocides that have followed, *The Disasters of War* posed fundamental questions concerning what today we call the ethics of representation.

Finally, we would do well to recall that there is a flip side to the moral darkness of *The Disasters of War*. Critique inevitably carries with it an implicit notion of a better state of affairs, and hovering over each of Goya's prints is the idea that the travesties depicted are not unavoidable, the idea that one day things might be otherwise. His project is in many ways a wager that making the atrocities of war more public might contribute to curtailing their repetition in the future. From our contemporary vantage point, this idea might seem naïve, given the extraordinary history of wartime violence that followed Goya's era. Still, it is no coincidence that even today those who wage war work hard to keep the kinds of truth Goya delivers out of public sight. Censorship, propaganda, and information management routinely accompany war for a reason, and when truths such as those depicted in the *Disasters* leak out, popular support for the violence often declines. We are right to question the power of images to change our world, but we should not let our scepticism despair of such projects. Images by themselves may not be able to change the world, but the people who look at them most certainly can. In the end, if there is hope within the world of disasters Goya's work puts before us, it lies with us, the would-be witnesses, and with what we decide to do after our journey through his images of war has come to an end.

Notes

Introduction

Given the breadth and richness of the bibliography on Goya and the *Disasters*, I do not aim to give readers an exhaustive account of all prior scholarly work on the print series, but rather a sampling of key interpretations within the critical tradition, from the 1800s to recent years. For a more extensive, annotated critical bibliography of the *Disasters*, see Blas, Aguilar, and Matilla, volume 2, on whom I have relied at length. My emphasis on the experience of viewing and reading has a strong phenomenological dimension. Of particular interest are the differing phenomenologies of visual images and the verbal texts that accompany them. For an overview of phenomenological approaches to the arts, see Magliola. For recent discussion of the importance of the distinctive phenomenology of the visual arts, see Crowther. Particularly useful is Crowther's critique of what he terms *semiotic reductionism*, in which "the picture is reduced to a kind of visual text, with its own distinctive made qualities (qua drawing, painting sculpture, photography or whatever) marginalized" (13). For the dating of the *Disasters* I follow Tomlinson (*Graphic*).

The 1863 edition contained eighty prints; two additional prints not included at the first printing were subsequently added to the end of the series. The most widely circulating edition of the *Disasters* today is the 1967 Dover paperback edition, which contains outright mistranslations of several captions. In the notes that follow I will periodically reference the Dover edition translations in order highlight how a more nuanced understanding of Goya's captions enriches the viewing and reading experience considerably. Nineteenth-century critics most commonly referred to the captions as *leyendas* (legends) rather than *títulos* (titles). Williams offers a nice summary of the importance of the captions within the *Disasters* more generally: "To the *Disasters* engravings, the captions are essential. They serve not to clarify but to unhinge. They deepen paradox, sharpen contradiction" (8). Wolf similarly notes that "the relationship of word to image is rich in associations" (40). Recent coverage of Goya in the Spanish press has signalled the verbal component of his artistry as an understudied dimension of his work.

Lafuente writes suggestively on the expressive dimensions of sequence:

> Goya conceived the series with a spirit we can rightly call poematic. If in the internal development of the *The Disasters* such an intention can become obscured or undermined by reiterations, trivialities, or unclear references (for there is a bit of everything in his prints), taking everything into account one cannot deny it [i.e., the poematic intention] in a collection of engravings that begins with the deep notes of *Sad Presentiments* and ends with the hopeful chords of *This is What is True.* (Heras Bretín 49)

Glendinning ("El asno") similarly observes that one of the principal differences between the *Disasters* and the *Caprichos* is the importance of sequence as well as the textual and conceptual links between prints. To date, there is no strong consensus over how much importance to grant the captions and the sequence in interpreting the prints. This book attempts to extend the line of inquiry opened by Lafuente and Glendinning by fleshing out the rich range of effects that Goya achieves through the interplay of image, caption, and sequence. It aims to make clearer the broader phenomenon that Tomlinson has identified across Goya's oeuvre:

> The creation of meaning through interrelated images distinguishes Goya's invention, as illustrated by series of decorative paintings and cabinet paintings, by the etchings of *Los Caprichos* and three series of etchings to follow, and ultimately by the paintings he created on the walls of his country house between 1820 and 1823. (*Goya: A Portrait* 102)

Several prints include earlier numbers that have been crossed out, pointing to an earlier ordering of the prints, which Goya reworked later. See Tomlinson (*Goya's War*) for a recent reconstruction of that early sequence, which is much more strongly thematic, and more closely follows the chronology of the prints' making. My hypothesis is that the second order, which has become standard since the 1863 edition, reflects a different organizational principle. Rather than speaking to the history of their making, the sequence of prints organizes the viewing experience in terms of a witness's voyage through the war years. Lafuente speculates that it may have been Goya's friend Juan Agustín Ceán Bermúdez who prompted the artist to reorganize the prints (*Los Desastres* 54). The Céan Bermúdez album, which consists of a complete bound set of prints with pencilled captions, was used as a model by the Royal Academy of San Fernando in the preparation of the 1863 edition. Some have suggested that Ceán Bermúdez may have penned the captions, but there is little proof to substantiate the speculation. The "voice" of the captions is entirely consistent with the wit, sarcasm, and word play one finds in the *Caprichos*, where the captions' authorship is not in question. Independent of definitive attribution, the captions with which the prints became public and circulate today are very much a part of the experience of viewing and reading them.

Wolf offers the most useful commentary on witnessing as a central concern in the *Disasters*, noting that the artist "understood the complex psychological and sociopolitical implications of being in the position of the witness. His ability to articulate this complexity in art contributes in large measure to its power" (37). My approach builds on this insight and expands it, to show that a central part of Goya's art deals with the ethical quandary of "witnessing" through art. For detailed reconstruction of Goya's biography during the war years, see Dufour. The definitive, tour de force biography of Goya is Tomlinson (*Goya: A Portrait*). Some of Goya's earliest critics called attention to the ambiguities of time and space in the *Disasters*. Mélida writes, for example: "Goya's work is difficult to interpret because one can barely fix with any exactitude the place and time where the action that takes place are represented; and yet he transports one perfectly to the theatre of events. He puts before one's eyes everything that the historian does not tell" (267). A considerable swath of art historical inquiry has nevertheless involved the attempt to find specific historical events to which the prints might refer.

Licht suggests that the *Disasters* have a "camera shutter," photographic quality (128), and Basels, Bordes, and Matilla offer a more recent exploration of the analogies between war photography and the *Disasters*. What Goya shares with much of the photojournalism of war is the moral denunciation of the violence. There is, however, a very important difference between the indexical dimension of photography and Goya's conception of images. Williams puts it succinctly: "This is *not* 'reportage' in any sense. The whole series is a carefully composed exercise" (6). Scholars have noted that Goya's art deliberately engages with the bimodal nature of aesthetic perception in pointed ways. Tomlinson, for example, observes that Goya's painting "insinuates the inherent ambivalence of painted representation as both artistic creation and historically situated narrative. He warns us against seeing painting merely as narrative (that is, in terms of the event represented)" (*Goya in the Twilight* 22). In a more philosophical register, Cascardi has recently underscored the way Goya's art foregrounds the artifice of the image as part of a broader project of enlightened critique: "Goya came relatively early in his career to reflect on the means by which any view of the world, including any view put forward under the guise of 'art,' is constructed – 'invented' rather than 'natural'" (11). See Wollheim for discussion of the distinction between "seeing in" and "seeing as" in pictorial representations. For recent reappraisals of Wollheim and his impact on pictorial theory, see Van Gerwen. My interest in what follows is to examine the way *The Disasters of War* engage Wollheim's "two folded" nature of pictorial representation in pointed ways, and often with surprising effects.

The double consciousness of aesthetic perception has been a mainstay of philosophical aesthetics since the eighteenth century. For a recent overview of the subject, see Church (246–58). Central to my discussion of aesthetic double consciousness is the emergence of the category of "illusion" within pictorial theory during the second half of the eighteenth century. Hobson has tracked the shift in terms of a general, eighteenth-century movement away from appearance conceived as *aletheia*, or revealing, to appearance understood in terms of illusion. In a more historical vein, Vega (*Ciencia*) has mapped what she calls the "triumph of illusion" within the visual culture of the second half of Spain's eighteenth century. For a broader overview on the subject, Gombrich remains a classic.

Beginnings

For examination of the poetics of beginnings and their role in the production of meaning, see Said. Technically speaking, the title page is a *paratext*, "a threshold, or … a 'vestibule' that offers the world at large the possibility of either stepping inside or turning back" (Genette 2). Goya's working title was *Fatal Consequences of the Bloody War in Spain with Bonaparte. And other emphatic caprichos in 85 prints. Invented, drawn and engraved by the original painter D. Francisco de Goya y Lucientes. In Madrid.* For most viewers today, however, the academy's title has become the de facto "vestibule" through which they enter the work. Vega notes that the Academy's title may have been part of a broader attempt to "universalize" Goya by verbally relating his work to Callot's *Miseries of War* and by distancing the series from the polemics surrounding Goya's patriotism. She also draws attention to Print 30, *Ravages of War*, as a possible influence ("Las estampas" 65–6). While there has been much speculation as to the reasons Goya did not publish the prints during his lifetime, to date no documents have provided a definitive answer. As an artwork, *The Disasters of War* resists conventional taxonomies. The print series is a collection of pictorial images, but it is also a collection of the verbal texts that accompany those images, and the relationship between what we see and what we read is a key component of the viewing experience. Technically speaking, there is no narration, no storyteller and no story, in the sense in which verbal narration is commonly understood. Nor are there equivalents to "character" or "plot" which develop over time.

See Blanchot for one of the most sustained twentieth-century philosophical inquiries into disaster and the impossible necessity of its representation. Goya's work will repeatedly pose the problem of limits (artistic, ethical, moral, philosophical) in attempting to depict war's horrors, and many issues central to subsequent twentieth-century debates on violence and representation – particularly those stemming from Holocaust studies – find early expression in the *Disasters*. Adorno's dictum on the barbarity of poetry "after Auschwitz" is a point of reference in debates on the limits of representation. For an overview of these debates in the context of the Holocaust, see Friedländer. For advocates of non-aesthetic approaches to the testimony of atrocity, see Lanzmann and Lang. For defences of aesthetic form in the testimony of catastrophe, see Chambers or, more recently, Trezise. For discussion of art and literature as vicarious forms of witnessing in the context of the Holocaust, see Weissman. Cascardi links the question of limits in the *Disasters* to an aesthetics of the sublime (229–68).

Preface

The future-orientation of much of Goya's work is captured succinctly by Licht: "Goya, more than any artist before or since, unable as he was to bring much of his most important work to his contemporaries, tacitly appointed future generations as his legitimate heirs" (10). If the *Disasters* were out of step with nineteenth-century Spanish culture, it was largely because of their strongly anti-nationalist tenor. Lafuente notes that, for the period, "Goya is alone in his anti-heroic interpretation of war" (*Los Desastres* 20). See Hobsbawm for an overview of nationalism in a broad nineteenth-century context. For nationalism in Spain during the 1800s, see Alvarez Junco. For analysis of the political uses of the uprisings of the Second of May within Spanish nationalist discourse, see Demange. For reflection on the War of Independence within modern Spanish culture more broadly, see Alvarez Barrientos.

The Academy's romantic and patriotic Goya echoes common appraisals of Goya's work at the mid-century. See Smith for an account of the reception in Madrid of the first edition. For a more extensive account of the shifting historical reception of Goya, see Glendinning (*Goya and His Critics* 69–102). As Schulz summarizes, "in place of the mid-nineteenth-century myth of Goya as an untutored and isolated genius … [more recent] advocates of the 'enlightened Goya' gave both the artist and his work a much-needed historical context" (9). For analysis of Goya's work in the context of the particularities of the Spanish Enlightenment, see Tomlinson (*Goya in the Twilight*). The most meticulous reconstruction to date of Goya's activities during the War of Independence is Dufour. Tomlinson summarizes Goya's position upon the return of Ferdinand VII:

> Although Goya passed the inquiry of the "purification" process and retained his title and salary as First Court Painter, Ferdinand VII seems to have preferred the work of the younger Vicente López. Goya turned to portraits and to apparently uncommissioned works … He also continued to work in etching, no longer depicting scenes of war and political satires but the more benign theme of the history of the bullfight in Spain, announced for sale in 1816 as *La Tauromaquia*. (*Goya's War* 110)

For the history of the so-called *afrancesados*, with many of whom Goya converged in Bordeaux, see Juretchke, Artola (*Los afrancesados*), and López Tabar. On the experience of exile and its relationship to Spanish culture more generally, see Kamen.

For discussion of author images and their regulatory functions, see Barthes, Foucault, or, more recently, Gallop. My interest here is to underscore how the image of the artist can shape the interpretation of the work, and conversely, how the work itself inevitably bears on the image of the artist. The varying degrees of aesthetic absorption that accompany the perception of artworks have been central to debates in aesthetics since Kant. Stecker (39–64) provides a useful overview of recent discussions. For discussion of the philosophy and psychology of aesthetic absorption, see Benson. For extensive discussion of the problem of absorption as a subject in painting, see Fried. My reference to the *Disasters* as a form of play draws on Gadamer: "when we speak of play in reference to the experience of art, this means neither the orientation nor even the state of mind of the creator or of those enjoying the work of art, nor the freedom of subjectivity engaged in play, but the mode of being of the work of art itself" (101).

Print 1

Sedlmayr reads the secularization of Agony in the Garden as part of a broader crisis of classical humanism: "It is that sheet from the *Desastres de la Guerra* which shows man kneeling in despair before the darkness of the void. But here there are no ministering angels" (121). Many viewers have seen in Goya's work an ironic stance vis-à-vis religious sentiment. "There is no evidence in his biography or his works that he ever had even the most distant personal experience of [the transcendent]. The only reality he knew was that of the world around him; and the longer he lived the more frightful did that world seem" (Huxley 10). Within the *Disasters*, the absence of any sense of transcendence marks an important shift from earlier, baroque depictions of violence: "Goya's martyrdoms distinguish themselves by not being sacrificial in nature. No purpose is being served by all this anguish and blood. All things and all occurrences are equal in value and have no way of revealing a higher purpose in either death or life" (Licht 192). Wolf similarly observes: "The association of contemporary events with religious history was deeply embedded in Spanish rhetoric of the time; Goya used this rhetoric only to expose it for what it was" (47). Bozal argues that this is part of Goya's "turn away from the aesthetics of the sublime" (*Goya y el gusto* 171–257). Goya's decidedly worldly approach to violence may also be related to his understanding of the way martyrdom narratives have historically accompanied and helped to fuel war. It is precisely in the name of otherworldly values that wartime sacrifice is usually organized. Much of the demystifying force of Goya's images is achieved by rendering violence without symbolic references to such values.

Mélida interprets the man in the foreground as a representation of the Spanish *pueblo*, abandoned by its leaders, and he suggests that the background figures are the "monsters and chimeras" of the impending French invasion (269). Such an approach understands the image primarily as a historical allegory. As an allegory of presentiment itself, this first print also signals a form of artistic self-reflexivity – art reflecting on the problem of representation – that we will see repeatedly throughout the *Disasters*. Lafuente compares the print to the first notes of a symphony (*Los Desastres* 49). He relates the background "monsters" to *Capricho* 43, suggesting that they are emblems of the irrationality of war (*Los Desastres* 133). For further reflection on the inaugural functions of the print, see Dérozier, who shows how Goya departed from his preparatory drawings in order better to adapt the image to its position (970–2). Vega has confirmed that the sense of historical foreboding to which the print alludes can in fact be found in the literature that preceded the uprisings of 1808. She has also dated the making of the print to the same period in which Goya was making the allegorical "caprichos enfáticos" ("Fatales" 26–8). Matilla underscores the difference between this first print and the openings of other, more properly commemorative print collections:

> In contrast to commemorative print series … in which the immediate political antecedents of the conflict were presented … Goya breaks radically with these traditional methods of narrative propaganda and centers his lens on the feeling of abandonment that weighs on contemporary man, alone and kneeling, before the dark tragedy that approaches. (*Goya en tiempos* 280–1)

Licht notes:

> Technically and formally this plate is among the more conventional of the series. The nocturnal mood is achieved by the traditional method of massive cross-hatching. In many ways this image stands under the sign of Goya's revered master, Rembrandt. Only the spectral use of double-images (insubstantial faces and animal figures that float about in the darkness and are hardly recognizable unless one turns the page on its sides) links this plate with the world of nightmare visions that first appear in the *Caprichos*. (176)

Hughes writes of the main figure: "He is Job on the dunghill of Spain; he is also taken from the familiar pose of Christ in agony in the olive grove of Gethsemane … Like the rebel in the white shirt facing French muskets in the Third of May, he is the Spanish people battered but not broken, face-to-face with a disastrous and heroic future that will be revealed in the plates to come" (273–5). Little of what follows the opening of the *Disasters*, however, can adequately be described as a heroic future. Baucom reads the strange sense of time produced by the caption as a function of imperial war itself: "the bleak, foreboding message of Goya's opening plate is that in the disasters that imperial war visits upon the world, time-present and time-future become time-past" (186). While the speculation is suggestive, the seemingly strange mixing of times in this print relies primarily on the underlying differences between the time frame inhabited by the notional viewer, on one hand, and the time frame one might want to attribute to the central figure on the other. What is future for him is past for us. Miller proposes that the central figure is a prophetic "seer," and that he is in effect a model of the kind of vision that informs the *Disasters* more generally: "If the gaze and the voice that inhabit these images can be ascribed to anyone, it would be to the unidentified 'seer' who appears in the opening plate" (92). Such an interpretation seems to minimize the important differences between "vision" on one hand and the "presentiments" named in the caption on the other. In addition, as we will see in subsequent *Disasters*, few captions can be attributed easily to a single voice. For analysis of Goya's relationship to belief and secularization as represented in the aesthetics of his religious paintings, see Cascardi (15–54).

Print 2

Many viewers have underscored the novelty of Goya's depicting wartime violence at close range. See, for example, Bozal (*Imagen* 207). Tomlinson notes that the earliest prints Goya made took a more distant perspective: "During the three years that he worked on the scenes of war and famine, his perspective shifted from a bird's-eye view to close in on imagined confrontations between enraged adversaries and the aftermath of extreme cruelty" (*Goya: A Portrait* 423). For recent histories of the Peninsular War/Spanish War of Independence, see, among others, Alvarez Barrientos, Artola (*La Guerra*), Aymes, Esdalie, and Fraser. See Bell, for a history of the Napoleonic Wars as the touchstone for modern warfare. For a recent study of the *Disasters* within the framework of Clausewitz's conception of "absolute war," see Santiáñez. Beruete was one of the earliest to characterize the soldiers as "automatons" in contrast to the Spanish partisans in this image (72). Lafuente sees the partisans as an "elemental, spontaneous" force (*Los Desastres* 58). Dérozier notes that the caption is ambivalent, either an expression of doubt about the irrational, reactionary nature of the anti-Napoleonic struggle or a commentary on the passions of the people, which trump enlightened reason (841–2). Lecaldano sees the print as an expression of the "rage and terror" of the people in their moment of uprising (13). Vega concurs with previous scholars that this print and the next one depict the uprisings of the Second of May ("Fatales" 30).

My own position, given Goya's decision not to evoke a time or place in his caption, is that the print maintains a more ambiguous relationship to the events of the Second and Third of May. The historical particularities that might have inspired this image and the next are not the primary concern, which centres on the question of war's justifications. The self-cancelling logic of violence in the name of enlightened reason is a striking gloss, *avant la lettre*, of the critique of instrumental reason adduced by Horkheimer and Adorno in *Dialectic of Enlightenment* at the close of the Second World War. The question of Goya's patriotism is long, vexed, and closely connected to his activities during the war. Tomlinson offers a useful synthesis: "Patriotism may well have led the artist to Zaragoza in 1808 … but … there is reason to doubt that his patriotism remained unchanged. In evaluating the series' evolution we discover that the appeal to the viewer becomes increasingly emphatic as the frame closes in on the subject and narrative disintegrates" (*Graphic*, 34). For detailed biographical analysis of Goya's activities during the war years, see Dufour. Within the *Disasters*, patriotism and the violence it can engender are most often an object of critique. Matilla has recently called attention to the differences between actions in the foreground and background of this print:

> in addition to the brutal contrast visible in the foreground … Goya sketches the other side of the conflict with considerable detail in the background … so we can see between the legs of the *manolo* in the centre of the composition a group of Spaniards knifing a French soldier, and less clearly, on the left, another Spaniard armed with a knife threatening the shadow of soldier. (*Goya en tiempos* 282–3)

Print 3

Mélida understood the deeply anti-patriotic message imparted by turning from Print 2 to Print 3, and it prompted him to criticize what he saw as Goya's excessive scepticism: "The people must undoubtedly have committed acts of ferocity with no justification; but from criticizing this to denying that reason was on their side there is a big difference" (269–70). Dodgson notes that the print explores the same theme as Print 2, but he does not comment on the reversal. For Sayre, the image "expresses the patriotic intensity of the Spanish cities and provinces who, with neither Spanish army nor national government, rose up one by one against the French invaders of 1808" (131). Dérozier sees in the depiction of the axeman's face the kind of animalized caricature that often appears in the *Caprichos* (843–4).

Matilla elaborates, noting that Goya consistently shows "moral deformation through satirical or grotesque faces, as he had done in the tapestry cartoon *La boda* [The Wedding] or in numerous prints from the *Caprichos*" (*Goya en tiempos* 284–5). Hughes comments that the axeman's pose is similar to the one we find in Goya's painting *La Fragua* (*The Forge*): "Only the weapons and targets differ: the smith's hammer about to fall on a red-hot iron billet, the patriot's axe about to chop into the soldier" (275). Vega finds echoes of the painting *Corral de locos* (*Courtyard of Lunatics*) in Goya's portrayal of the same man ("Fatales" 26).

In claiming that nothing can justify the violence, Goya counters the centuries-long tradition of *jus ad bellum* or "just war" theory. For an overview of the tradition, see Johnson. Together the prints also dismantle the friend-enemy distinction that twentieth-century political theorists such as Carl Schmitt would much later take to be the basis of political life as such, and in this regard Prints 2 and 3 mount a powerful critique not only of Napoleonic imperialism and Spanish nationalism, respectively, but also of the violence of political sovereignty itself. This is the dimension of Goya's critique that remains so thoroughly contemporary and pertinent to our own times. The *Disasters* are uncanny in the Freudian sense of the "strange familiarity" that informs the viewing experience. My discussion of the double temporality of images – their belonging to the past and to the present of viewing/reading – draws on Walter Benjamin, for whom "image is that wherein what has been comes together in a flash with the now to form a constellation" (463). The intuitive understanding that the sort of violence depicted in Goya's prints is ongoing today is reinforced by the increasingly porous boundaries between "wartime" and "peacetime" since the Second World War. For analysis of the concept of wartime and its mutation over the second half of the twentieth century, see Dudziak. For reflection on how the *Disasters* can enrich theoretical understanding of what it means to be an enemy, see Baucom.

Print 4

See Cook for broad-ranging discussion of women and war. For a historical overview of women's participation in the war in Spain, see Fernández. Lafuente notes that Goya's frequent representation of women serves to emphasize the popular rather than professional dimensions of the struggle against Napoleon's forces (*Goya* 25). Historical testimonies have emphasized the participation of women in the uprising of the Second of May, 1808, leading Lecaldano to speculate that this print may depict an episode from that struggle. For the history of women's participation in the War of Independence and the myth making that immediately surrounded them, see Castells. For analysis of Goya's depiction of women, see Tomlinson (*Goya: Images* 15–69). Working with Bakhtinian notions of polyphony, Tomlinson has also underscored the many voices that "speak" through Goya's art: "The author's voice – in *Los Caprichos* and in Goya's oeuvre as a whole – is subsumed by a multitude of other voices: the traditions of art addressed, the personalities of the subjects portrayed, the projected desires of the patrons or intended public" (*Goya in the Twilight* 7). If this is broadly true of his oeuvre, it becomes quite literally so for the verbal artistry that is part of the *Disasters*. Many of Goya's captions are deliberately crafted in open-ended ways. The question of who "speaks" is left unresolved, thus prompting an exploration of the possibilities (i.e., Goya as artist, a figure within the scene depicted, the anonymous voice of a bystander, the viewer, etc.). For discussion of voice in relation to witnessing, see Wolf.

The lack of strong visual hierarchy typical of Goya's compositional style accentuates the ambiguities of voice and address. Licht observes that, "in the *Disasters*, the entire field of the plate is potentialized, and every form within this field … plays a part that becomes progressively equal in value to every other form within the same field" (191). Tomlinson similarly observes that "Goya creates a composition devoid of hierarchy, which in turn enables him to intimate a variety of relationships among its constituents without giving priority to any" (*Goya in the Twilight* 71). When coupled with deliberately open-ended captions, the result is an invitation to examine the various ways in which Goya's words engage his images. I will often return to the question of voice and address over the course of the book.

Most critical analyses of this print have taken the caption's assertion of womanly courage as a straightforward affirmation. Mélida comments on the women: "The artist has wanted to signify that the French, taking advantage of the weakness of the sex, took out their vengeance on them for the aggressions of the men; the majority of the time they nevertheless found their just punishment, as occurs in the scene represented" (270). Hoffman sees the depiction of women in a generally positive light that departs from Goya's portrayals of most other figures in the series (125–6). By contrast, Volland underscores the misogynistic underpinnings of most of Goya's depictions of women in the series. Vega notes the way Goya's depiction of women combatants challenges but also reaffirms the patriarchal discourse of the day ("Las estampas" 84). Drawing on Lafuente, Glendinning ("El asno") discusses this print and the one that follows as examples of the textual and conceptual links that Goya often establishes between prints.

I draw attention to the irony that emerges from the discrepancy between what we see in the image and what we read in the caption because an ironic understanding of the print is in keeping with what I take to be Goya's morally consistent vision throughout the series. Irony, sarcasm, and wit are key features of his captioning in the *Disasters*, as they were in his earlier *Caprichos*. Hughes makes similar observations: "Part of the brilliance of this series, strange as it may seem at first, is to be found in its ambivalence. Its sympathies oscillate without settling into the kind of plain resolution that one expects from propaganda" (292). The phenomenon Hughes mentions is further amplified by ambivalences in voicing and address.

Print 5

Recent work in the social sciences on the relationship between war and gender offers a useful lens for thinking about gender in the world of the *Disasters*. For Goldstein, for example, war- and gender-systems are mutually constitutive (59–127). In this sense Goya's prints seem prescient in capturing what Goldstein describes as the "reciprocal causality" that binds war and gender together; that is, the way war strongly influences peacetime gender roles, and the way those roles in turn structure wartime violence (6). As later prints will make clear, conventional notions of the masculine and the feminine organize much of the violence, whether women are present or not. The violence is often openly phallic, and the victims, regardless of their biology, are symbolically – and often literally – feminized.

Mélida notes that in this print the tables have turned with respect to Print 4: the women do not defend themselves but now attack, and the woman with child and lance "takes heroism to the point of barbarism" (270). Brunet does not comment on the shift in emphasis from Print 4 to Print 5 but rather sees both prints as examples of "the fury with which the women fight against French soldiers" (50). Lafuente notes the strongly symbolic dimensions of the mother and child: "one of the most accomplished symbols of the Spanish war against the French invader" (*Los Desastres* 59). For Lecaldano the mother and child are among the "crudest of the series" (20). Hoffman points to the erotic undertones of scenes of struggle between men and women (126–7). Volland comments extensively on the animalization of the women as instinctive creatures propelled primarily by maternal fury (157–61); while she attributes the animalization to Goya, it seems important to leave open the possibility that the image aims to show how *war* animalizes these women.

Print 6

Murray et al. provide a useful overview of the standard wartime medical care from the mid-eighteenth into the early nineteenth centuries:

> The primary emphasis was on removal of bullets within easy reach and avoidance of primary wound closure. If a wound was to be closed, an onion was placed in the wound before closure, and the wound reopened at 24 to 48 hours. The wound was expected to develop swelling and pus by the fourth day postinjury, which were thought to be signs of proper wound "digestion" necessary for healing. Amputation continued to be the therapy for compound fractures. Superficial burns were treated with wine and deep full-thickness burns with hog's lard ... Wound care during the War of 1812 (1812–1815) continued to emphasize early amputations to shorten hospital stays, to reduce the risk of infection, and to reduce the trauma caused by transportation on horse-drawn vehicles. Management continued to rely upon incision and removal of foreign bodies, with fasciotomy to prevent further tissue damage. During the Napoleonic Wars (1803–1815), amputations were also the standard of care. It was reported that Napoleon's surgeon, Dominique-Jean Larrey, could perform 200 surgeries a day, or one every 7.2 minutes. (S222)

Early commentary on this print (Mélida 270, Brunet 50, Yriarte 117, Dodgson 1) suggests that the agonizing officer is General Claude François Dupré, who was mortally wounded at the Battle of Bailén in July of 1808. It is not until the 1950s, with Lafuente's commentary, that a more generic understanding of the print emerges: "Goya presents us with the small and pitiful incident of a battle that never passes into the history books ... it could have been him [Dupré] or any of the thousands of French officers who fell" (*Los Desastres* 59). More recently, Vega conjectures that the battlefield might be related to events in Zaragoza. She concurs, however, with a more general approach to the print's meaning: "it tries to reveal the anonymous, lacklustre deaths of so many distinguished military men who, arriving to gather honours, were left buried in unknown fields of the Iberian Peninsula" ("Las estampas" 90).

The caption has been read primarily as the expression of Goya as chronicler-artist. Lafuente notes, for example, that Goya directs the words of the caption "dryly and rudely" (*Los Desastres* 59). We return once again to the problem of moral consistency. If the *Disasters* are, in Hughes's words, "the greatest anti-war manifesto in the history of art" (304), it seems highly unlikely that captions expressing battlefield fervour (Prints 2, Print 7) or hatred (Print 6) are straightforward expressions of the artist's sentiments. Irony, sarcasm, or other forms of double voicing are far more plausible. Such readings are consistent with the legacies of eighteenth-century wit and the Spanish *conceptista* tradition that Stoichita and Coderch (192–218) have underscored in their approach to the captions to the *Caprichos*. For analysis of Goya's reflections on the eros and violence of image making, and of art more generally, see Ciofalo (111–42).

Print 7

Nineteenth-century scholars (Piot, Mélida, Brunet, Muñoz) routinely identify the woman as Agustina of Aragón. Lafuente follows this interpretation, but he notes that "even in this case we must observe that this print, the glorification of an individual feat, presents the heroine with her back almost entirely turned to us and her face hidden, by which heroism is impersonalized" (*Los Desastres* 51–2). Sayre suggests that the print is loosely based on an engraving ("Batería del Portillo") from Juan Gálvez and Fernando Brambila's 1812 series, *Ruinas de Zaragoza* (134–5). Dérozier believes that in expressing admiration for Agustina, Goya makes manifest his conflicted feelings about the war (849–51). More recent interpretations have built on Lafuente's intuitions concerning the generic status of the woman. Vega sees the print as an abstraction of womanly heroism, arguing that the figure should not be presumed to be Agustina of Aragón ("Grande Hazaña!" 293–6). Hughes sees the image as a straightforward assertion of feminine courage:

> It is the only conventionally "heroic" plate in the whole series – heroic in that the artist presents a character as entirely courageous and worthy of admiration, neither helpless victim, nor a person driven by terror to involuntary acts of courage, nor a bestial and atrocious intruder; in short as a citizen in full command of her humanity. (288)

Tomlinson, however, underscores important departures from the conventional visual rhetoric associated with feminine courage:

> There is no reason to doubt that Agustina, portrayed in several popular prints of the period, inspired Goya's etching; yet it is significant that she is left unidentified.

> Avoiding conventional formulae for heroic portrayals, which depend on recognition and veneration of the individual (and risk reduction to cliché when this is lost), Goya forces the viewer to reconstruct the heroic deed. The woman is turned from us, her head, neck and shoulders obscured in shadow. (*Graphic* 29)

More recently, Matilla underscores the point:

> The conceptual background of this print is radically different [from standard representations of Agustina de Aragón] precisely because of its generic and emblematic meaning. Goya explicitly renounces the representation of concrete personages and situations. (*Goya en tiempos* 286–7)

An ironic understanding of the print is consistent with Goya's demystification of wartime mythologies more generally, with the critique of war throughout the *Disasters*, and with the moral conviction that informs his work as a satirist (in the *Carpichos* and the *Disasters*). Goya himself was not a witness to Agustina's heroism, but rather received the *story* of Agustina. It is consequently not difficult to imagine that he would have been attuned to the patriotic myth making that infused her story. A sarcastic understanding of the caption is also consistent with the anti-nationalist stance revealed in Prints 2 and 3, and Goya's anti-propagandistic stance more generally. For a biography of Agustina of Aragón, the process by which she was mythologized, and the political uses to which her image was put well into the twentieth century, see Queralt del Hierro.

Print 8

Edwards reminds present-day readers of the everyday intimacy between humans and horses throughout much of history and well into the 1930s. He also underscores the socially symbolic meanings of horses:

> Among the population at large the division between owners and non-horse owners marked a real division in society … Horses were expensive to keep and, if under-used economically, were among the first "luxury" items to go in a depression. Owners themselves were graded. Contemporaries could immediately assess a person's social status by his or her horse: its appearance; how it was used or ridden; and the way it was "dressed" (trained and presented). (Edwards, Enenkel, and Graham 5)

Brunet describes the scene as follows: "The French dragoons beating a retreat and leaping over a stream; one of the riders falls from his horse" (50). Lafuente notes that "in order to give us an idea of a battle, Goya uses a procedure analogous to what a modern film-maker might do: an episodic foreground, the rider who falls from his horse … an individual accident in a cavalry charge" (*Los Desastres* 60). Sayre relates the print's style to the *caprichos enfáticos* and, citing Lafond, sees parallels with Jacques Gamelin's depiction of wartime horses in *Neouveau recueil d'osteologie et de myologie* (1779): "besides the similarity of composition, the two prints share a sense of the confusion and dust of battle, and a fluidity of design" (137). This print is an exception to Hughes's observation that Goya "tended to avoid doing horses, and there are very few of them (and those, only in the background) just where you might expect to see them in quantity, among the plates of the *Desastres*" (278).

Many readers have been perplexed by the ambiguity of the caption. In Spanish, verb endings generally indicate grammatical person, but in the third person, which Goya often uses, the verb form allows for many possibilities (he, she, it, you.) Lecaldano observes, "what Goya wanted to affirm *always happens* is not clear; perhaps the horse's fall, or maybe he wanted to insinuate that often a small incident can frustrate the most customary magnificent actions" (23). Dérozier sees the print as a parody of traditional representations of the field of battle (852). Vega relates the print to the defeat of the French at the Battle of Bailén, suggesting that the fallen rider also symbolizes crushed pride ("Las estampas" 96). Standard translation of the caption into the English "It always happens" misses the connotations of the original *suceder*, which contains the idea of succession or following.

Prints 9, 10, and 11

For the history of wartime violence against women as well as the slow and tenuous emergence of rape as a war crime within international law, see Askin (18–46). For commentary and analysis of rape as a constant across virtually all modern wars, see Branche and Virgili. Citing a wide range of historical sources, Sayre (137) and Vega ("Las estampas" 98–100) document how common rape was during the war in Spain. See Dwyer for recent discussion of the role of massacres and atrocities within Napoleonic warfare. Herrera provides a useful overview of nineteenth-century perceptions of rape. Ciofalo says, "The notion of secrecy, deeds committed beyond the light of day, rape among them, courses through *Los Desastres de la Guerra* … Most of all, under archways. These are the places Goya sought to shine his light" (123). Nineteenth-century readers (Piot 361–2, Brunet 50) assumed that the old woman in Print 9 was the victim's mother. Hoffman sees the image as an ironic reworking of the triad (man, prostitute, madam) that appears with frequency in the *Caprichos*. He interprets the watermill as a symbol of heaviness, incarceration, and self-sufficiency (127). Lafuente observes, "for the soldier free of command, a woman is prey, part of the booty of war, but Goya wants to tell us that Spanish women are not easy to dominate" (*Los Desastres* 140). In light of the sequence, however, it seems unlikely that Goya is mythologizing feminine resistance. For Volland, the young woman's demeanour is ambiguous because of the embrace (152–3), but this interpretation overlooks the caption, which leaves no doubt concerning either woman's desires. Matilla attributes two different functions to the watermill: "it situates the action in a rural space, and symbolically it represents the violence, which turns unendingly" (*Goya: Luces* 208).

Of Print 10 Lafuente observes: "Goya wants to impress us … with the bestial presentation of these bodies in a harsh, desperate struggle; the confusion of soldiers and women within a scrambled commotion shows one more aspect of battle with no end" (*Los Desastres*

141). Dérozier interprets the swords and cap on the ground as a commentary on the abandonment of the key features of the identity of professional soldiers (854). Lafuente underscores Goya's frequent use of arches or other, similar structures in order to create a cave-like effect (*Los Desastres* 142). Bozal takes Lafuente's intuition further in his analysis of archways and their significance in the construction of "parabolic" pictorial space (*Imagen* 216). For Cascardi, Goya's approach to space similarly involves the "destruction of the logic of special organization" (264) as part of a broader phenomenon in which "the encounter with the absolute destruction of war … provides the impetus for a new visual language" (268).

Hoffman detects possible echoes of Poussin's *Massacre of the Innocents* in Print 11, and he notes that the head thrown back in anguish was a sign of pathos within the gestural language of late eighteenth-century painting. Approaching the depiction of the central woman within the framework of eighteenth- and early nineteenth-century misogyny, Volland calls attention to the passive, sensual, "pre-orgasmic" expression of the central victim (139–41). Hughes highlights Goya's focus on body tension: "The design is like the quadrant of a clock face: half of a low arch through which light shines, and a man and a woman, brightly lit, stretched across it at forty-five degrees, like a minute hand … There is brutal tension in their arms, which create the unifying diagonal of the design" (292). Noting the violence of separating mother from child, Vega captures the sense of the caption most fully: "not even for those reasons of humanity did [the soldiers] contain themselves" ("Las estampas" 103).

The cumulative effect of the three prints, which together underscore the inevitability of wartime rape, comes close to the conclusions of recent scholarship on the subject of war and rape. Seifert observes, for example: "War is a ritualized, finely regulated game … When looking back through history we find much to suggest that within this ritual one rule of the game has always been that violence against women in the conquered territory is conceded to the victor … We have no evidence that any negotiations have ever been carried out to halt this outrage against women" (58, quoted by Miller, 182). Hughes comments that Print 11 is "compositionally the most developed of the three rape scenes, an image that shows to a sublime degree what power Goya could develop when his talent for showing awful events in terms of utter compositional starkness was fully at work" (292). The caption to Print 11 has been widely mistranslated as "Nor these" and "Neither these," which misses the way the Spanish original conveys the idea of "Not even under these circumstances." Poor translations have also made it difficult to appreciate the way this print culminates the complex, three-print reflection Goya has organized.

Print 12

Compare the differing nuances of "For that you have been born," with the emphasis on *that*, and the more widely circulating English translation, "This is what you were born for." Mélida is critical of the deeply anti-patriotic sentiment expressed by the caption: "of course one has been born to die, but when one gives one's life for one's homeland, even though its defence is a duty for every citizen, the sacrifice deserves a different appraisal" (271). Yriarte notes the philosophical depth of the print, characterizing it as "a shout of shame," and he underscores the particularly caustic tenor of the caption: "Do you feel the scorn in the philosopher's words, whose heart rebels and whose reason is indignant?" (118). Beruete considers that because of its caption "this composition is one of the saddest and most pessimistic pages one can imagine" (74). Lecaldano similarly qualifies the print as "one of the most disturbing compositions of the series, which Goya makes even more bitter with the caption: the poor have not been born to live and work but rather to die unjustly and senselessly, before their time" (31). Lafuente sees the dark column in the sky as part of the "cave effect" that often appears in the *Disasters*. For Dérozier the sarcastic critique of wartime death applies equally to the Spanish and the French (857–8).

There is no critical consensus concerning the living figure. Mélida (271) suggests that he vomits blood, while Brunet (50) takes him to be nauseated, and the two interpretations – in one he is dying, in the other he is retching – continue to coexist within the critical literature. Sayre associates the image with the mass deaths that accompanied the 1809 outbreak of typhus fever, and she notes the way Goya's use of lavis in the sky aims to create "a hazy atmosphere and to define more clearly the volume and placement of the figures. Their reality is thus increased, and our emotional response to the scene is heightened" (144). Hughes comments on the standing figure: "He is leaning forward, racked with nausea at the sight, puking right on the corpses. The daring of this image can perhaps be assessed from the fact that, a century later, during World War II, neither British nor German censors would have permitted a newspaper to publish a photo of a corpse – much less a heap of corpses, and still less a man vomiting on them" (297). Vega conjectures that the dead are "neither soldiers nor guerrilla fighters but rather poorly armed countrymen … who became involved in the fight" ("Las estampas" 106). She also suggests that the print is a tacit indictment of "the disregard and ingratitude of rulers towards those who have fallen in defence of their cruel régimes" (*Francisco* 33).

Print 13

The nineteenth-century reception of this print has had a strong influence on subsequent interpretations. Responding to the caption, Mélida writes, "and so bitter! To see himself detained and tied, while in his very sight his enemies violate his own wife after perhaps having plundered him, is truly horrible" (271). Dodgson, Lafuente, and Lecaldano offer similar readings. Volland approaches the woman's portrayal as a passive victim in terms of misogyny (147–9). Vega offers an interpretation of the print that departs considerably from the longstanding assumption that it is another scene of impending sexual violence. She argues instead that the body language and facial expressions of the central figures do not strongly suggest a sexual content. Based on details of the preparatory drawing, she speculates that the print may be the depiction of the final moments of the fall of a city. The arches would in this reading be those of a town square as soldiers ransack it ("Las estampas" 109).

The fact that Goya did not include details from the drawing, however, might just as easily speak to his intention to keep the print from being approached as a loco-descriptive image. Following a very different psychological tack, Ciofalo suggests that the archways in the image are reminiscent of a skull's eye-sockets, and that the entire scene may be a representation of

Goya's mind, "the world's first anatomically inside-out self-portrait" (134). Bozal has undertaken the most extensive analysis of Goya's use of archways in the *Disasters*: arches create an oppressive parabolic sense of space, they define and juxtapose two different (interior/exterior) spaces, and they prompt the viewer to construct pictorial space in the image (*Imagen* 216).

Prints 14 and 15

The part-for-whole function of pictorial space in Goya's *Disasters* has struck many viewers, and it is due largely to the predominance of the "open form" that characterizes Goya's approach. For discussion of the distinction between "open" and "closed" form, see Wölfflin (124–48). Along similar lines, Licht observes:

> Goya's space no longer grows from a fixed center, and without a fixed center we cannot take our bearings in the directionless world he shows us. In plate 15 of the *Disasters*, as well as in most subsequent pictures, there is the emphatic notion that the event not only is insane in its blind cruelty but that also it occurs in a universe equally bereft of reason, direction or meaning. It is an abyss that stretches to all sides of us and even opens menacingly behind. (188)

Crowther offers a useful synthesis: "it is clear that as well as drawing attention to what is contained within the frame and affirming the separateness of pictorial from 'real space,' the frame has a profoundly aesthetic function … the frame itself … can be a kind of explicit symbolic affirmation that this is an artistic image rather than just a piece of pictorial information" (59). Butler offers commentary along the same lines: "the frame tends to function, even in minimalist form, as an editorial embellishment of the image" (8). For more philosophical reflections on framing, see Derrida and Simmel. For a summary of approaches to framing within contemporary aesthetics, see Savedoff.

The most common English translation of the caption to Print 14 is "The way is hard," which misses the word play in Spanish. Mélida (271), Brunet (51), Muñoz (368), Beruete (75), Sayre (146), and others propose that Print 14 depicts punishment for a massacre in Valencia. Lecaldano suggests that those being executed are French (37). Dérozier argues that the victims are most likely *afrancesados* (860–1), and Vega posits that they are in fact Spanish *guerrilleros* (*Francisco* 33–4), noting that both Print 14 and Print 15 involve the depiction of distinct temporal moments ("Las estampas" 112). Emphasis on placing the image historically tends to come at the expense of the moral dimensions of Goya's critique. Gassier suggests possible links between Print 14 and Callot's *La Pendaison* and *Les Supplices* (174). Lafuente associates the "hard step" with many of the forms of death throughout the series (*Los Desastres* 61). Commenting on Print 14, Licht offers an insightful contrast between Goya and Callot:

> We are not told, as we were by Callot … that the men who have been hanged or are about to be executed deserved their punishments because of their crimes. Nor does

> Goya go to the other extreme of enlisting our sympathy by telling us that they were unjustly sentenced and executed. Both these appeals would depend on a stable and reliable standard of justice … We are not given the chance to judge the case. Either every fiber within us calls out to stop the killing, or else we seek cowardly refuge by trying to get the facts straight. (184)

Wolf notes that images of benediction in Goya often underscore "the hypocritical terms in which the sacred blessing is administered" (45). She cites Print 14 as an example of the way Goya routinely "subverts the meaning of traditional Christian iconography," which was a mainstay of wartime propaganda (45–6).

Many critics have associated Print 15 with *Executions of the Third of May, 1808*. For Brunet the caption to Print 15 is reminiscent of the caption to *Capricho* 24, "There was no remedy [No hubo remedio]" (51). Beruete notes the "surprising tragic effect" of the truncated rifles, which Goya uses relatively frequently (75). Lafuente underscores the way the framing augments the impersonal nature of the killing: "a man, blindfolded and tied to a post, guerrilla or prisoner, awaits in darkness for the gunshot of the squad. In order for the scene to acquire greater impersonality, we only see the muzzles of the rifles from which they are about to discharge their deadly fire" (*Goya* 25). Bozal has commented extensively on the repetition of trees, poles, posts, benches, beams, and stakes within the *Disasters*: "One must point out the resemblance between trees and poles, also between trees and gallows, and even between trees and 'the stick' for the condemned, which turns into the neck-cuff of the garrotte" (*Goya. Nuevas* 129–30).

Print 16

In an early example of a critical tradition that has often minimized the role of Goya's captions, Carderera suggests that the images speak for themselves: "What would the epigraphs have added to this scene in which bandits rob piled cadavers of their last clothes?" (243). He poses the question rhetorically, but there is a revealing answer to his query. The caption sets up the narrative content of the image in terms of taking advantage, in both the moral and material sense. This would not be the case with a different caption, or if the image stood on its own. For Mélida and many others the soldiers are Frenchmen and the victims are Spanish (272). Lafuente underscores the lack of respect for the dead: "After death, plundering; the fallen are deprived even of their undergarments by victorious soldiers, a lamentable operation that Goya presents here in all of its repugnant crudeness" (*Los Desastres* 145). Sayre offers an alternative reading: "Neither the Spanish civilians nor their soldiers were well equipped to fight. Descriptions abound regarding lack of supplies. Here Spanish soldiers are depicted stripping their dead of usable clothing" (150). Dérozier emphasizes the disappearance of respect for human dignity (864–5). Williams notes the word play: "*Se aprovechan*, runs one caption; it could mean 'they take advantage' or 'they're of use to each other'" (8). Vega addresses the significance of the stripping, and of nudes more generally, in the *Disasters*: "Nudity was a form of punishment based on humiliation, which … was reinforced even more in the eighteenth century due to the importance that fashion had within social relations." Echoing earlier observations by Pérez-Sanchez, she sees in the scene a secularization of the Deposition: "those soldiers that plunder the dead for their garments … have their referent in the ones that in the end raffled away Christ's … The secularization of painting offered new themes for the depiction of nudes" ("Las estampas" 118). For discussion of the problem posed by the beauty of male nudes, see Prints 18, 37, and 39.

Print 17

For an overview of the major historical shift in military organization, tactics, and command and control during the Napoleonic Wars, see Rothenberg. This print was initially published out of sequence owing to a misreading of the numeration. In the first edition it appeared in position 77 rather than 17. Mélida noted that the position made little sense (280). Early viewers like Brunet were confused by the subject matter: "We are not able to say what this drawing refers to" (51). Lafuente was the first to articulate fully the interpretation that would subsequently become standard: "The invaders themselves *do not agree*; they fight and disagree with one another; this print by Goya, in this part of the series, has the mission of reflecting that irritation, weariness and discouragement that Napoleon's generals experience in the face of a strange and disconcerting war" (*Los Desastres* 146). In another moment he suggests that the leaders may not necessarily be French: "those who *do not agree* are, without a doubt, two commanders in disagreement about the development of the operation; this disagreement was almost constant in our war of Independence, in the French as well as the Spanish command" (146). Sayre similarly notes that the nationality of the army cannot be determined, and she calls attention to the depiction of the soldiers on the right, noting that the bright white background "consumes and dematerializes the soldiers caught in its light" (152). For Dérozier, the print is a critique of the ineptitude of commanders, whether French or Spanish (866). Vega comments on the importance of the composition and its relationship to the caption: "it is evident that there are two clearly differentiated parts that underscore the epigraph that Goya wrote" ("Las estampas" 121). She conjectures that "perhaps Goya wants to reflect the profound differences that existed … between those officers who knew and obeyed the rules of war, and those others who paid no attention" (*Goya grabador* 33). She also considers the horse in the foreground to be the true protagonist of the scene, not only because of its gaze, but also because of the detailed attention to form with which Goya has rendered it ("Las estampas" 121).

Print 18

Scholarly discussion of repetition in the series has approached the topic primarily in terms of themes. Lafuente notes, for example, that "Goya often offers us … repeated versions of one tragic motif, sometimes with an insistence that seems excessive," and he proposes seven kinds of scenes that are repeated: rape, piled bodies, firing squads, the wounded, executions, flights from violence, and hunger (*Los Desastres* 51). My comments on repetition aim to shift critical focus onto its effects on the viewing experience. While Goya's many returns to a theme mean one thing at the level of the making of the *Disasters*, the effect of repetition for viewers moving through the series is of a different order. Repetition is, among other things, a device that conveys the idea of frequency within the broader illusion of moving through the war years. For an overview of repetition as an expressive device, see Enos (600).

Mélida offers a revealing example of the prevalence of nineteenth-century "miasmatic" medical theory: "a mound of naked cadavers covers the ground, and they infest the air with the miasmas produced by their decomposition" (272). Symmons, Hoffman, and Bozal have studied parallels between this print and John Flaxman's illustration of Canto 29 in Dante's *Inferno*. For Hoffman, Goya's images are far more harsh, presaging scenes from the concentration camps of the Second World War (130–1). Bozal comments on the universalizing effects created by the way Goya has pared away anecdotal details that were originally in the preparatory drawing (*Imagen* 201–3). Sayre relates the scene to the problem of the disposal of bodies during the war, especially during the first and second sieges of Zaragoza. She observes that "the hazy atmosphere strongly suggests the sun's heat, its deteriorating effects on the corpses, and the resulting nausea of the two searching among the dead" (153). Matilla interprets the caption as follows: "in this case Goya changes the verb 'to eat' [from the proverb] to 'to bury,' but the meaning of the title is quite similar; nothing can be done." He goes on to note that the ambiguous blend of mourning and nausea appears to have come to Goya after the preparatory drawing, where the couple is more clearly grieving (*Goya en tiempos* 318–21). Hughes discusses this print as an example of the role of disgust in the print series: "Two survivors, hand and handkerchiefs stuffed to their faces to block the stench of decay, scan a heap of stripped bodies, now beginning to rot, in the hope of finding a friend or a relative. You probably won't, Goya implies, and if you do, it won't matter; the dead are dead, so just get them in the hole" (297).

The sculptural quality of Goya's male nudes has drawn the attention of many scholars of the *Disasters*. Tomlinson offers the following synthesis:

> The carefully delineated nudes refer back to the academic studies after antique casts that Goya, like all other academically trained artists, would have drawn in earlier years. Given the grotesque subject, it is perhaps with a certain irony that the artist meticulously defines these idealized figures through the use of stippling and dry point. The reference to the antique is significant … we sense Goya's own admission that the reason and beauty epitomized by the classical tradition have been defeated. (*Graphic* 31)

To the extent that classical beauty is not entirely defeated – i.e., the bodies are disturbing precisely because they remain beautiful – Goya also seems to pose the broader question of beauty and its relationship to violence. For an artist who deliberately departs from the pictorial idealization of warfare (Bozal, *Goya y el gusto* 171–257), the question becomes an abiding concern in the series. In this sense, the *Disasters* presage one of the central questions that would emerge in the wake of the Second World War and the Holocaust: What role can art and the aesthetic play in conveying extraordinary historical violence? For a recent overview of the subject of "unwanted beauty" in the context of Holocaust studies, see Kaplan. As emphasis on the singular nature of the Holocaust yields to new approaches that probe its place within a broader, deeper history of historical atrocity (see, for example, Rothberg, Silverman, and Sanyal), the *Disasters* may become an object of renewed interest for comparative studies.

Prints 19 and 20

For an introduction to the human face and its significance across cultures, see Bates and Cleese. For a classic overview of the face in Western art, see Brophy. There is a strong ethical charge to Goya's emphasis on the faces of suffering victims. For the philosopher Immanuel Levinas, for example, the face is the fundamental locus from which all ethical imperatives proceed. Within Goya's *Disasters*, the suffering faces of victims often make an ethical demand on the viewer, a demand that is complicated by awareness of the difference between the encounter with actual faces and the perception of faces in an artistic image. At the same time, my reference to the "democratization" of suffering is intended to underscore the political dimensions of making such suffering visible.

If, as Jacques Ranciere suggests, the political can be thought of in terms of a "distribution of the sensible" – here the visible – the *Disasters* are an exemplary attempt to bring "the part that has no part" within representations of war into visibility. In a similar vein, if one of the standard features of wartime propaganda is to make some lives (and deaths) count more than others, Goya's relatively egalitarian approach to the representation of suffering takes on additional significance. For a recent exploration of the manipulation of visibility during times of war, see Butler. Goya's depictions of wartime indifference to the suffering of others can usefully be conceived in terms of "moral damage," a term that has recently emerged within clinical psychology to describe the effects of war on veterans who return to civilian life. See Litz et al. for an overview.

Interpretation of this print since the first edition shows considerable range. Mélida observes, "this print could represent a Mameluke officer [who] with his presence impedes his subordinates from carrying out the barbaric scene they are getting ready to represent" (272). Beruete reads the caption as follows: "At the foot of some ruins Mamelukes try to force some women, having killed a young man who accompanied them. But the Spanish must be getting closer, for a French officer arrives and says … 'there is no longer any time'" (77). Lecaldano offers a similar reading (52). For Lafuente, Goya intimates that the male companion who has fallen is about to be castrated (*Los Desastres* 148). Tomlinson elaborates the idea further: "by setting her [the woman's] arm against that of the second soldier behind, Goya emphasizes her futile attempt to prevent him from castrating his unconscious victim, an act of aggression that alludes graphically to the woman's own imminent violation" (*Graphic* 30). Sayre comments on the way Goya links the central woman and her male companion through tone: "[the] same pale tone is found on the breeches of the victim at the right … his shirt and the face and sleeve of the horror-stricken woman facing the soldier remain white, linking these two Spaniards by means of identical tonalities" (157). For Dérozier, the print is a subtle critique of Spanish resistance to the French, which caused unnecessary death and destruction in many cities (869–70). Vega corrects earlier identification of the soldiers as Mamelukes – "these are clearly Polish soldiers" – and, following Sayre, she links this print with a working proof [*Infame provecho*] that did not make it into the collection ("Las estampas" 127).

Commenting on Print 20, Brunet notes "the bravery and resignation of the faces of these people who do their duty" (51). Lafuente comes closer to the modern consensus on this print: "One does not stop fighting. Having finished the action, those who have not died, although they may be wounded, must be cured to start again" (*Los Desastres* 149). After review of the preparatory drawings for this print, Sayre suggests that the image may have initially been inspired by Goya's visit to Zaragoza after it had been besieged. She also notes that subsequent preparatory drawings attest to Goya's desire to make the image more generic, so that it could allude to anywhere in Spain (159).

Prints 21, 22, and 23

Beruete is at a loss about the meaning of Print 21: "One can neither understand the composition nor its relationship to the legend" (77). Lafuente suggests that the dead are fallen guerrilla fighters, but similarly observes, "the title of the print, stoic and contemptuous, does not make clear Goya's intention in applying it to this scene" (*Los Desastres* 150). Lecaldano speculates that "perhaps Goya means that leaving them [the cadavers] there or transporting them to another place makes no difference because they are dead and nobody can give them back their lives" (59). Wolf relates the woman who covers her eyes to other witness figures in the *Disasters* who signal the difficulty of looking (43). More recently, Vega observes that the laconic caption, the indeterminate pictorial space, and the lack of any preparatory drawings make this print especially difficult to interpret. She speculates that the dead might be patients from a hospital that was destroyed during the first siege of Zaragoza ("Las estampas" 134). The most commonly circulating literal translation into English, "It will be the same," does not convey the notion that "It will make no difference" as clearly as the original Spanish. In English the verbal and conceptual connections between the three captions are also far less obvious.

Mélida is of the opinion that in Print 22 "the grouping and postures of the cadavers are more spontaneous and natural" than in Print 21: "it perfectly reproduces confusion and disorder, a consequence of defeat" (273). Lafuente writes, "again [we see] the unfortunate group of the dead fallen next to their arms in a tragic and mixed up pile" (*Los Desastres* 150). For Gassier the bodies in this print are reminiscent of the fallen in *Executions of the Third of May, 1808* (232–3). Print 23 prompts Lafuente to observe that the "repeated scene and legend indicate that Goya wants to give us the idea that all of Spain is strewn with desolation and death" (*Los Desastres* 151). Many scholars have noted important differences between the preparatory drawings and the final versions of Prints 22 and 23. The changes confirm Goya's tendency to remove details in order to imbue the prints with a more generic or universal meaning. Vega notes that in both preparatory drawings Goya "has eliminated all action" – a living crowd in Print 22, and ongoing battle in Print 23 – "in order to reinforce the sense of silence and abandon" ("Las estampas" 138).

Prints 24 and 25

The common English translation of the caption to Print 24, "They'll still be useful," misses the pun on the Spanish verb *servir* (i.e., to serve in the military and, at the same time, to be of use). The gap between the sentiments portrayed in these images and the ironic tone of the captions is typical throughout the *Disasters*. While the majority of Goya's prints correspond to the visual codes of the pathetic (see Bozal, *Imagen* 171–257), his captions deliberately disrupt visual pathos through critical verbal commentary. Mélida reacts strongly against the caption's implicit dismantling of patriotic sacrifice: "It is not this selfish view that must have moved our fathers to gather and heal the wounded, no, but rather the charity so deserved by those who risked their lives in defence of the homeland; but Goya worried little about that" (273). Lafuente understands what Mélida appears to have missed: that Goya's tone in Prints 20, 24, and 25 is "laden with bitter irony" (*Los Desastres* 61). Of Print 24 he observes, "again [we encounter] Goya's harsh and blunt lashing" (153). Lecaldano glosses the caption more extensively: "field workers have arrived in time to lend aid to Spanish soldiers wounded in combat. They will hide them, they will treat them, and who knows if they will save them. But this is not a humanitarian gesture. The objective is that, put back on their feet in whatever way, they can continue to be useful for fighting" (65). Vega associates the image with events in Zaragoza ("Las estampas" 141).

In turning to Print 25, Mélida offers an example of the way sequence can suggest narrative continuity: "Some of those gathered in the field are now being treated, others find themselves on the ground awaiting their turn" (273). Beruete comments on the connection between the two prints, noting way Print 25 "completes the thought that *these wounded too*, once healed, will be able to go to the front once more and *they will still be able to serve*" (79). Lafuente describes the hospital scene in terms of its "heterogeneous confusion" (*Los Desastres* 153). Matilla notes that the caption is particularly cutting, given the fact that none of the figures in this scene are in fact ready to return to service (*Goya en tiempos* 84–6). Vega conjectures that the figure behind the man convalescing in bed may be the artist himself: "Next to his pillow emerges a head whose features immediately remit to Goya himself, in a kind of doubling that recalls the preparatory drawings for *The Dream of Reason* … That series [the *Caprichos*] began with a self-portrait; in contrast, in the *Disasters* it is not possible to affirm his presence as strongly" (*Francisco* 53). If it is Goya, the print would offer one more example of self-reflexivity in the series. For extensive discussion of self-portraiture in Goya, see Ciofalo.

Print 26

"And he is right" – Mélida writes of the caption – "the execution by firing squad of all those women, children and defenceless men is a barbarity whose sight is damaging. The various emotions that weigh on the victims are presented with much passion and mastery" (274). Beruete makes the connection to earlier execution scenes: "A composition similar to number 15, admirable for its action and movement, for the expression of the tragedy represented there, and for the sentiment that it reveals. Indeed, a scene so terrible that it *cannot be looked at*" (78). Lecaldano and Hoffman also note the similarities with Print 15, and Hoffman sees affinities with other images: the covered woman embracing the child is reminiscent of *Capricho* 3, and the woman with her head thrown back recalls the ecstatic expression of Bernini's *St. Theresa* (131). Volland compares this same figure with the central male victim in *Executions of the Third of May, 1808*, concluding that, in contrast to men, women in the *Disasters* give themselves over to death willingly as sexual objects that sacrifice themselves for the homeland (142–4). If this is the case, however, one would need to reconcile such a reading with Goya's critique of the killing. At stake is the question of whether Goya espouses misogynistic premises in the *Disasters* or registers a broader cultural misogyny as part of his critical reflection.

Williams comments about the victims, "They are ordinary … their probably unremarkable lives are ending now in brutal, wanton, faceless killing. They die without heroism or dignity and yet there is something inexpressible about the manner of their dying which makes it an obscenity" (1). Wolf comments on the theme of looking, and she sees this print as a counterpoint to Print 44, *Yo lo vi* (I saw it) (43). Extending Lafuente's observations regarding Goya's penchant for "cave-like" settings (*Los Desastres* 96), Bozal argues that the use of domed structures such as caves and archways prompts viewers to "construct the image" (*Imagen* 216). Vega notes that the victims' clothing signals that they are of relatively high social status, and she suggests that they are *afrancesados* ("Las estampas" 146). It seems, however, that Goya has deliberately composed the image so as not to indicate the side of the conflict to which victims and perpetrators belong. There are no soldiers' uniforms, and the clothing of the victims does not indicate their political affiliations. Moral commentary again trumps politics and history.

Many scholars have commented extensively on what Goya might actually have seen during the war years, and a good number have taken the caption to this print as an affirmation that the prints are largely testimonial. This argument does not stand up for very long, however, if one considers the kind of violence Goya depicts. Hughes makes the point that questions concerning the possibilities of Goya's actual witnessing miss a more important dimension of the *Disasters*: "Never mind that not everything, or even not much, that is depicted in them happened in front of Goya's eyes. He was the artist who invented a kind of illusion in the service of truth: the illusion of being there when terrible things happen" (272). My comments on the print suggest that it deliberately reminds viewers of the illusory status of the image by carefully leaving the threat out of the frame.

Print 27

For historical documentation on nineteenth-century military regulations governing burial, see Vega ("Las estampas" 149). For an overview of the nineteenth-century transition from miasmatic theories of disease to modern germ theory, see Magner (305–31). Early scholars of the *Disasters* note the interpretive challenges posed by this print. Mélida registers the ambiguity of the caption:

> In order to understand the true meaning of this word [*caridad*], it would be necessary to know the sense with which Goya used it, for with respect to the composition it could just as soon be praise as an epigram [i.e., criticism]. Some men … occupy themselves with throwing cadavers that have remained in the field and have been stripped of their clothes into a pit. No doubt it is to bury them, but the way they are doing it and the idea that they themselves may have been the plunderers, along with the habitual sarcasm of the legends, give rise to the doubt that we have noted. (274)

Brunet similarly observes that this is one of Goya's "most sarcastic and ironic" captions (52), while Beruete is left with questions: "One cannot understand this composition well. Is it that these four men are charitably burying the dead, or are they four outlaws who are hiding them after having plundered them? By their attitudes I think the latter" (79). For Lafuente the print is less ambiguous: "these naked dead, thrown into the pit, pushed in with lances or grabbed by the legs disrespectfully, are not treated with much *charity* by their buriers" (*Los Desastres* 154). By contrast, Gassier sees no irony in the caption: "Goya has found the briefest and most surprising title in existence: Charity, as if to proclaim his unbreakable faith in man and in human fraternity, which is stronger than wars and death" (*Dibujos* 240–1). Commenting on the callous facial expressions of the workers, Sayre summarizes the radical diminishment of moral feeling that Goya's *Disasters* often convey:

> The face of the man in the cocked hat is set apart from the white sky by a tone of lavis. The expressionless face of the observer standing with folded arms, drawn with dots like the corpses, and the face of the man next to him are white against the toned background. By this means Goya focuses attention on their expressions so that one is instantly aware that they no longer remember that the dead were once their friends and neighbors. They push them into a common grave with neither feeling nor compassion … So … in the *Desastres* does war exercise its inexorable power. (165–8)

Gassier, Wilson-Bareau, and Dérozier each note that the figure in the background may be Goya (Dérozier 882–3). For more extensive interpretation of Goya's self-portrait in this print, see Ciofalo 84–8. Cascardi notes that the darkness of the pit suggests "that the graves are bottomless – that there is no measure by which the earth can contain the suffering of those who have been killed by the violence of war. There is no consolation in burial" (253).

Prints 28 and 29

The Spanish word used for the caption to Print 28, *Populacho*, is commonly translated as "Rabble," but its etymology (from Lat. *populus*) and its association with *pueblo* link the expression more closely to a pejorative expression for "the people" than "rabble" does in English. Matilla notes that a secondary meaning of *populacho* is simply "crowd" or "mob" (*Goya en tiempos* 314), with less emphasis on social class than "rabble." Mélida (274), Brunet (52), Dodgson (4), and Lecaldano (78) all refer to the victim in Print 28 as the Marquis of Perales. Lafuente again represents a turning point in the print's interpretive history when he argues against searching for a specific historical reference in the print: "Without a doubt the victim is a Frenchman or an *afrancesado* … this print has been related to the Marquis of Perales … Unfortunately similar incidents took place in almost every Spanish province, and in Madrid itself it was repeated with commissioner Viguri, who was labelled an *afrancesado* and friend of Godoy's" (*Los Desastres* 155). Gassier notes that the caption confirms Goya's rejection of violence, whatever its form (242). Dérozier observes that the nationality of the victim matters little; the point of the print is to critique the rage of the mob, much as Goya had done in the case of crowds gathered for Inquisitorial violence in the *Caprichos* (884). Hoffman comments on the implied sexual sadism of the image and relates it to other artists of the period (132–3). Tomlinson explains the strong links between Print 28 and prints from *La Tauromaquia*:

> The theme of *Rabble*, in which cruelty becomes public spectacle, parallels that of plate 12 of *La Tauromaquia* … In *Rabble* we even find the man employing the crescent-shaped *media-luna*, a device used in the bullfight to hamstring the animal. Although each of these etchings is usually studied only within the context provided by its immediate series, they are clearly linked in their depiction of the rabble's niggardly bravura, tested only when victory is assured by the enemy's disadvantage. (*Graphic* 33)

Hughes underscores that the caption to Plate 28 counters the common myth that Goya was a populist: "The title of the image is one contemptuous word, spat on the page … This is not the utterance of a sentimental populist. Goya has no doubt, and leaves us none, that the patriots can be as brutal, sadistic, and depraved as the invaders; and sometimes he leaves open the question of which are the murderers and which the victims" (293).

Mélida (274), Brunet (52–3), Muñoz (337), and Beruete (18) speculate that the victim in Print 29 is General Filangieri. As with the previous print, Lafuente argues that the reference is less historically specific: "the list of those who fell victim to the popular furor, which was always ferocious and almost always unjust, is too long to attempt any kind of identification" (*Los Desastres* 156). He observes that the change in judgment from one print to the next is an intentional attempt to disconcert the viewer (*Los Desastres* 61). Sayre notes the exceptional nature of the man who looks down the rope at his victim: "In contrast to the brutal enemy soldiers of 33 and 37 … this particular Spaniard evinces some sympathy" (170). Lecaldano suggests that the caption to Print 29 may represent the speech of the "rabble" as it tries to legitimate itself (78). Dérozier offers a similar reading: "Is he not trying to attenuate the reach of the first caption by echoing, and not without irony, the justifications that spectators of good society could apply to themselves?" (885–6). Wolf emphasizes the contrast between the two men who pull (35).

Print 30

"In a bombardment, perhaps of Gerona, a house collapses and engulfs within its ruins, men, women, children, furniture and everything it contains. The horrible disorder of a misfortune of this scale is perfectly interpreted" (Mélida 274). Lafuente underscores the novelty of the subject: "I believe it is the first time in the history of art that a scene of bombardment in which the civilian population is victim is presented with this astonishing immediacy" (*Los Desastres* 156). He is also among the first to address the disturbing facets of Goya's depictions of feminine victims:

> I have pointed out … the pleasing quality that Goya puts into the depiction of the female body, even in these scenes of tragedy and devastation. This element, typical of the artist, who was never indifferent to the eternal feminine and which I have described as *sensuality in the terrible*, can similarly be seen … in other prints of the *Disasters* (prints 11, 13, 41, 50). (*Los Desastres* 156)

Sayre relates the scene to accounts of the explosion of a powder magazine that demolished most of a city block during the first siege of Zaragoza (172). Dérozier similarly suggests that Zaragoza is the most likely historical reference, and she interprets the print as a symbolic commentary on the irrationality and chaos of war (887–8). Gassier notes the similarity between the caption and the title of Callot's *The Miseries of War*. Hoffman sees a metaphorical expression of the idea of a fallen humanity in the print, and he reflects on the conjuncture of death and the erotic, contrasting Goya's treatment of the subject with Gilroy and Hogarth (134–5). Echoing several scholars who have been struck by the strong sense of immediacy of the print, Vega observes that the scene represents "a domestic interior – bourgeois by the type of furniture – at the precise moment when the upper floors are collapsing: some lie on the ground, others continue to fall … and Goya underscores that idea of immediacy and surprise by putting in the foreground the mother who was nursing her child when the floor came down" ("Las estampas" 158). Volland sees necrophilia in the depiction of the mother and considers it part of a broader trend in Goya to treat dead women as sexual objects (151–2). Matilla posits an extremely innovative approach to the subject:

> Goya is going to opt for an absolutely novel image in which he will show us an impossible vision, for he situates himself in the interior of the bombed building itself and at the precise moment in which it crumbles from the effect of the explosion. Only through art is it possible to show the viewer an image like this one, capturing an event that takes place in one tenth of a second. (*Goya en tiempos* 297)

Hughes calls the scene "an appalling fragmentation, a jumbling of bodies and furniture, that seems like a prophecy of the effects of aerial bombardment of high-explosive shelling on a gutted house" (276).

Print 31

Perhaps in part because of its ambiguities, appraisals of the print's quality have generally been negative. Mélida considers it "among the weakest of the collection, despite the author's having used all kinds of techniques in its execution" (274). Brunet and Muñoz concur. Beruete observes that "it is an ugly composition of bad taste that does not produce the desired effect of terror" (81). Lafuente echoes earlier sentiments: "In my opinion it is one of the worst engravings of the series, like some others that have these big figures with weak, ragged drawing. In addition, the group on the left is confused and poorly resolved" (*Los Desastres* 157). Lecaldano adds, "It is one of the least convincing compositions, in which the generality of the events is not able to communicate atrocity, but it is saved thanks to the hirsute figure in the foreground" (82). Common to such appraisals is the sense that the image leaves things unresolved. To my knowledge there has been little inquiry into whether this might be by design.

Until recently, the scholarly consensus was that the image represents French atrocities committed against the Spanish. Piot offers an early interpretation along this line: "Soldiers who have just executed three individuals hanged from a tree on the right; one of them, in front, puts his saber back into its sheath" (361–2). Vega is the first to venture an alternative interpretation: "Goya reflects … the tragedies that those who were considered *afrancesados* or of French origin lived through. The wild-eyed soldier takes out his sword with angry resolve to cut the ropes with which the bodies appear hanged from the tree" ("Fatales" 35–6). Contemporary textual accounts of atrocities committed against Francophiles provide the context for her interpretation. She notes, in addition, that the lack of tension in the legs of the hanged man suggests that the soldier holding them is not pulling but rather preparing to break the body's fall ("Fatales" 36). The difficulties the image poses regarding the affiliation of the victim are in keeping with the way Goya's work often poses complex moral questions, regardless of who commits the atrocities. The "thing" that is "harsh" in this image speaks beyond the two sides of the conflict. Some of the standard translations of the caption into English include "This is too much!" and "That's tough," both of which approximate Goya's original but do not convey the same ambiguity over just what the "thing" is.

Print 32

Huxley draws attention to the symbolism of damaged trees and foliage and considers this one of the more harrowing images in which a withered tree plays a central role (7–8). Lafuente does the same, noting a connection between the trunk in this image and the role of foliage in Goya's 1813 paintings, *The Making of Bullets* and *The Making of Gun Powder in the Sierra de Tardienta.* Bozal also includes this print in his discussion of trees and plant life in the *Disasters* (*Imagen*, 207; *Goya. Nuevas*, 129–30). Lecaldano is, to my knowledge, the first to comment on the possible addressees of the caption: "[the victim] asks about the why of such a fate; all of this contrasts with the indifference of the tormentors, who also are not up to answering the terrible question" (84). Symmons notes compositional parallels between this image and Flaxman's illustration for Canto 22 of Dante's *Inferno.*

Dérozier calls attention to the caption's link with Print 2 ("With reason or without it"), arguing that while reason may have offered Goya some solace initially, at this point in the series he despairs of it (892). This interpretation seems a misreading, given that Print 2 in combination with Print 3 simply does not communicate belief in reason. If there is a crisis in Goya's commitment to the ideals of enlightened rationalism, it is on display from the outset of the series. Licht has developed at length the parallels that Goya seems to suggest between the tree trunk and the leg of one of his assailants:

> Here the insentient tree trunk is given the same moral importance as the soldier who brutally shoves his foot against the garroted man's shoulder. The tree becomes an accomplice to murder … But there is more. The strokes of the burin used for the description of the form and surface of the tree trunk are exactly duplicated in the left leg of the soldier who pushes forward with his left foot … Leg and tree are (visually) equally responsible for the death of the partisan. (193)

Wolf comments that in Prints 32 and 33, as well as in later allegorical prints, "the line that divides the audience and the performance … can be unstable" (42). Vega notes that the print belongs to the most intense catalogue of horrors in the series (Prints 31 to 40), which she relates to Giovanni Batista Casti's poetic work *Gli Animali Parlanti* ("Fatales" 35–6). For more extensive theoretical deliberation on the relationship between war and forms of violence that exceed the will to kill, see Miller.

Print 33

Lecaldano underscores the way Goya's rendering of the soldiers calls attention to their impassive demeanour: "Here it is not about the fury that leads to delirious actions, but rather about cold, blind determination. Goya condemns those who act and those who do not oppose themselves to the act" (84). Bozal observes that Goya's composition emphasizes the proximity of perpetrators and victims: "Tormentors and executioners are so close to their victims that they almost form the same group" (*Imagen* 207). Wolf remarks on the secularization of the iconography of martyrdom in images such as this one (46–7). Licht sees in the non-naturalist elements of the image evidence of a broader tendency in the *Disasters*:

> Frequently, under the impact of the chaos, forms lose substance and voids gain density for no apparent reason. Returning to Plate 33, we find that a spectral form, resembling in silhouette the French Mamelukes uniform, rises just above the blade of the executioner's sword. Are we to think of this shape as a person, as the shadow of a person, or as a capricious form denoting some other, enigmatic presence? At the same time, an unexplained shape appears between the two spectators in the upper left portion of the plate. Here instead of the space that ought to separate the shoulder of

> the man in the white headpiece from the chest of the man in the black cap, we find a mass of etched lines that are identical with those used to describe the tree. (200)

While one can interpret such details expressively, with Licht, as saying something about the warped perceptions of the world that accompany wartime violence, my point is that such elements almost by definition puncture naturalist illusion for a moment, reminding viewers that, for all of its gruesomeness, what is before them is an image.

Vega speculates that the mutilations in Prints 32 and 33 might be understood as vengeance for earlier atrocities committed against the French or their Spanish supporters, the *afrancesados* ("Fatales" 35–6). While such information can inform our understanding of the war years historically, the captions to these prints, which easily could have signalled such content – we might imagine *Cruel venganza!* ("Cruel vengeance!") – do not speak to motivations. The motivations of perpetrators, like reasons and justifications, are often ancillary to Goya's concerns. Volland cites this print as an example of a broader tendency she sees in the *Disasters*. Whereas female victims, she argues, tend to retain their sexual allure in Goya's prints, male victims are much more frequently rendered as asexual, feminized, or castrated (168–71). This may be the case, but male victims are often also presented in statuesque forms that raise unsettling issues concerning attractive images of victims more generally. The victim in this image is in effect "feminized," as Volland contends, but the narrative content of the scene and Goya's pictorial approach to his subject are two separate matters. Nothing in the way Goya renders the dead man's body suggests that *the artist* has a feminizing agenda.

Cavarero provides a useful analysis of mutilation as an assault on the dignity of the human being "in its being as singular body": "Death may transform it [the body] into a cadaver, but it does not offend its dignity or at any rate does not do so as long as the dead body preserves its figural unity … [Mutilation] aims to destroy the uniqueness of the body, tearing at its constitutive vulnerability. What is at stake is not the end of human life but the human condition itself, as incarnated in the singularity of vulnerable bodies" (8). In prints such as this one, Goya seems to anticipate such insights by pointedly gesturing to the fact that "more" can in fact be done to the enemy after his or her death. Miller draws on several of Goya's prints in order to argue that our tendency to conceptualize war primarily in terms of killing and death misses something fundamental about the nature of its violence: "There is an element in war, lying precisely in its relationship with violence, that remains uncontrollable, or more precisely that associates the essence of warfare with an excess of the means over their hypothetic finality, making warfare exceed its own definitions and essence" (28). This print, which is Goya's most explicit verbal meditation on excess, does not form part of Miller's reflections, but to view the forty-seven *Disasters* on war horrors in sequence is to move progressively closer to these sorts of truths about war.

Prints 34, 35, and 36

Piot notes the range of emotions in the crowd in Print 34: "some cry and some hold their heads in their hands." He associates the spectacle in Print 35 with the kinds of reprisals that took place routinely in Valencia (361–2). Most other nineteenth-century commentary is restricted to technical details. To my knowledge, Lafuente was the first to draw attention to the affinities between Print 34 and one of Goya's earliest prints, *El agarrotado* (The Garrotted Man). He reads the caption to Print 34 as a commentary on the arbitrary and unjust nature of the sentence the condemned have received: "in the harshest moments of the French occupation, starting with the sorrowful days that followed the 2nd of May, it was enough for a weapon to be found in the pockets of a Spanish countryman for him to be condemned to the death penalty" (*Los Desastres* 159). He also notes that the caption in Print 35 may refer to the fact that, while some of the executed men wear their arms around their necks (thus attesting to their crime), others do not: "others were executed with dark and unclear pretexts, and in truth *one cannot know why*" (*Los Desastres* 160). For a historical overview of executions by garrotte in Spain, see Sueiro.

Glendinning draws attention to the verbal link between Prints 34 and 35. Building on earlier comments by Lafuente, Sayre expands on Southey and Lovett in order to confirm the history of the French prohibition against carrying arms (175). Lecaldano highlights the way the details of the face in Print 34 convey the victim's agony (86). Wolf discusses Print 34 as an example of Goya's abiding interest in the psychological effects that viewing suffering has on onlookers: "a whole range of expressions can be made out in the sketchily but carefully drawn faces in the crowd" (43). Bozal argues that tree trunks, branches, and sticks belong, symbolically, to the same world as gallows, garrottes, and other implements of violence (*Goya: Nuevas* 129–30). Vega draws on contemporary wartime accounts in order to corroborate the laws prohibiting arms as well as the punishment. For her, the victims in both prints have been rendered to suggest that they posed little or no threat but were simply unlucky ("Fatales" 36). She additionally reminds readers that pocket knives – the putative crime in Print 34 – were everyday implements, particularly among the common people ("Las estampas" 170).

Piot is one of the earliest scholars to draw attention to the soldier's expression in Print 36: "A soldier is in front of a hanged man whom he appears to contemplate with pleasure" (361–2). Beruete considers the rendering of the soldier a grotesque detail that detracts from the detailed rendering of the hanged man (82). Lafuente reminds readers that historical accounts of the period often referenced the way bodies were left to hang along Spain's roadways: "trees offered their harvest of death; patriots whom the French army hanged with the least pretext" (*Los Desastres* 160). For many, the soldier's nationality is Polish; others refer to him as French. Emphasis on nationality tends to miss the moral rather than nationalistic framework that informs the *Disasters* more generally. Sayre sees a contrast between the soldier's expression in this print and the expressions of the soldiers in Print 33. If there is a contrast, however, it is the contrast between indifference in the earlier print and apparent bemusement in this one.

Lecaldano suggests that it is boredom in the soldier's face and compares him to a workman waiting to go home (90). Dérozier notes that this print serves as a transition from Prints 34 and 35, which in her view reference Inquisitorial violence, and the prints that will follow, where the gruesome extremes of bodily violence become more pronounced

(897). Hoffman links the soldier's pose to Goya's famous *Capricho* 43 ("The Dream/Sleep of Reason Produces Monsters"), which also draws on the melancholy pose (135). Bozal makes a similar connection: "a 'dreaming' executioner contemplates his work and reminds us of the other dreamer, whose sleeping reason produced monsters" (*Imagen* 208). Wolf underscores the parallels between the soldier and the notional viewer: "In Goya's print, the single soldier, viewed close up and individualized, in combination with the technical subtlety of the etched lines and aquatint tone, seduces us to became as transfixed as the soldier: we are simultaneously fascinated and repulsed" (38). Licht comments: "The soldier … looking up at his handiwork with the self-satisfied, quasi-innocent smile of a simpleton who has done his job and confidently expects his share of praise is a ferocious indictment of murder excused by being commanded" (196). Vega notes: "The violence of the scene does not arise … from the death, nor from the face of the hanged man, nor from the abuse of nature. One finds the violence in that figure that placidly rests to contemplate the reality before his eyes." She goes on to suggest that Goya is invoking the tradition of the *miles gloriosus* or "swaggering soldier," and that the expression on the soldier's face signals pride in his work ("Fatales" 37–8). Together, the three prints discussed here are a fine example of the conceptual richness of Goya's work that can be lost when individual *Disasters* are discussed without reference to their position in the series. Print 36, for example, has often been reproduced without its caption or discussion of its role as the culminating moment in a three-print sequence.

Print 37

Lafuente comments on the caption as follows: "This is worse, one hundred times worse than death for the poor tortured victim – it seems here that he is a Spanish guerrilla fighter – and worse too for the moral appraisal of the executioners. The impressive print … puts before our eyes the refinement of human cruelty which is capable of advancing beyond death" (*Los Desastres* 77). Glendinning cites this print as an example of the textual links that often bind prints together ("El asno" 228). Sayre connects the print with reports of the kinds of reprisals imperial troops took after residents of the town of Chinchón killed French soldiers in December of 1808 (177). Lecaldano suggests that the scene is "worse" because death is coupled with torture and the purposeful exhibiting of the body (93). Hoffman sees parallels between the cut branch and the severed arm; he notes that often Goya will link the human form to trees in order to produce an "Überfigur" (136). Bozal makes similar observations, underscoring the relationship between the tree and the body: "the tree, itself tortured, becomes an element of torture: terrible nature has its way with the tortured man, as if horror were the only world possible. The union [between human and nature] that could produce joy has been inverted completely" ("El arbol" 129–30).

Volland cites the image as an example of the misogyny she attributes to Goya, arguing that the artist can only imagine male victims in feminized (i.e., castrated or penetrated) form (175–7). She seems in this regard not to distinguish between the gendered dimensions of the wartime violence Goya depicts, on one hand, and Goya's approach to gender as an artist on the other. Licht notes that "even deprived of its arms the figure retains a certain gesture, a certain eloquence. The exhaustion of the dimmed eyes, the mouth gone rigid in the last scream of pain, and the general contrapposto of the figure maintain a tenuous relationship with earlier, more classical conceptions of the human figure" (196). Vega describes the visual citation of the Belvedere Torso in detail:

> If we separate the trunk [of the body] from the head – which seems stuck on and not attached naturally – and from the legs, we realize that one of the eighteenth-century models of reference, the Belvedere Torso, has been transferred from the realm of beauty to the scene of torture. This classical sculptural monument, which Goya himself drew during his trip to Italy, is moulded delicately: with light dotting he introduces brief but eloquent shadows that convey the smoothness of the polished marble … This effect of sculpted stone is intensified by the way he has mutilated the forearm. ("Las estampas" 177)

Cascardi observes of Prints 33, 37, and 39 that, through visual reference to statuary, Goya takes aim at classical ideals of beauty, which are "subjected to ruination" (264). With the exception of Lafuente, who explores two possible ways of understanding the caption, there has been relatively little commentary on the complexities of its address (i.e., the question of for whom "This is worse.") Similarly, to my knowledge, there has been almost no commentary on how the visual citation of the Belvedere Torso within the image bears on one's understanding of the caption. Regardless of how one approaches the question of why "This is worse," the print is a good example of the complex conceptual work Goya's captions often elicit.

Print 38

Mélida misconstrues Goya as a partisan patriot based on the caption: "Readers will have noticed that in all the legends to these prints Goya shows himself to be more supportive of the national cause. The truth is that the scenes represented in them are so cruel, so inappropriate for civilized armies, that they cannot help but excite the indignation of even the coldest spirit" (274). Such an interpretation, however, runs counter to the basic moral position – clearly expressed in Prints 2 and 3 – that Goya advances across the series. Muñoz disparages the quality of the print and similarly argues for a nationalist interpretation of the caption: "We only applaud the noble enthusiasm for the national cause and the hatred for the Vandalic invader that palpitates in the work" (381). There is nothing within the series, however, that would prompt readers to conclude that the French were distinctively more barbaric than the Spanish during the war. The patriotism of early critics seems to have muted their sensibility to Goya's humanitarian denunciation of the violence on both sides of conflict. For a useful overview of the history of the concept of barbarism in Europe, see Boltesi.

Beruete comments that despite many technical infelicities, Goya was successful in conveying the victim's "efforts and desperation," even as his back is turned to viewers (83).

Lafuente sees "an execution with large, not excessively careful figures. Now we have a firing-squad execution, in the middle of a field, doubtless the consequence of a guerrilla action" (*Los Desastres* 162). Lecaldano speculates that firing at the victim's back intentionally dishonours him, suggesting that he may have been a traitor (94). Dérozier observes that the caption highlights Goya's "moral indignation" (900). Bozal includes this image in his discussion of trees and plant life more generally in the *Disasters* (*Imagen* 207). Licht notes that "the exclamatory *Barbarians*! (Bárbaros!) of the caption stands in strongest contrast to the calm, almost playful professionalism of the marksmen" (196). Vega draws on historical accounts that refer to the routine practice of executing prisoners if they were unable to keep pace with their captors on the march. She observes that "the ignominious way in which the victim has been tied to the tree, which is the only way to keep his body upright," suggests that the execution in this print is likely to be an illustration of the practice ("Las estampas" 181).

Print 39

A common mistranslation of the caption to this print has been "A great deed! – *against* the dead!," which misses the instrumentalization of the body parts for purposes of display as conveyed by the original Spanish – *Con muertos!* ("With the dead!"). Brunet praises Goya's execution, which he believes makes up for the lower quality of the previous print (54). Muñóz considers the print to be of exceptionally high quality: "The drawing is perfect. Through dry point, the author has given the bodies great relief, and with the aquatint in the background a pleasant tone" (382). Beruete sees a strong thematic and technical relationship between Print 37 and Print 39, and many subsequent scholars have concurred (83). For Lafuente the identity of the victims is somewhat uncertain: "We do not know, by the way, if it is Frenchmen or Spaniards who committed the fierce savagery of dismembering in this way one of the cadavers that hang from a tree in Print 39, although by the features of the torn off head, by its broad cheeks and mustached face [stereotypically French features] we suppose that the atrocity can be attributed to Spanish guerrilla fighters" (*Los Desastres* 163).

Lecaldano notes that "The body-parts hang like the wasted parts of men who shortly before were palpitating, thinking beings" (96). Dérozier sees this print as the climax of the sequence that begins with Print 31 (901). For Tomlinson, the evocation of classical norms of beauty signals Goya's understanding that classical modes of representation cannot account adequately for his subject matter. Vega finds echoes of Tytios or Marsyas in the inverted victim on the left, and she links the victim in the centre to one of Goya's prints on torture, "La seguridad del reo no exige tormento" (The securing of the convict does not call for torture). She also notes the way the reference to classical statuary in the inverted torso "prompts reflection" ("Grande" 305–7). Hughes makes similar observations: "This is a sickeningly effective play on the neoclassical cult of the antique fragment. Bits and pieces of human bodies … are hung on a tree, to terrify the passerby. They remind us that, if only they had been marble and the work of their destruction had been done by time rather than sabers, neoclassicists like Mengs would have been in esthetic raptures over them" (295).

Licht discusses the mutilations in Print 37 and Print 39 as examples of Goya's approach to the human figure: "The body of man, for untold centuries represented as an object of reverence, is for the first time rendered as corrupt and repulsive, bereft of nobility, and bearing no trace of the spirit that once inhabited it … In plate 39, we have arrived at a point at which the human body turns to carrion that is no different from the carrion of animals" (196). While his comments are persuasive, viewers who proceed through the series in sequence may well recall that long before Plate 39, Goya has repeatedly underscored war's capacity to turn the human body into an object of revulsion (see, for example, Plate 12, Plate 18, or the piled bodies of the dead in Plates 22 and 23). At the same time, even in this culminating print, the bodies of the victims are more than mere carrion. The citation of classical statuary and the ambivalence of the caption's address, which applies to the scene and to the image Goya has made, are examples of the way Goya reflects on the relationship between his own "doing" as an artist and the violent, artistic "doing" of the perpetrators.

Print 40

Almost from the outset, critical commentary on this print has been at somewhat of a loss to explain its meaning. Mélida notes that it is virtually impossible to unravel the allegorical meaning of the image (275), and Brunet similarly observes the difficulty of interpreting the print (54). Beruete believes that the allegory refers to a concrete historical personage who has been lost to later generations; he also notes the strangeness of a masculine figure wearing what appears to be a skirt (83). Dodgson sees a connection between the beast in this print and a very similar "monster" at the end of the entire series, Print 81. Based on the similarities, he interprets the creature as an allegorical representation of war (6).

Lafuente develops an extensive interpretation along similar lines. He sees the creature as a representation of the "Great Beast" of the Apocalypse, understood as war. For him the caption alludes to the human figure, understood as a representation of the Spanish people: "The attacker's victory seems anything but sure, but whatever the case, *he gets something out of it*, and that is what Goya has wanted to express" (*Los Desastres* 64–5). Precisely because the outcome of the struggle is not clear, however, it seems more likely that the caption is intentionally open-ended and equally applicable to both sides of the struggle. Gassier is baffled by the allegory: "Is it about the struggle against obscurantism, or to the contrary, about submission to the dark powers that govern the world? One more ambiguity posed by Goya" (248–9). Lecaldano follows Lafuente: "perhaps Goya has wanted simply to represent the people, who with such poor means but thanks to their ardour are able to land a blow against the war-monster, making it not impotent, but at least weaker" (100). It seems difficult, however, to imagine Goya rallying behind the Spanish people, given his extraordinarily critical portrayal of "the people" as both willing spectators and perpetrators of horrific violence in many earlier prints.

Vega has developed the most extensive interpretation of the print as a representation of Great Britain. Drawing on historical accounts of the day, she reminds readers that Spain's official ally raped and pillaged Spanish towns with almost as much frequency as the French imperial army. In light of this context, she takes the beast to be "the English Bulldog that gets something out of the Peninsular War" (*Francisco* 39). While the reconstruction of Great Britain's role in the Peninsular War is rich and suggestive, there is little about the image itself to suggest that the beast should be understood as a bulldog. My interpretation of the print as a bitter acknowledgment that "something is to be gained," despite the catastrophes of war, is premised on the idea that Goya is morally consistent across the series. In earlier *Disasters* (Prints 16 and 24, for example), Goya also comments caustically on the material interests that drive war.

Prints 41, 42, and 43

Early commentary on Print 41 (Mélida, Brunet) tries to link the scene with a specific historical event: the sacking and burning of the town of Torquemada by the French General Lesalle's troops. Beruete comments on Goya's success in rendering the running figures, praising "the spontaneity of this group in which terrified individuals flee, they run, they fall, and in horror they get away from the catastrophe" (84). Lafuente notes that the print belongs to a cluster of images dedicated to fleeing victims (Prints 41–5), and he draws attention to Goya's masterful manipulation of tonal contrast (*Los Desastres* 164). Sayre sees in the print a possible reference to the bombardment of Zaragoza. Both Lafuente and Lecaldano, however, mention that while the sacking of Torquemada could be a reference, such events were so frequent that it makes little sense to try to pin down one particular episode. The critical consensus concerning the generic rather than loco-specific thrust of the *Disasters* is now a mainstay of its critical reception. Vega notes that if the print does refer to Zaragoza, it departs from conventional depictions of the city, which focused on its ruins as a testament of heroic resistance ("Fatales" 35).

Mélida was quick to associate Print 42 with Goya's frequent satires of the clergy (276). Brunet similarly draws attention to Goya's tendency towards caricature in his depictions of the religious establishment (54). Muñoz notes, "the stupid facial expressions of the religious men provoke more hilarity than compassion in the midst of their tragedy" (382). Lafuente observes that both Prints 42 and 43 take up the same theme: "these are friars fleeing in an open field. The flight could just as easily refer to the proximity of the enemy as it could symbolize the French hostility to religious orders, which lead to the intruder king's decree dismantling them" (*Los Desastres* 66). Lecaldano suggests that the image is showing a world turned on its head: "professional men of peace have been transformed, and they propagate violence" (106). Vega notes that because of its possible allegorical registers, these images might well be categorized as "caprichos enfáticos" ("Fatales" 39–40.).

Prints 44 and 45

Brunet takes Print 44 to be based on something Goya actually saw, while noting that the image combines "the grotesque" (i.e., the priest) and "the pathetic" (i.e., the mother and child) (54). Beruete also understands the caption as a straightforward assertion by

Goya: "The engraver saw the scenes, he felt them, and afterwards – a marvellous artist – he endowed his creations with the intense emotion that he felt" (85). Lafuente is similarly convinced: "we are impressed by Goya's quasi-documentary affirmation … that in the epigraph [i.e., the caption] assures us of the faithful testimony he offers us" (*Los Desastres* 89). He and others speculate that the artist would likely have been able to witness such a scene during his trip to Zaragoza in the fall of 1808.

Dérozier argues that "I saw it" ought to be read as a reference to the priest's behaviour in what amounts to a moral calling out of the self-interested stance of the clergy during the war (907). Wolf is the first to more fully explore the ambiguity of the "it" mentioned in the caption, noting that it could equally name what the mother and child are looking at or what Goya himself witnessed. She links the caption to similar affirmations elsewhere in Goya, including *Tauromaquia* 21 and *Album C* 87 (39–40). Cascardi observes: "we do not really know whether these words give voice to what the crowd has seen and attempts to name – the invisible thing from which it flees – or whether the words articulate what the artist claims to have witnessed" (127). Vega draws on historical sources to substantiate the frequency with which civilian populations were displaced during the war ("Fatales" 27). For Hughes, the anticlerical, satirical thrust of the print is somewhat at odds with the claim made in the caption: "*Yo lo vi.* 'I saw it,' he inscribed under plate 44 … in which refugees from a country village are fleeing from the advance, unseen by us, of the French soldiers; but one can't help wondering if he did see that fiercely satirical conjuncture of the mother urging her terrified child to follow her and not look back, and the village priest on the left, clutching the possessions most dear to him, a bulging money bag" (272). It is not simply the satirical facets of the print that complicate the meaning of the caption. Like other *Disasters* that thematize looking in their captions – see Print 26, for example – Goya's withholding of the source of the terror underscores the artifice of the composition.

Appraisals of Print 45 generally find it technically less successful than Print 44. Sayre's analysis of the second print suggests that Goya executed it some ten years after Print 44 (187). If that is the case, the two prints together offer a wonderful example of the expressive effects of Goya's captions, which in this case make complex conceptual links between two *Disasters* made many years apart. As Lafuente notes, together the two prints highlight the very different circumstances under which civilians fled: "In some cases villagers warned in time move to safety without too much urgency, taking with them what they can of their meagre belongings" (*Goya* 66).

Prints 46 and 47

Mélida considers Print 46 to be of inferior quality, and he conjectures that the caption, "This is bad," could be an expression of Goya's own negative aesthetic judgment about his work. Leaving aside the question of the print's quality, Mélida's comment makes clear that early nineteenth-century scholars of the *Disasters* understood that Goya's captions might address not only the scene depicted but also the image *qua* image. Brunet picks up the same idea: "Goya, unhappy with his own work, refers to it this way in his title" (55). The most common English translation of the caption is "This is bad." Lafuente draws attention to the general context: "In this print Goya underscores the French army's wrath at the religious orders based on their profound anticlericalism, on one hand, and on the attraction of looting convents, which contributed to the numerous killings of monks" (*Los Desastres* 167).

Glendinning cites Prints 46 and 47, among others, as examples of *Disasters* that are linked to one another grammatically ("El asno"). Lecaldano notes that these two prints seem to soften Goya's usual anticlericalism (116). Dérozier similarly comments that, coming in the wake of the earlier, critical images of monks fleeing, the two prints mark a shift in Goya's attitude (909). The softening of Goya's critical stance vis-à-vis the clergy is all the more striking precisely because it comes in the closing images of the forty-seven-print sequence on violence. Vega draws extensively on historical sources that attest to the widespread plundering of churches and convents. She underscores the way Print 47 emphasizes the material dimensions of the looting rather than their sacrilegious tenor ("Fatales" 40).

Afterword

See Licht (182–3) and Basels, Bordes, and Matilla for approaches to the *Disasters* as quasi-photographic. Ciofalo emphasizes the artist's subjective vision in his exploration of Goya's self-portraits, and Bozal (*Goya y el gusto*) understands the warping of pictorial space as an ultimately more realistic rendering of wartime than conventional pictorial perspective. Bouvier links the visual codes of the *Disasters* to wartime trauma. An important intervention that resituates Goya within the complexities of the Spanish Enlightenment is Tomlinson (*Goya in the Twilight*). For a more recent, philosophically oriented discussion of Goya's oeuvre within the coordinates of enlightened critique, see Cascardi. Particularly apposite to the *Disasters* as I have discussed them in this book is his observation that, in Goya, "the work of art is at once *like* the world and fundamentally unlike it" (98). Following Santiáñez, Cascardi suggests that war's destruction operates not only at the level of the represented but also at the level of Goya's visual idiom itself, where we find "a destruction of the logic of spatial organization, and with that, a destruction of compositional principals" (266). For the relationship between the emerging sciences of the 1700s and the understanding of images as illusions, see Vega (*Ciencia*). For a classic overview of Roman satire, see Knoche. For discussion of the tradition of eighteenth-century visual satire, see Mansfield and Malone.

Bibliography

Adorno, Theodor. *Prisms*. Cambridge, MA: MIT Press, 1983.

Alvarez Barrientos, Joaquín. *La Guerra de la Independencia en la cultura española*. Madrid: Siglo XXI de España Editores, 2008.

Alvarez Junco, José. *Mater dolorosa: la idea de España en el siglo XIX*. Madrid: Taurus, 2001.

Artola, Miguel. *Los afrancesados*. Madrid: Alianza, 2008.

– *La Guerrra de la Independencia*. Madrid: Espasa Calpe, 2011.

Askin, Kelly Dawn. *War Crimes against Women: Prosecution in International War Crimes Tribunals*. The Hague: M. Nijhof, 1997.

Aymes, Jean René. *La Guerra de la Independencia en España (1808–1814)*. Madrid: Siglo XXI de España editores, 2008/Lleida: Milenios, 2009.

Barthes, Roland. "The Death of the Author." In *Image-Music-Text*, 142–8. New York: Macmillan, 1978.

Basels, Sandra, Juan Bordes, and José Matilla. *Goya, cronista de todas las guerras: "Los Desastres" y la fotografía de guerra*. Las Palamas: Centro Atlántico de Arte Moderno, 2009.

Bates, Brian, and John Cleese. *The Human Face*. New York: Dorling Kindersley, 2001.

Baucom, Ian. "The *Disasters of War*: On Inimical Life." *Polygraph* 18 (2006): 167–90.

Bell, David. *The First Total War: Napoleon's Europe and the Birth of Warfare As We Know It*. New York: Houghton Mifflin, 2007.

Benjamin, Walter. *The Arcades Project*. Cambridge, MA: Belknap Press, 2002.

Benson, Ciaran. *The Absorbed Self: Pragmatism, Psychology and Aesthetic Experience*. New York: Prentice Hall, 1993.

Beruete, Aureliano. *Goya grabador*. Madrid: Blass, 1918.

Blanchot, Maurice. *The Writing of the Disaster*. Trans. Ann Smock. Lincoln: University of Nebraska Press, 1995.

Blas, Javier, Isla Aguilar, and José Matilla. *El libro de los desastres de la guerra*. 2 vols. Madrid: Museo Nacional del Prado, 2000.

Boltesi, Maria, ed. *Barbarism Revisited: New Perspectives on an Old Concept.* Leiden: Brill/Rodopi, 2015.

Bouvier, Paul. "'Yo lo vi.' Goya Witnessing the Disasters of War: An Appeal to the Sentiment of Humanitarianism." *International Review of the Red Cross* 93.884 (2011): 1107–33.

Bozal, Valeriano. "El arbol goyesco." In *Goya, nuevas visions. Homenaje a Enrique Lafuente Ferrari*, ed. Isabel García de la Rasilla and Francisco Calvo Serraller, 129–30. Madrid: Fundación Amigos del Prado, 1987.

– *Goya. Nuevas visiones.* Madrid: Amigos del Museo del Prado, 1987.

– *Goya y el gusto moderno.* Madrid: Alianza, 1994.

– *Imagen de Goya.* Barcelona: Lumen, 1983.

Branche, Raphaëlle, and Fabrice Virgili. *Rape in Wartime.* New York: Palgrave Macmillan, 2013.

Brophy, John. *The Face in Western Art.* London: Harrap, 1963.

Brunet, Pierre Gustave. *Etude sur Francisco Goya: sa vie et ses travaux.* Paris: Aubry, 1865.

Butler, Judith. *Frames of War: When Is Life Grievable?* London/New York: Verso, 2009.

Carderera, Valentín. "François Goya: sa vie, ses dessins et ses eaux-fortes." *Gazette des Beaux-Arts* 15 (1863): 243–4.

Cascardi, Anthony. *Francisco de Goya and the Art of Critique.* New York: Zone Books, 2022.

Castells, Irene, Gloria Espigado, and María Cruz Romero. *Heroinas y patriotas. Mujeres de 1808.* Madrid: Cátedra, 2009.

Cavarero, Adriana. *Horrorism: Naming Contemporary Violence.* New York: Columbia University Press, 2007.

Chambers, Ross. *Untimely Interventions: AIDS Writing, Testimonial, and the Rhetoric of Haunting.* Ann Arbor: University of Michigan Press, 2004.

Church, Jennifer. *Possibilities of Perception.* Oxford: Oxford University Press, 2013.

Ciofalo, John. *The Self-Portraits of Francisco Goya.* Cambridge: Cambridge University Press, 2000.

Cook, Bernard. *Women and War: A Historical Encyclopedia from Antiquity to the Present.* Santa Barbara: ABC-CLIO, 2006.

Crowther, Paul. *Phenomenology of the Visual Arts (Even the Frame).* Stanford: Stanford University Press, 2009.

Demange, Christian. *El dos de mayo. Mito y fiesta nacional (1808–1958).* Madrid: Marcial Pons, 2004.

Dérozier, Claudette. *La guerre d'Independence espagnol a travers l'estampe (1808–1814).* Vol. 2. Lille: Université Lille III, 1976.

Derrida, Jacques. *The Truth in Painting.* Chicago: University of Chicago Press, 1987.

Dodgson, Campbell. *Los Desastres de la Guerra.* Oxford: Oxford University Press, 1933.

Dudziak, Mary. *War-Time: An Idea, Its History and Its Consequences.* Oxford: Oxford University Press, 2012.

Dufour, Gerard. *Goya durante la Guerra de la Independencia.* Madrid: Cátedra, 2008.

Dwyer, Philip. "'It Still Makes Me Shudder': Memories of Massacres and Atrocities during the Revolutionary and Napoleonic Wars." *War in History* 16.4 (2009): 381–405.

Edwards, Peter, Karl Enenkel, and Elspeth Graham, eds. *The Horse as Cultural Icon: The Real and Symbolic Horse in the Early Modern World.* Boston: Brill, 2012.

Enos, Theresa, ed. *Encyclopedia of Rhetoric and Composition: Communication from Ancient Times to the Information Age.* New York: Garland, 1996.

Esdalie, Charles. *Fighting Napoleon: Guerrillas, Bandits and Adventurers in Spain (1808–1814).* New Haven: Yale University Press, 2004.

Favret, Mary. *War at a Distance: Romanticism and the Making of Modern Wartime.* Princeton: Princeton University Press, 2014.

Fernández, Elena. *Mujeres en la guerra de la independencia.* Madrid: Silex, 2009.

Foucault, Michel. "What Is an Author?" In *Textural Strategies: Perspectives in Post-Structuralist Criticism*, ed. Josué Harari, 141–60. Ithaca: Cornell University Press, 1979.

Fraser, Donald. *Napoleon's Cursed War: Popular Resistance in the Spanish Peninsular War (1808–1814).* London/New York: Verso, 2008.

Fried, Michael. *Absorption and Theatricality: Painting and Beholder in the Age of Diderot.* Berkeley: University of California Press, 1980.

Friedländer, Saul. *Probing the Limits of Representation: Nazism and the "Final Solution."* Cambridge, MA: Harvard University Press, 1992.

Gadamer, Hans Georg. *Truth and Method.* London/New York: Continuum, 2011.

Gallop, Jane. *The Deaths of the Author: Reading and Writing in Time.* Durham, NC: Duke University Press, 2011.

Gassier, Pierre. *Dibujos de Goya. Estudios para grabados y punturas.* Barcelona: Noguer, 1975.

Genette, Gerard. *Paratexts: Thresholds of Interpretation (Literature, Culture, Theory).* Cambridge: Cambridge University Press, 1997.

Glendinning, Nigel. "El asno cargado de reliquias en los *Deastres de la Guerra* de Goya." *Archivo Español de Arte* 25.139 (1962): 221–30.

– *Goya and His Critics.* New Haven: Yale University Press, 1977.

Goldstein, Joshua. *War and Gender: How Gender Shapes the War System and Vice Versa.* Cambridge/New York: Cambridge University Press, 2001.

Gombrich, E.H. *Art and Illusion: A Study in the Psychology of Pictorial Representation.* Princeton: Princeton University Press, 1960.

Goya, Francisco. *The Disasters of War.* New York: Dover, 1967.

Heras Bretín, Rut. "Los escritos de Goya en sus dibujos: intencionados, literarios, y muy misteriosos." *El Pais*, 20 February 2020. Accessed 25 March 2020. https:elpais.com/cultura/2020/02/05/actualidad/1580865157_712725.html.

Herrera, Heidi. "She Does Not Want: Wartime Rape in Goya's Disasters of War." *AWE (A Woman's Experience).* Vol 5, Article 5. Accessed 4 April 2020. https://scholarsarchive.byu.edu/awe/vol5/iss1/5.

Hobsbawm, Eric. *Nations and Nationalism since 1780: Programme, Myth, Reality.* Cambridge: Cambridge University Press, 1990.

Hobson, Marian. *The Object of Art: The Theory of Illusion in Eighteenth-Century France.* Cambridge: Cambridge University Press, 1982.

Hoffman, Werner. *Goya. Das Zeitalter der Revolutionen. 1789–1830.* Hamburg/Munich: Hamburger Kunsthalle/Prestel Verlag, 1980.

Horkheimer, Max, and Theodor Adorno. *Dialectic of Enlightenment. Philosophical Fragments.* Stanford: Stanford University Press, 1987.

Hughes, Robert. *Goya.* New York: Knopf, 2003.

Huxley, Aldous. *The Complete Etchings of Goya with Foreword by Aldous Huxley.* London: Allan Wingate, 1959.

Jauss, Hans. *Toward an Aesthetic of Reception. (Theory and History of Literature).* Minneapolis: University of Minnesota Press, 1982.

Johnson, James. *Just War Tradition and the Restraint of War: A Moral and Historical Inquiry.* Princeton: Princeton University Press, 1981.

Juretchke, Hans. *Los afrancesados en la Guerra de la Independencia: su génesis, desarrollo, y consecuencias históricas.* Madrid: Rialp, 1962.

Kamen, Henry. *The Disinherited: Exile and the Making of Spanish Culture (1492–1975).* New York: HarperCollins, 2007.

Kaplan, Brett. *Unwanted Beauty: Aesthetic Pleasure in Holocaust Representation.* Urbana: University of Illinois Press, 2007.

Knoche, Ulrich. *Roman Satire.* Trans. Edwin Ramage. Bloomington: Indiana University Press, 1975.

Lafuente Ferrari, Enrique. *Los Desastres de la Guerra de Goya y sus dibujos preparatorios.* Barcelona: Instituto Amatller de Arte Hispánico, 1952.

– *Goya: "El 2 de Mayo" y "Los fusilamientos de la Moncloa."* Barcelona: Juventud, 1946.

Lang, Berel. *Holocaust Representation: Art within the Limits of History and Ethics.* Baltimore: Johns Hopkins University Press, 2003.

Lanzmann, Claude. "Holocauste, la représentation impossible." *Le Monde*, 3 March 1994: 7.

Las Casas, Fray Bartolomé de. *Brevísima relación de la destrucción de las Indias.* Madrid: Cátedra, 2006.

Lecaldano, Paolo. *Goya. I Disastri della Guerra.* Milan: Arnoldo Mondadori, 1975.

Licht, Fred. *Goya.* New York: Abbeville Press, 2001.

Litz, Brett, et al. "Moral Injury and Moral Repair in War Veterans: A Preliminary Model and Intervention Strategy." *Clinical Psychology Review* 29 (2009): 695–706.

López Tabar, Juan. *Los famosos traidores: los afrancesdos durante la crisis del Antiguo Régimen.* Madrid: Biblioteca Nueva, 2010.

Lovett, Gabriel. *Napoleon and the Birth of Modern Spain.* New York: New York University Press, 1965.

Magliola, Robert. *Phenomenology and Literature: An Introduction.* West Lafayette, IN: Purdue University Press, 1977.

Magner, Lois, ed. *A History of Medicine*. New York: M. Dekker, 1992.

Mansfield, Elizabeth, and Kelly Malone, eds. *Seeing Satire in the Eighteenth Century*. Oxford: Voltaire Foundation, 2013.

Matilla, José Manuel. *Goya: luces y sombras*. Madrid: Museo del Prado, 2012.

– "Tristes presentimientos de lo que ha de acontecer." In *Goya en tiempos de guerra*, ed. Manuela Mena Marques. Exhibition catalogue. Madrid: Museo del Prado, 2008.

Mélida, Enrique. "Los Desastres de la Guerra. Colección de 80 láminas inventadas y grabadas al agua fuerte, por Don Francisco de Goya." *Arte en España. Revista quincenal de las artes del dibujo* 2.19–20 (1863): 266–81.

Miller, Steven. *War after Death. On Violence and Its Limits*. New York: Fordham University Press, 2014. Digital.

Montaigne, Michel. *The Complete Essays*. New York: Penguin, 1993.

Muñoz, Cipriano (Conde de la Viñaza). *Goya, su tiempo, su vida y sus obras*. Madrid: M.G. Hernández, 1887.

Murray, Clinton, Mary Hinkle, and Heather Yun. "History of Infections Associated with Combat-Related Injuries." *Journal of Trauma, Injury, Infection and Medical Care* 64.3 (March Supplement 2008): S221–S231.

Piot, Eugene. "Catalogue raisoneé de l'oeuvre gravé de Francisco de Goya y Lucientes." *Cabinet de l'amateur et de l'antiquaire. Revue des tableaux et des estampes anciennes, des objets d'art, d'antiquité et de Curiosité*. 4 vols. Paris: Bureau du Journal, 1842–6.

Pérez Sánchez, Alphonso, and Eleanor Sayre. *Goya y el espíritu de la ilustración*. Exhibition catalogue. Madrid: Museo del Prado, 1989.

Queralt del Hierro, María Pilar. *Agustina de Aragón: la mujer y el mito*. Madrid: La Esfera de los Libros, 2008.

Ranciere, Jacques. *The Politics of Aesthetics: The Distribution of the Sensible*. London/ New York: Continuum, 2006.

Rothberg, Michael. *Multicultural Memory: Remembering the Holocaust in the Age of Decolonization*. Stanford: Stanford University Press, 2009.

Rothenberg, Gunther. *The Art of Warfare in the Age of Napoleon*. Bloomington: Indiana University Press, 1981.

Rousseau, Jean-Jacques. *The Basic Political Writings*. Ed. Donald A. Cress. London: Hackettt, 2012.

Said, Edward. *Beginnings: Intention and Method*. New York: Columbia University Press, 1985.

Santiáñez, Nil. *Goya/Clausewitz: Paradigmas de la guerra absoluta*. Barcelona: Alpha Decay, 2009.

Sanyal, Debarati. *Memory and Complicity: Migrations of Holocaust Remembrance*. New York: Fordham University Press, 2015.

Savedoff, Barbara. "Frames." *Journal of Aesthetics and Art Criticism* 57.3 (1999): 345–56.

Sayre, Eleanor. *The Changing Image: Prints by Francisco de Goya*. Boston: Museum of Fine Arts, 1974.

Schmitt, Carl. *Political Theology: Four Chapters on the Concept of Sovereignty*. Cambridge, MA: MIT Press, 1985.

Schulz, Andrew. *Goya's Caprichos: Aesthetics, Perception and the Body*. Cambridge: Cambridge University Press, 2005.

Sedlmayr, Hans. *Art in Crisis: The Lost Center*. Chicago: Henry Regnery, 1958.

Seifert, Ruth. "War and Rape: A Preliminary Analysis." In *Mass Rape: The War against Women in Bosnia-Herzegovina*, ed. Alexandra Stiglmayer. Lincoln: University of Nebraska Press, 1994.

Silverman, Max. *Palimpsestic Memory: The Holocaust and Colonialism in French and Francophone Fiction and Film*. New York: Berghahn Books, 2013.

Simmel, Georg. "The Picture Frame: An Aesthetic Study." *Theory, Culture and Society* 11 (1994): 11–17.

Smith, Alan. "La recepción de la primera edición de *Los desastres de Guerra* en el Madrid del jóven Galdós." *Bulletin of Spanish Studies* 86.4 (2009): 459–74.

Sontag, Susan. *Regarding the Pain of Others*. London: Penguin Books, 2019.

Southey, Robert. *History of the Peninsular War*. London: J. Murray, 1823.

Stecker, Robert. *Aesthetics and the Philosophy of Art: An Introduction*. Lanham: Rowman and Littlefield, 2010.

Stoichita, Victor, and Anna Coderch. *Goya: The Last Carnival*. London: Reaktion Books, 1999.

Sueiro, Daniel. *Los verdugos españoles, história y actualidad del garrote vil*. Madrid: Alfaguara, 1971.

Symmons, Sarah. "John Flaxman and Francisco de Goya: Infernos Transcribed." *Burlington Magazine* 113.822 (September 1971): 508–12.

Tomlinson, Janis. *Goya: A Portrait of the Artist*. Princeton/Oxford: Princeton University Press, 2020.

– *Goya in the Twilight of Enlightenment*. New Haven: Yale University Press, 1992.

– *Goya's War: Los Desastres de la Guerra*. Claremont, CA: Pomona College Museum of Art, 2013.

– *Graphic Evolutions: The Print Series of Francisco Goya*. New York: Columbia University Press, 1989.

Tomlinson, Janis, ed. *Goya: Images of Women*. New Haven: Yale University Press, 2002.

Trezise, Thomas. *Witnessing Witnessing: On the Reception of Holocaust Survivor Testimony*. New York: Fordham University Press, 2013.

Van Gerwen, Rob, ed. *Richard Wollheim on the Art of Painting: Art as Representation and Expression*. Cambridge: Cambridge University Press, 2001.

Vega, Jesusa. *Ciencia, arte e ilusión en la España ilustrada*. Madrid: Consejo Superior de Investigaciones Científicas, 2010.

– "Las estampas de los *Desastres de la Guerra*." In *Estudios: Desastres de la Guerra*. Madrid: Planeta, 2008.

– "Fatales consecuencias de la Guerra, por Francisco de Goya pintor." In *Francisco de Goya grabador. Instantáneas: Caprichos*. Madrid: Caser, 1992/Madrid: Turner, 1992.

– *Francisco de Goya grabador: instantáneas. Caprichos*. Madrid: Caser, 1992.

– "Grande Hazaña! Con Muertos!" In *Goya y el espíritu de la ilustración*, ed. Alphonso Pérez Sanchaez and Eleanor Sayre. Exhibition catalogue. Madrid: Museo del Prado, 1988.

Volland, Gerlinde. *Männermacht und Frauenopfer: Sexualität und Gewalt bei Goya*. Berlin: Reimer, 1993.

Weissman, Gary. *Fantasies of Witnessing: Postwar Efforts to Experience the Holocaust*. Ithaca: Cornell University Press, 2004.

Williams, Gwynn. *Goya and the Impossible Revolution*. London: Pantheon, 1976.

Wilson-Bareau, Juliet. "Goya: *The Disasters of War*." In *Disasters of War: Callot, Goya, Dix*, 27–56. Manchester: National Touring Exhibitions, 1998.

Wolf, Reva. "Onlooker, Witness and Judge in Goya's Disasters of War." In *Fatal Consequences: Callot, Goya, and the Horrors of War*, 37–52. New Hampshire: Hood Museum of Art, 1990.

Wölfflin, Heinrich. *The Principles of Art History*. New York: Dover, 1950.

Wollheim, Richard. *Art and Its Objects*. Cambridge: Cambridge University Press, 1980.

Yriarte, Charles. *Goya: sa biographie, les fresques, les toiles, les tapisseries, les eaux-fortes et le catalogue d l'oeuvre*. Paris: Henry Plon, 1867.

Index

Adorno, Theodor, 228, 232

afrancesados: considered traitors to Spain, 17, 18–19, 250; mutilation, 254; victims of execution, 81, 160, 241, 248, 252

agarrotado, El (The Garrotted Man) (Goya), 255

Agony in the Garden, analogy, 21–2, 23, 229–30, 231

Agustina of Aragón (*La Artillera*), *48*, 50–1, 236–7

Album C (Goya), 261

Algún partido saca (He [or it] gets something out of it) (Print 40), *192*, 193, 195–7, 259–60

allegory, 195, 196–7, 204, 230, 259

Also. See *Tampoco* (Print 36)

Amarga presencia (Bitter presence) (Print 13), *76*, 77–9, 110, 240–1

animali parlanti, Gli (Casti), 253

aprovechar, 94–5, 242

Así sucedió (That's how it happened) (Print 47), *214*, 215, 216–17, 262

asymmetrical warfare, 100

Aún podrán servir (They will still be able to serve) (Print 24), *128*, 129, 131–4, 150, 247

Bailén, Battle of, 235–6, 238

barbarism, 189, 257

Bárbaros! (Barbarians!) (Print 38), *186*, 187–9, 257–8

Basels, Sandra, 227

battlefields: disagreement, 101, 243; hangings, *174*, 175, 178–9, 255–6; killing by partisans, *28*, 29–32, 232–3; mass graves, 105, *140*, 141; military divisions, 100–1; moving the wounded, *128*, 132; strategy and tactics, *98*, 99–100; successes, 99; tending to the wounded on, *42*, 43–6, *114*, 115–17, 125, *130*, 131, 235–6, 245, 246; witnessing, 100, 101, 104–5, 107, 116. *See also* corpses

Baucom, Ian, 231

beasts, allegory of struggle with, *192*, 193, 195–7, 259–60

beauty: in classical sculpture, 104, 105; contrasted to atrocity, 104–5, 143, 155, 182, 244–5, 257, 258

Because of a knife. See *Por una navaja*

beginnings: collection opening prints, 230; decision-making in creative expression, 11; *incipit* (it begins here), 11; shaping engagement of the arts, 12, 15, 19; sources of *Disasters*, 11–12; title pages, 12, *13*, 14, 228. *See also* presentiment

Belvedere Torso, 182, *183*, 257

Benjamin, Walter, 233
Beruete, Aureliano, 231, 240, 241–2, 245–50, 252, 255, 257, 258–60
Bien te se está (It serves you right) (Print 6), *42,* 43–6, 68, 117, 150, 235–6
Bitter presence. See *Amarga presencia*
Black Paintings (*Pinturas negras*) (Goya), 36, 220
boda, La (The Wedding) (Goya), 233
bodies: backs to executioners, 188, 257, 258; bestial presentation, 238; body–tree relationship, 188, 256, 258; depiction, 23, 251; faces of attendants, 133, 134, 245, 246, 249; faces of perpetrators, 110–11, 149, 150, 159–60, 163, 168, 250, 253; faces of victims, 109–10, 115, 117, 125, 132, 134, 137, 139, 142, 163–4, 248, 255; faces of women, 36; grotesque faces, 205, 215, 232–3; hands and feet, 29, 43, 44, 65, 104, 105, 137, 154, 203, 253; injuries, 133–4; naturalistic details, 116; necrophilia, 154, 251; nudity, 104, 143, 155, 204, 242–3, 244, 254; signs of pathos, 239; of soldiers, 94; of the wounded, 115, 132, 133–4. *See also* mutilation
bombardment of civilians, *152,* 153–6, 251
Bonaparte, Joseph, King of Spain, 3–4, 18
Bordes, Juan, 227
Bouvier, Paul, 262
Bozal, Valeriano, 230, 239, 241–2, 244, 248, 252–3, 256, 258, 262
Brunet, Pierre Gustave, 235, 237, 240–3, 246, 249–52, 258, 259, 260, 261
burials, *140,* 141–3, 249
Bury and be quiet. See *Enterrar y callar*
Butler, Judith, 241

Callot, Jacques, 241
cannons, 49, 50, 55, 78, 117
capital punishment. *See* executions
caprichos, Los (Goya): compared to *Disasters,* 205, 221, 232–3, 247, 248, 250, 256; language of captions, 226, 234, 236, 242; sequence, 226; triad of man, prostitute, and madam, 238
captions: absence of historical context, 126, 147, 232; addressing the dead, 105–6; ambiguity of language, 26–7, 78–9, 111–12, 138–9, 238, 249; ambiguity of voice, 5, 37, 44–5, 74–5, 116, 233–4; authorship, 226; back-and-forth associations, 62–3; caption–image interplay, 5, 23, 40, 46, 58, 79, 94–5, 100, 225; colloquial speech, 45, 73, 124; in context of print sequence, 5, 29–30, 40, 50, 78, 89, 124–5; disrupting visual pathos, 247; double voicing, 23, 37, 46, 50, 54, 75, 139, 148; effect on viewing experience, 5, 23, 59, 95, 112, 138, 242; Goya's artistry, 4, 17, 23, 225; irony, sarcasm, and wit, 5, 45, 55, 74, 142, 221, 234, 236, 240; open-ended, 37, 78, 85, 89, 112, 233–4, 259; praise in preface, 17; prompting self-reflection, 79, 112; reflecting on Goya's practices, 90, 101; as signs on the condemned, 178; as titles, 22; translations, 5, 40, 67, 84–5, 225, 239; use of term, 10, 225; wordplay, 55, 101. *See also* images; religious allusions; sequence; *individual prints*
Carderera, Valentín, 242
Caridad (Charity) (Print 27), *140,* 141–3, 148, 248–9
Cascardi, Anthony, 227, 228, 239, 249, 257, 261, 262
Catholic Church: escape by clerics and monks, *200, 202,* 203, 204–5, 260; executions of church officials, *186,* 188; Goya's anticlericalism, 83, 85,

188, 204, 209, 216, 262; Inquisition, 204; murder of friars, *212,* 213, 215–17, 261–2; plunder, *214,* 215, 216–17, 262; priests, 82, 83, 85, 148, 204, 209, 261; relationship with Napoleonic regime, 66–7, 204; role in the uprising, 66–7, 148, 188; symbolism in prints, 66, 67. *See also* religious allusions
Cavarero, Adriana, 254
caves, 138, 239, 240, 248
Ceán Bermúdez, Juan Agustín, 226
charity, 142–3, 249
Charity. See *Caridad*
children, depicted, *38, 64, 136, 152, 208*
Ciofalo, John, 238, 240–1, 262
Clausewitz, Carl von, 4
clothes: plundered, *92,* 93–6, 242–3; trousers stripped, 147, 178–9; of victim, 87
Coderch, Anna, 236
Comer y callar (proverb), 106
composition: arches and archways, 66, 77–8, 109, 133, 138, 215, 239, 240–1, 248; diagonal line, 29, 53, 61, 65, 66, 83, 100, 132, 147–8, 163, 239; image–caption interplay, 101, 243; intersecting straight and curved lines, 66; landscapes, 116; naturalism vs. abstraction, 116–17, 132–3; reinforcing sense of movement, 66, 134, 142, 205, 260; repetition, 89, 178, 242; scale, 95; spaces beyond image, 82–3, 84, 87–8, 139, 209–10, 211, 242, 261; spatial symbolism, 82; starkness, 239; temporal dimensions, 89, 94; in thematic clusters, 124; visual hierarchy, 234; V-shape, 160; with watermill, 58, 238; X-shape, 93, 95. *See also* images; space; *individual prints*
conceptista tradition, 236
Con razón o sin ella (With reason or without it) (Print 2), *24,* 25–7, 231–2; anonymity of perpetrators, 51; anti-nationalist stance, 237; role in sequence, 30, 62, 78, 253
convenir, use of term, 101
corpses: antiheroism, 73, 168; on battlefields, *102,* 103–7, *118, 120, 122*; burials, *140,* 141–3, 249; buried and forgotten, 106, 107, *140*; contrasted to classical sculpture, 104–5, 155, 182, *183,* 257; decomposition, 73, 105, 141, 244; detailed depiction, 87, 104, 142; effects of bombardment, 153–6, 251; feminine, 251; heaped, *70,* 71–5, 123–4, 125, 131, 142, 239–40, 246–7; mistreatment, 141–3, 249; plundered, *92,* 93–6, 242–3; recurrence, 243–4; sexual propriety, 154–5, 251; witnessing, 73–4; at Zaragoza, 153, 244, 246
Corral de locos (*Courtyard of Lunatics*) (Goya), 233
courage: defined, 37, 40; of viewer, 37; of women combatants, *34,* 35–7, *48,* 49–51, 234, 236–7
Crowther, Paul, 225, 241
Curarlos y a otra (Cure them, and on to another) (Print 20), *114,* 115–17, 245, 246; ironic tone, 150, 247; role in sequence, 117, 125, 131

Dérozier, Claudette, 230, 232, 236, 238–43, 246, 249–53, 258, 261–2
desjarretadora, 147, 250
Disasters of War, The (*Disasters*): audience, 27, 45; Céan Bermúdez album, 226; compared to *Los caprichos,* 205, 221, 232–3, 247, 248, 250, 256; demystification of national myths, 16–17; dimensions, 10; ethical quandaries of making, 8, 11–12, 79, 90–1, 182, 194, 222, 223; first edition

(1863), 4, 6, 9, 10, 225, 226, 243; first edition preface, 16, 17–18, 19, 27; first edition title and title page, 12–14, *13,* 228; focus of, 3, 4, 7–8, 14, 94, 155; as form of violence, 90–1; historical context, 11–12, 16–17, 228, 229; pictorial illusion, 8, 227; poematic intention, 226; points of entry into, 6, 228; reception, 220; satire, 36, 221–2; thematic groups, 4, 9, 219; time and space of, 8, 31, 227, 262; title, 14–15, 72, 156, 228, 251; variation, 167; war realism, 219–20; whole series as artwork, 5–6, 228; working title and proofs, 12, 72, 228, 246–7. *See also* captions; Goya, Francisco de; images; sequence; violence; wars; witnessing; *individual prints*

disastre, use of term, 12

diseases, 4, 141, 188

Dodgson, Campbell, 232, 250, 259

Duro es el paso! (Hard is the step!) (Print 14), *80,* 81–5, 110, 241–2

Edwards, Peter, 237

Enlightenment (in Spain), 18, 220–1, 262

Enterrar y callar (Bury and be quiet) (Print 18), *102,* 103–7, 142, 143, 150, 243–5

Escapan entre llamas (They escape among flames) (Print 41), *198,* 199, 203–5, 260

escape: by civilians among flames, *198,* 199, 203–4, 260; by civilians from violence, *206,* 207–11, *208,* 260–1; by clerics, *200,* 201, 203, 204–5, 260, 261; by monks, *202,* 203, 205, 260, 262

Esto es malo (This is bad) (Print 46), *212,* 213, 215–17, 261–2

Esto es peor (This is worse) (Print 37), *180,* 181–5, 256–7, 258

Estragos de la guerra (Ravages of war) (Print 30), *152,* 153–6, 228, 237, 251

ethics of representation, 223

executions: Battle of Valencia, 81, 241, 255; captions' meaning, 84–5, 89–90, 241; as deterrent, 178, 193, 255; faces of perpetrators, 88, 137, 164, 179, 252, 255–6; by firing squad, *24,* 25–7, *86,* 87–91, *136,* 137–9, *186,* 187–9, 231–2, 241, 242, 247–8, 257–8; as form of wartime killing, 82; by garrotting, *170, 172,* 175–8, 254–5, 256; by hanging, *80,* 81, 87, *158,* 159–61, 252; by hanging and strangulation, *162,* 163–5, 252–3; by hanging on battlefield, *174,* 175, 178–9, 255–6; historical context, 81, 87, 241; inevitability, 87, 89–90; injustice of, 241, 242, 255; justifications, 176, 177, 178, 179; places of occurrence, 138; psychological torment, 82, 89; recurrence, 163, 243–4; of stragglers, 188, 258; as visual spectacles, 83, 90, 175, 177–8, 254–5; witnessing, 83–4, 88, 90–1, 241–2

Executions of the Third of May, 1808 (Goya), 3, 25, 242, 246, 248. *See also* executions

famine, 4, 6, 9, 219

Ferdinand VII, King of Spain, 7, 18, 229

Filangieri, Carlo (general), 250

First World War, deaths, 3

fragua, La (*The Forge*) (Goya), 233

framing: effect of, 232, 242; as expressive device, 84, 88; outside the frame, 49, 71, 83, 88, 112, 149, 209–10, 211; reminder of artifice, 139, 241. *See also* composition

Fuerte cosa es! (A harsh thing it is!) (Print 31), *158,* 159–61, 252

Gadamer, Hans Georg, 229
Gamelin, Jacques, 237
Gassier, Pierre, 241, 246, 249, 250, 251, 259
gender, 36, 40, 41, 234–5
Genette, Gerard, 228
Glendinning, Nigel, 226, 234, 255, 256, 262
Goldstein, Joshua, 234
Goya, Francisco de: about, 12; activities during war years, 7, 8, 18, 220–1, 232, 248; anticlericalism, 83, 85, 188, 204, 209, 216, 230, 262; artistry, 4–5, 17, 23, 225; chronicle-artist, 236; court painter, 7, 12, 18–19, 54, 221, 229; final years and death, 16, 18; humanitarianism, 7; later works, 229; moral self-reflection, 10, 177; patriotism, 232; portraitist, 110; as portrayed in *Disasters'* title page and preface, 17–18, 19, 228, 229; self-portraits in *Disasters,* 143, 247, 249, 262; study of male nudes, 244; support of enlightened reform, 7, 18, 221; as war realist, 219. See also *caprichos, Los; Disasters of War, The*
Grande hazaña! Con muertos! (A great deed! With dead men!) (Print 39), *190,* 193–4, 258–9
guerrilleros: about, 26; mutilation as deterrent, 181, 256; victims of execution, 178, 241, 258; violence by, 258

Hard is the step!. See *Duro es el paso!*
Harsh thing it is!, A. See *Fuerte cosa es!*
healing: hospitals, *130,* 133–4, 247; pointlessness, 137–8; for redeployment, *114,* 116, 125, *130,* 131, 134, 137, 141, 235
He deserved it. See *Lo merecía*
He [or it] gets something out of it. See *Algún partido saca*
heroism: antiheroism of corpses, 73, 168; antiheroism of divided military command, 100–1; impersonalized, 236; in light of print sequence, 55; and nationalism, 50; in war art, 55; of women, 40, 50–1, 236–7. *See also* courage
Hinkle, Mary, 235
Hobson, Marian, 227
Hoffman, Werner, 234, 235, 239, 244, 248, 250, 251, 256
Holocaust, 228, 244–5
Horkheimer, Max, 232
horses, *52,* 53–5, 101, 235, 237–8, 243
hospitals, *130,* 133–4, 247
Hughes, Robert, 231, 233, 234, 236, 238–40, 244, 248, 250–1, 258, 261
Hugo, Victor, 82
Huxley, Aldous, 252

images: backgrounds, 35, 44, 51, 58, 59; conveying invisible feelings, 22–3; effect of double-images, 231; foregrounds, 44, 237; as form of violence, 9, 46, 178; image–caption interplay, 5, 6; interior scenes, *130,* 133; lack of historical reference, 8, 51, 126, 240, 244; lack of pictorial realism, 95–6, 169, 188, 220, 253, 262; limits of portraying violence, 8; minimal attention to place, 35, 126; perspective, 220, 231, 232; photographic quality, 8, 227; relevance, 31, 233; skies, 71, 89, 100, 117, 138, 181, 188, 240, 243; use of term, 10; variation and repetition, 187–8; visual hierarchy, 234; as visual text, 225; as well-crafted illusions, 8, 222, 227. *See also* captions; composition; sequence; techniques; *individual prints*
Inferno (Dante), 244, 253
Inquisition, 204

I saw it. See *Yo lo vi*
It all goes a jumble. See *Todo va revuelto*
It always happens. See *Siempre sucede*
It serves you right. See *Bien te se está*
It will be the same thing. See *Será lo mismo*

Judith and Holofernes (Goya), 36
just war theory, 233

Lafuente Ferrari, Enrique, 225–6, 228, 230, 232–3, 235–43, 245–52, 255–62
Last Day of a Condemned Man, The (Hugo), 82
Lecaldano, Paolo, 232, 233, 235, 238, 239, 241, 245–53, 255–62
Levinas, Immanuel, 245
leyendas (legends). *See* captions
Licht, Fred, 227, 228, 230–1, 234, 241, 253, 256–9
llevar el agua a su molino (to take advantage of a situation), 58–9
Lo merecía (He deserved it) (Print 29), *146,* 147, 149–50, 250

Making of Bullets, The (Goya), 252
Making of Gun Powder in the Sierra de Tardienta, The (Goya), 252
manhood, destruction of, 168–9
Marquis of Perales, 147, 250
martyrdom, 21–2, 39, 194, 219, 230, 253
Massacre of the Innocents (Poussin), 239
Matilla, José Manuel, 227, 230, 232–3, 237–8, 244, 247, 250–1
medical care, 235. *See also* healing
Mélida, Enrique, 227, 230, 232, 234–5, 239–47, 249, 252, 257, 259 61
Miller, Steven, 231, 254
Miseries of War, The (Callot), 251
mismo, Lo (The same thing) (Print 3), *28,* 29–32, 110, 232–3; role in sequence, 62, 78, 253
mismo en otras partes, Lo (The same thing in other parts) (Print 23), *122,* 123, 125–6, 246–7
misogyny, 248, 256–7
mob violence, *144, 146,* 147–50, 249–50
moral damage, 245
morality, 164–5, 177, 216, 217, 219
moral self-reflection: on being a witness, 73, 101, 164, 169; discomfort at viewing, 68, 79; by Goya, 10, 177; on making and viewing war images, 222; on meaning of violence, 51. *See also individual prints*
mujeres dan valor, Las (The women give courage) (Print 4), *34,* 35–7, 62, 78, 233–4. See also *Y son fieras*
Muñoz, Cipriano, 241, 250, 252, 257, 258, 260
Murray, Clinton, 235
mutilation: castration, *166,* 167–9, 178–9, 193, 245; and classical male nudes, 194; as deterrent, 169, 177, 258; dismemberment, *190,* 193–4, 258–9; impalement, *180,* 181–5, 256–7; sexual nature, 168, 181, 254; as spectacle, 182; undoing body's dignity, 168, 254

Napoleonic Wars: about, 72, 220–1; barbarism, 189, 257; deaths, 3; framed as wars of emancipation, 26; and justification of imperialism, 27, 31, 189, 233; Mamelukes of the Imperial Guard, 245, 246, 253; medical care, 235; presentiment of, 22; strategy and tactics, 99–100. *See also* battlefields; Peninsular War; soldiers
nationalism: anti-nationalist stance, 30, 237; critiqued in *Disasters,* 16–17, 228, 233, 257; effect on Europe, 221; and heroism, 50; narrative, 16–17; violence in the name of, 7, 30, 31

nature: as instrument of violence, 181, 255; tree–body relationship, 188, 256, 258; tree "decorated" with body parts, *190*, 193, 194, 258; tree depictions, 95–6, 115, 138, 181, 252, 253, 254; war's effects on, 95–6, 115, 181
necrophilia, 154, 251
Neither do they. See *Tampoco* (Print 10)
Ni por ésas (Not even like that) (Print 11), *64*, 65–8, 78, 110, 239
No quieren (They don't want to) (Print 9), *56*, 57–9, 62, 67, 78, 238
No se convienen (They do not agree) (Print 17), *98*, 99–101, 243
No se puede mirar (One cannot look) (Print 26), *136*, 137–9, 247–8
No se puede saber por qué (One cannot know why) (Print 35), *172*, 173, 175, 176–8, 179, 254–6
Not even like that. See *Ni por ésas*
Nothing can be done, And. See *Y no hay remedio*

One cannot know why. See *No se puede saber por qué*
One cannot look. See *No se puede mirar*

Para eso habéis nacido (For that you have been born) (Print 12), *70*, 71–5, 239–40
paragone, 104
paso, 84–5
patriotism, 16, 17, 196, 232, 239, 247, 250. *See also* heroism
pendaison, La (Callot), 241
Peninsular War (1808–14): about, 3; Battle of Bailén, 235–6, 238; Battle of Valencia, 81, 241, 255; British involvement, 195–6, 259–60; civilian uprising, 3–4, 16, 66–7, 148, 188, 233, 246; deaths, 4, 124, 236, 240; disagreement in battle, 242; lack of supplies, 242; mother and child symbolism, 154–5, 235; partisans, 26, 232; perspectives, 26, 27; political aftermath, 4, 6, 7, 9, 219; reprisals at Chinchón, 256; soldiers as automatons, 100, 231–2; Torquemada, 260. *See also* battlefields; Catholic Church; executions; mutilation; nationalism; violence; Zaragoza, siege of
Perales, Marquis of, 147, 250
phenomenological dimensions, 225
pictorial theory, 227
Pinturas negras (Black Paintings) (Goya), 36, 220
Piot, Eugene, 252, 255
plundering: from Catholic Church, *214*, 215, 216–17, 262; clothes from corpses, *92*, 93–6, 242–3; perpetrators, 195
populacho, use of term, 249–50
Populacho (Rabble) (Print 28), *144*, 145, 147–9, 150, 249–50
Por qué? (Why?) (Print 32), *162*, 163–5, 252–3
Por una navaja (Because of a knife) (Print 34), *170*, 171, 175–6, 177, 178, 254, 255, 256
presentiment, *20*, 21–3, 31–2, 230, 231
prints, use of term, 10

Qué hay que hacer más? (What more is there to do?) (Print 33), *166*, 167–9, 253–4, 257
Qué valor! (What courage!) (Print 7), *48*, 49–51, 55, 62, 78, 236–7

Rabble. See *Populacho*
Ranciere, Jacques, 245
rape: bodies depicted, 238, 239; facial expressions, 109–10, 111, 245; and the feminine sacrosanct, 67; Goya's moral stance, 57–8; imagined outcomes of

struggle, 62, 67; perpetrators, 61–2, 65–6, 110–11, 195, 239, 245, 259; phallic pattern of thinking, 57, 168; places of occurrence, 65, 66–7, 68, 112, 238; prints, *56, 60, 64, 76, 108*; recurrence, 78, 243–4; sodomy, 147, 250; thematic clusters, 78, 79, 109; twofold view, 58–9, 66, 67–8; as unavoidable, 67, 111–12; in Western art, 58; witnesses, 79, 240; witnessing, 111, 112, 245; women's resistance, 59, 61–3, 65–6, 238; women treated as spoils of war, 57–8, 238, 239

Ravages of War. See *Estragos de la guerra*

reason (*razón*), 25, 26–7, 30, 41, 232. See also *Con razón o sin ella*

reforms, 7, 18, 221

refugees, *206,* 207–11, *208,* 260–1

religious allusions: Agony in the Garden, 21–2, 23, 229–30, 231; charity, 142–3, 148; Christian iconography in propaganda, 242; church and bell-tower in background, 65, 66; Crucifixion, 85; Deposition of Christ, 94, 243; Goya's ironic stance, 36, 230; Madonna and Child, 154; martyrdom, 219, 253; *memento mori,* 74, 75; paraphernalia worn by victims, 175; Pietà, 36, 94; Spanish Inquisition, 204; St. Sebastian, 193–4; *Via dolorosa,* 85. *See also* Catholic Church

Royal Academy of Fine Arts of San Fernando, 12, 14, 16, 17, 18, 226

Ruinas de Zaragoza (Gálvez and Brambila), 236

Sad presentiments of what is to come to pass. See *Tristes presentimientos de lo que ha de acontecer*

Same thing, The. See *mismo, Lo*

Same thing in other parts, The. See *mismo en otras partes, Lo*

satirical tradition, 36, 221–2

Sayre, Eleanor, 232, 236–8, 240–6, 249–51, 255–6, 260–1

Schulz, Andrew, 229

sculpture: Belvedere Torso, 182, *183,* 257; making, 182; male nudes, 143, 182, 194, 254, 258, 259; *paragone,* 104

Se aprovechan (They take advantage) (Print 16), *92,* 93–6, 110, 242–3

Second of May 1808 in Madrid, The (Goya), 3, 16, 232

Second World War, 4, 240, 244

Sedlmayr, Hans, 229–30

Seifert, Ruth, 239

self-reflection. *See* moral self-reflection

semiotic reductionism, 225

sequence: alternating violence and aftermath, 72, 117, 159; contributing to meaning, 31–2, 148; conveying complex ideas across image groups, 32, 234; conveying unremitting war logic, 131–2; effect of repetition, 103, 176, 187–8, 243–4; increasingly violent, 167; movement of the viewer, 6, 85, 131–2; narrative continuity, 247; and open-ended captions, 37, 112, 233–4, 259; organization, 4, 5–6, 8, 226, 230; perspective, 63, 232; poematic intention, 226; role of allegory, 196–7; thematic clusters, 78, 79, 109, 117, 125. *See also* captions; images; presentiment; *individual prints*

Será lo mismo (It will be the same thing) (Print 21), *118,* 119, 123–4, 125, 141, 246

sexual assault. *See* rape

Siempre sucede (It always happens) (Print 8), *52,* 53–5, 237–8

soldiers: as automatons, 100, 231–2; bodies, 94; crushed pride, 238; divisions within military command,

100–1; identity symbols, 239; Mamelukes of the Imperial Guard, 245, 246; *miles gloriosus,* 256; narratives of their dying, 53–4; plundering, *92,* 93–5, *214,* 215, 216–17, 262; soldier–victim relationship, 160–1, 252; taking advantage, 94–5, 217, 242; wounded, 115–17
So much and more. See *Tanto y más*
Sontag, Susan, 222
space: abstract, 8, 123, 142, 147, 215, 246; alternating settings, 159; echoing state of moral world, 96; and new visual language, 239; non-naturalistic, 59, 133, 260; open form, 241; reminding viewer of print's illusion, 35, 77–8, 124, 138; and witnessing, 111. *See also* composition
Spanish Inquisition, 204
Spanish partisans: depicted in *Disasters,* 29, 30, 189, 232; guerrilleros, 26, 160, 178, 181, 241, 256, 258; sympathy for, 27. See also *afrancesados;* nationalism; women; *individual prints*
St. Sebastian, 193–4
St. Theresa (Bernini), 248
Stoichita, Victor, 236
suffering: aftermath of conflict, 72; at Battle of Bailén, 235–6; and compassion, 46; democratized depiction, 110, 245; desensitization, 149, 187–8, 215; and enmity, 45, 236; facial expressions, 245; grief, 124, 246; justification, 45; medical care, 235; *paso,* 84–5; psychological torment, 82, 137; in war art, 110; of the wounded, *42,* 43–4, 45–6, 133
supplices, Les (Callot), 241
Symmons, Sarah, 244, 253

También éstos (These too) (Print 25), *130,* 131–4, 247
También esto (This too) (Print 43), *202,* 203, 205, 260
Tampoco (Also) (Print 36), *174,* 175, 178–9, 255–6
Tampoco (Neither do they) (Print 10), *60,* 61–3, 78, 238–9
Tanto y más (So much and more) (Print 22), *120,* 121, 123, 124–5, 246–7
Tauromaquia, La (Goya), 229, 250, 261
techniques: aquatint, 12, 44, 58, 256, 258; contrasts, 44, 53, 61, 77, 100; to convey movement, 53; cross-hatching, 231; dry point, 12, 244, 258; effect of sculpted stone, 257; engraving, 12, 44, 253; etched lines, 53, 61, 256; for facial expressions, 249; stippling, 244
That's how it happened. See *Así sucedió*
There is no longer any time. See *Ya no hay tiempo*
These too. See *También éstos*
They are wild beasts, And. See *Y son fieras*
They do not agree. See *No se convienen*
They don't want to. See *No quieren*
They escape among flames. See *Escapan entre llamas*
They take advantage. See *Se aprovechan*
They will still be able to serve. See *Aún podrán servir*
Third of May 1808, The (Goya), 231, 232
This is bad. See *Esto es malo*
This is worse. See *Esto es peor*
This too. See *También esto*
This too, And. See *Y esto también*
Todo va revuelto (It all goes a jumble) (Print 42), *200,* 201, 203, 204–5, 260
Tomlinson, Janis, 226, 227, 229, 231–7, 250, 258, 262
tone: abstract quality of darkness, 123, 133, 138; contrasting background and foregound, 138, 153; heightening difference, 100, 103–4; symbolic

dimensions, 43–4, 53, 66, 87, 117, 132; used to link figures, 245–6
total war, 4
transcendence, absence of, 230
trees. *See* nature
tres de mayo de 1808 en Madrid, El (*The Third of May 1808*) (Goya), 231, 232
Tristes presentimientos de lo que ha de acontecer (Sad presentiments of what is to come to pass) (Print 1), 6, *20,* 21–3, 229–31

Valencia, Battle of, 81, 241, 255
Vega, Jesusa, 227–8, 230, 232–4, 236, 238–43, 246–8, 251–62
viewing. *See* captions; images; sequence; witnessing
violence: aftermath, 72, 73–4; animalistic, 40–1; anonymity of perpetrators, 51; art–violence relationship, 105, 143, 178, 179, 182, 194, 217, 257, 259; vs. beauty, 104, 244–5; deadening of moral feeling, 111, 149, 164, 187–8; engendered by patriotism, 232; ethical challenges of making and viewing in images, 8, 9, 79; Goya's approach, 7, 10, 227, 230; guerrilla warfare's effect on French army, 26; images themselves as form of, 46, 90; justification, 27, 30, 164–5, 189, 233; memory and forgettery, 106; by Napoleon's troops, 4, 7, *24,* 26; of political sovereignity, 233; progressively greater in sequence, 167, 181; regardless of side, 30; as routine, 164; by Spanish guerrillas, 4, 7; unseen causes, 72; variations, 167. *See also* corpses; executions; mob violence; mutilation; rape; suffering
Volland, Gerlinde, 234–5, 238–40, 248, 251, 254, 256
war art, 55, 110, 219
warfare: asymmetrical, 100; by French armies, 25, 72, 99, 100; gendered nature, 40–1; myth of being civilized, 189; secular truth of, 219; by Spanish partisans, 26, *28,* 100; total war, 4; violence everywhere, 159. *See also* violence
War of 1812, medical care, 235
War of Independence, Spanish. *See* Peninsular War
wars: aftermath, 43–4, 72, *152,* 153–4, 251; allegorical representation, 195–7, 259–60; deadening of moral feeling, 111, 149, 164; demystification of wartime mythologies, 14, 101, 189, 219, 237; disruption of households, 210–11; driven by material interests, 196, 259–60; hope for the future, 223; and human purpose, 73–4, 239–40; justification, 26, 27, 30, 150, 196, 217; just war theory, 233; lack of redemption, 154; memory and forgettery, 103, 105–6, 142, 143; moral damage, 245; presentiment of, 22; propaganda, 223, 245; recurrence, 31; sense of time, 231; as series of disasters, 14; undoing of distinctions, 41, 156, 161, 219–20, 233, 252; war–gender relationship, 41, 234–5; wartime thinking, 57, 100, 116, 131, 150, 217. *See also* corpses; suffering; violence; *specific wars*
watermills, 58, 238
weapons: bayonets, 137, 138; cannons, 49, 50, 55, 78, 117; daggers, 196; death penalty for carrying, 176, 177, 255; *desjarretadora,* 147; knives, 176, 255; rifles, 87–8, 138, 242; swords, 99, 112, 159, 160, 168, 176, 181, 215, 252
Wedding, The (*La boda*) (Goya), 233

What courage!. See *Qué valor!*
What more is there to do?. See *Qué hay que hacer más?*
Why?. See *Por qué?*
Williams, Gwynn, 225, 227, 242, 248
Wilson-Bareau, Juliet, 249
With reason or without it. See *Con razón o sin ella*
witnessing: actual experience vs. an image, 8, 9, 10, 46, 68, 111, 116, 222–3; affected by sequencing, word play, and non-naturalism, 67, 139 156, 226, 243–4; attention drawn to artifice, 84, 88; the dead, 193–4; effect of allegory, 196–7; effect of repetition, 117, 176, 187–8; ethical quandary of witnessing through art, 227; Goya as witness, 143, 210, 247, 249, 262; Goya's understanding of, 226–7; illusion of, 8–9, 169; limits of, 105, 156; moral responsibilitiy, 84; time frame of viewer vs. figure in print, 112, 231; traumatic nature of, 6, 220; viewer's position, 6, 68, 79, 116, 139; witnesses within prints, 79. *See also* moral self-reflection; *individual prints*
Wolf, Reva, 225–7, 230, 242, 246, 248, 250, 253, 255–6, 261
Wollheim, Richard, 227
women: Agustina of Aragón, 50–1, 236–7; as Amazon-like, 39; as animalistic, *38,* 39–41, 235; combatants, 36, 39, 234, 235; courage, *34,* 36, 37, 40, *48,* 49–51, 63, 234; as dying martyrs, 39, 248; as feminine sacrosanct, 67; heroism, 40, 50–1, 236–7; involvement in violence, 41; misogyny, 248, 256–7; nudity, 155, 254; popular representation, 233; as protective mothers, 39, 65, 66, 154, 209, 210–11, 235, 251, 261; in Second of May uprising, 233; in wartime propaganda, 36. *See also* bodies; rape
Women give courage, The. See *mujeres dan valor, Las*
World War I, 3
World War II, 4, 240, 244

Ya no hay tiempo (There is no longer any time) (Print 19), *108,* 109–12, 245–6
Y esto también (And this too) (Print 45), *208,* 209, 210–11, 261
Y no hay remedio (And nothing can be done) (Print 15), *86,* 87–91, 138, 241, 242, 248
Yo lo vi (I saw it) (Print 44), *206,* 207, 209–10, 211, 248, 260–1
Yriarte, Charles, 239–40
Y son fieras (And they are wild beasts) (Print 5), *38,* 39–41, 62, 78, 234–5
Yun, Heather, 235

Zaragoza: Goya's trips to, 7, 50, 153, 232, 246, 261; as print background, 51
Zaragoza, siege of: Agustina of Aragón, 50–1, 236–7; bombardment effects, 251, 260; corpses, 153, 244, 246; treating the wounded, 247

Toronto Iberic

1 Anthony J. Cascardi, *Cervantes, Literature, and the Discourse of Politics*
2 Jessica A. Boon, *The Mystical Science of the Soul: Medieval Cognition in Bernardino de Laredo's Recollection Method*
3 Susan Byrne, *Law and History in Cervantes'* Don Quixote
4 Mary E. Barnard and Frederick A. de Armas (eds), *Objects of Culture in the Literature of Imperial Spain*
5 Nil Santiáñez, *Topographies of Fascism: Habitus, Space, and Writing in Twentieth-Century Spain*
6 Nelson Orringer, *Lorca in Tune with Falla: Literary and Musical Interludes*
7 Ana M. Gómez-Bravo, *Textual Agency: Writing Culture and Social Networks in Fifteenth-Century Spain*
8 Javier Irigoyen-García, *The Spanish Arcadia: Sheep Herding, Pastoral Discourse, and Ethnicity in Early Modern Spain*
9 Stephanie Sieburth, *Survival Songs: Conchita Piquer's* Coplas *and Franco's Regime of Terror*
10 Christine Arkinstall, *Spanish Female Writers and the Freethinking Press, 1879–1926*
11 Margaret Boyle, *Unruly Women: Performance, Penitence, and Punishment in Early Modern Spain*

12 Evelina Gužauskytė, *Christopher Columbus's Naming in the* diarios *of the Four Voyages (1492–1504): A Discourse of Negotiation*
13 Mary E. Barnard, *Garcilaso de la Vega and the Material Culture of Renaissance Europe*
14 William Viestenz, *By the Grace of God: Francoist Spain and the Sacred Roots of Political Imagination*
15 Michael Scham, Lector Ludens*: The Representation of Games and Play in Cervantes*
16 Stephen Rupp, *Heroic Forms: Cervantes and the Literature of War*
17 Enrique Fernandez, *Anxieties of Interiority and Dissection in Early Modern Spain*
18 Susan Byrne, *Ficino in Spain*
19 Patricia M. Keller, *Ghostly Landscapes: Film, Photography, and the Aesthetics of Haunting in Contemporary Spanish Culture*
20 Carolyn A. Nadeau, *Food Matters: Alonso Quijano's Diet and the Discourse of Food in Early Modern Spain*
21 Cristian Berco, *From Body to Community: Venereal Disease and Society in Baroque Spain*
22 Elizabeth R. Wright, *The Epic of Juan Latino: Dilemmas of Race and Religion in Renaissance Spain*
23 Ryan D. Giles, *Inscribed Power: Amulets and Magic in Early Spanish Literature*
24 Jorge Pérez, *Confessional Cinema: Religion, Film, and Modernity in Spain's Development Years, 1960–1975*
25 Joan Ramon Resina, *Josep Pla: Seeing the World in the Form of Articles*
26 Javier Irigoyen-García, *"Moors Dressed as Moors": Clothing, Social Distinction, and Ethnicity in Early Modern Iberia*
27 Jean Dangler, *Edging toward Iberia*
28 Ryan D. Giles and Steven Wagschal (eds), *Beyond Sight: Engaging the Senses in Iberian Literatures and Cultures, 1200–1750*
29 Silvia Bermúdez, *Rocking the Boat: Migration and Race in Contemporary Spanish Music*
30 Hilaire Kallendorf, *Ambiguous Antidotes: Virtue as Vaccine for Vice in Early Modern Spain*
31 Leslie Harkema, *Spanish Modernism and the Poetics of Youth: From Miguel de Unamuno to* La Joven Literatura
32 Benjamin Fraser, *Cognitive Disability Aesthetics: Visual Culture, Disability Representations, and the (In)Visibility of Cognitive Difference*
33 Robert Patrick Newcomb, *Iberianism and Crisis: Spain and Portugal at the Turn of the Twentieth Century*
34 Sara J. Brenneis, *Spaniards in Mauthausen: Representations of a Nazi Concentration Camp, 1940–2015*

35 Silvia Bermúdez and Roberta Johnson (eds), *A New History of Iberian Feminisms*

36 Steven Wagschal, *Minding Animals In the Old and New Worlds: A Cognitive Historical Analysis*

37 Heather Bamford, *Cultures of the Fragment: Uses of the Iberian Manuscript, 1100–1600*

38 Enrique García Santo-Tomás (ed), *Science on Stage in Early Modern Spain*

39 Marina Brownlee (ed), *Cervantes'* Persiles *and the Travails of Romance*

40 Sarah Thomas, *Inhabiting the In-Between: Childhood and Cinema in Spain's Long Transition*

41 David A. Wacks, *Medieval Iberian Crusade Fiction and the Mediterranean World*

42 Rosilie Hernández, *Immaculate Conceptions: The Power of the Religious Imagination in Early Modern Spain*

43 Mary Coffey and Margot Versteeg (eds), *Imagined Truths: Realism in Modern Spanish Literature and Culture*

44 Diana Aramburu, *Resisting Invisibility: Detecting the Female Body in Spanish Crime Fiction*

45 Samuel Amago and Matthew J. Marr (eds), *Consequential Art: Comics Culture in Contemporary Spain*

46 Richard P. Kinkade, *Dawn of a Dynasty: The Life and Times of Infante Manuel of Castile*

47 Jill Robbins, *Poetry and Crisis: Cultural Politics and Citizenship in the Wake of the Madrid Bombings*

48 Ana María Laguna and John Beusterien (eds), *Goodbye Eros: Recasting Forms and Norms of Love in the Age of Cervantes*

49 Sara J. Brenneis and Gina Herrmann (eds), *Spain, World War II, and the Holocaust: History and Representation*

50 Francisco Fernández de Alba, *Sex, Drugs, and Fashion in 1970s Madrid*

51 Daniel Aguirre-Oteiza, *This Ghostly Poetry: Reading Spanish Republican Exiles between Literary History and Poetic Memory*

52 Lara Anderson, *Control and Resistance: Food Discourse in Franco Spain*

53 Faith Harden, *Arms and Letters: Military Life Writing in Early Modern Spain*

54 Erin Alice Cowling, Tania de Miguel Magro, Mina García Jordán, and Glenda Y. Nieto-Cuebas (eds), *Social Justice in Spanish Golden Age Theatre*

55 Paul Michael Johnson, *Affective Geographies: Cervantes, Emotion, and the Literary Mediterranean*

56 Justin Crumbaugh and Nil Santiáñez (eds), *Spanish Fascist Writing: An Anthology*

57 Margaret E. Boyle and Sarah E. Owens (eds), *Health and Healing in the Early Modern Iberian World: A Gendered Perspective*

58 Leticia Álvarez-Recio (ed), *Iberian Chivalric Romance: Translations and Cultural Transmission in Early Modern England*
59 Henry Berlin, *Alone Together: Poetics of the Passions in Late Medieval Iberia*
60 Adrian Shubert, *The Sword of Luchana: Baldomero Espartero and the Making of Modern Spain, 1793–1879*
61 Jorge Pérez, *Fashioning Spanish Cinema: Costume, Identity, and Stardom*
62 Enriqueta Zafra, *Lazarillo de Tormes: A Graphic Novel*
63 Erin Alice Cowling, *Chocolate: How a New World Commodity Conquered Spanish Literature*
64 Mary E. Barnard, *A Poetry of Things: The Material Lyric in Habsburg Spain*
65 Frederick A. de Armas and James Mandrell (eds), *The Gastronomical Arts in Spain: Food and Etiquette*
66 Catherine Infante, *The Arts of Encounter: Christians, Muslims, and the Power of Images in Early Modern Spain*
67 Robert Richmond Ellis, *Bibliophiles, Murderous Bookmen, and Mad Librarians: The Story of Books in Modern Spain*
68 Beatriz de Alba-Koch (ed), *The Ibero-American Baroque*
69 Deborah R. Forteza, *The English Reformation in the Spanish Imagination: Rewriting Nero, Jezebel, and the Dragon*
70 Olga Sendra Ferrer, *Barcelona, City of Margins*
71 Dale Shuger, *God Made Word: An Archaeology of Mystic Discourse in Early Modern Spain*
72 Xosé M. Núñez Seixas, *The Spanish Blue Division on the Eastern Front, 1941–45: War Experience, Occupation, Memory*
73 Julia Domínguez, *Quixotic Memories: Cervantes and Memory in Early Modern Spain*
74 Anna Casas Aguilar, *Bilingual Legacies: Father Figures in Self-Writing from Barcelona, 1975–2005*
75 Julia H. Chang, *Blood Novels: Gender, Caste, and Race in Spanish Realism*
76 Frederick A. de Armas, *Cervantes' Architectures: The Dangers Outside*
77 Michael Iarocci, *The Art of Witnessing: Francisco de Goya's* Disasters of War